Between Care and Justice

SUNY series in Contemporary Italian Philosophy
_____
Silvia Benso and Brian Schroeder, editors

Between Care and Justice
The Passions as Social Resource

Elena Pulcini

Translated and Annotated by
Silvia Benso and Antonio Calcagno

SUNY
PRESS

Published by State University of New York Press, Albany

Tra cura e giustizia. Le passioni come risorsa sociale by Elena Pulcini
© 2020 Bollati Boringhieri editore, Torino

© 2024 State University of New York

For information, contact State University of New York Press, Albany, NY
www.sunypress.edu

Library of Congress Cataloging-in-Publication Data

Names: Benso, Silvia, translator. | Calcagno, Antonio, translator.
Title: Between care and justice : the passions as social resource / Translated and
    annotated by Silvia Benso and Antonio Calcagno
Description: Albany : State University of New York Press, [2024] | Series:
    SUNY series in Contemporary Italian Philosophy | Includes bibliographical
    references and index.
Identifiers: ISBN 9781438497860 (hardcover : alk. paper) | ISBN 9781438497884
    (ebook) | ISBN 9781438497877 (pbk. : alk. paper)
Further information is available at the Library of Congress.

10 9 8 7 6 5 4 3 2 1

Contents

Translators' Acknowledgments   vii

Author's Acknowledgments   ix

Introduction   1

1. Beyond *Homo Oeconomicus*: Empathy and Moral Sentiments   7

2. Care *versus* Justice or Care *and* Justice?   23

3. The Passions of Justice: Not Only Compassion   39

4. The Passions of Care: For *Good* Care   57

5. Global Perspectives: Care and Justice Confronting the
   Challenge of the Spatially *Distant Other*   69

6. Global Perspectives: Care and Justice Confronting the
   Challenge of the Temporally *Distant Other*   89

7. For an Emotive Subject: Taking Care of the Passions   125

Notes   155

Index   207

Translators' Acknowledgments

Elena Pulcini was both a brilliant philosopher and a warm, kind person. Her untimely death left many friends, philosophers, students, and admirers bereft of her wisdom and insight. We are honored to present here a translation of her last major philosophical treatise—a work that encapsulates many years of thinking and social and political engagement with our contemporary world and all of its pressing challenges.

This translation would not have been possible without the help of Elena Pulcini's family, and we are grateful for their continued support. We also wish to acknowledge the generosity and patience of Flavia Abbinante of Bollati Boringhieri. She helped promote and secure the rights for this translation. We are also grateful to Dr. Michael Rinella of the State University of New York Press. His generous persistence and openness, especially during and following the pandemic, have helped bring this volume to press. Finally, we thank the editorial, production, and marketing teams at SUNY Press, including Diane Ganeles, for all their help.

This volume is dedicated to the memory of our friend, teacher, and fellow philosopher Elena Pulcini. May her ideas continue to transform the world and humanity she loved.

Silvia Benso and Antonio Calcagno

Author's Acknowledgments

This book had a long gestation period, during which the many places of discussion and elaboration of individual themes helped develop and clarify its theoretical framework. This work also advanced thanks to the often impervious and feverish confrontation with current events and the rapid changes they introduced. It therefore remains impossible to thank the people who, time and again, have enriched my journey with precious direct or indirect stimuli. I limit myself here, then, to mentioning some contexts and places of collaboration, which constitute for me (even in the role of coordinator) constant points of reference for the main thematic nodes of my reflection: the international network of Care Ethics, founded in Utrecht by Joan Tronto, within which I have shared, also as a member of the board, fruitful exchanges, in particular, with my Canadian friend and colleague Sophie Bourgault; the friends of MAUSS (Mouvement anti-utilitariste en sciences sociales), directed by Alain Caillé, who also inspired the "convivialist" project of which I have the pleasure of being a part; and SIP (Society for Italian Philosophy), expertly coordinated by Silvia Benso (USA) and Antonio Calcagno (Canada). I also thank the thirty-year-old Critical Theory Seminar (Gallarate and Cortona), a venue for exchanges and even clashes, which are always fruitful; and also the group of colleagues and friends in political philosophy (the Department of Political and Social Sciences of the University of Florence and the Laboratory of Philosophy of the Global Age, which I founded), including Dimitri D'Andrea and Mirko Alagna, with whom I have shared, especially in recent years, a full roster of seminars and debates, preserving a rare space for authentic discussion.

I also owe a lot to all the groups, associations, and cultural institutions with whom and in which I have held a great number of workshops and conferences over the years: they have made accessible and opened new perspectives on the world, through other languages and points of view, which philosophy should no longer do without in order to live up to the radical transformation we are now experiencing. I have learned from ecology and feminism, psychoanalysis and pedagogy, literature and cinema.

Special thanks goes to Leonard Mazzone, who had the patience to read and comment, with the depth that characterizes him, the entire book, and to my husband, Dario Squilloni, for his availability to discuss from time to time the various stages of the evolution of this book, for bearing my anxieties, which are only justified by my own philosophical passion.

Finally, I would like to thank Bollati Boringhieri, to which I feel connected, especially on account of my relationship with Alfredo Salsano, whom I had the privilege of meeting before his death. I hope that our collaboration will continue to be intense and lasting.

Elena Pulcini

Introduction

Why do we *care* for others even when we are not connected by personal relationships? Why do we fight for *justice* even when it does not concern us directly? In short, what are the motivational foundations that push us to act ethically and adopt socially empathic behaviors?

Since its inauguration a few decades ago, with the publication of Carol Gilligan's book *In a Different Voice*, the debate on care and justice has taken on such proportions as to discourage any new attempt to address its complex and multiple implications, be they psychological or political, ethical or legal.[1] One could legitimately affirm that all possible ethical and normative responses to the social pathologies and great challenges of our time can be summarized in these two paradigms: on the one hand, we need justice in order to face up to inequality and exploitation, humiliation and poverty; on the other, we are discovering the urgency of care to combat atomism and indifference, the erosion of the social bond, the neglect of the living world, and the dramatically declining conditions of the environment. In other words, any unilateral and oppositional vision between the two ethical perspectives—of which we find undeniable traces in current reflections[2]—needs to be overcome in order to propose a clearer and more reciprocal integration between the two.

I would like to point out, however, that I will address the topic from a specific point of view that appears barely present in the contemporary debate: that is to say, from the point of view of a form of *moral psychology*[3] that not only reaffirms the importance of emotions on a cognitive level but also questions the emotional roots of ethics, thereby allowing us to tackle the problem of the affective motivations[4] behind both the demand for justice and the disposition to, and practice of, care. Reflecting on the role that passions and feelings play in both ethical perspectives is,

1

in other words, a *via regia*, a royal path. By following it, not only can we rethink them beyond stereotyped images but we can also fearlessly undermine even their potentially negative aspects and fully enhance their emancipatory aspects and unexpected twists.

First of all, let us think about the idea of *justice*. What the theorists of care have in common in this regard (from Gilligan to Held, from Kittay to Tronto)[5] is the radically critical approach to liberal theories of justice and, in particular, to the model proposed by John Rawls in *A Theory of Justice*.[6] They contest not only the undisputed and alleged hegemony of this model over the span of modernity, but also its abstract and rationalistic character, which has ended up obscuring other possible ethical (and political) perspectives. In other words, to the justice paradigm, founded on the values of an abstract individualism, of rationality, and of the subject's autonomy and independence, they oppose the care paradigm, based on the values of concreteness and affectivity, interdependence and relationality.

Insofar as it denounces the one-sidedness of the ethical paradigm of modernity, this is, undoubtedly, the strong point of care ethics. Yet, in my view, it also represents its weak point, since it ends up boxing the idea of justice into its prevailing and consolidated image, precluding the possibility of a different theory of justice. To propose the relationship between care and justice in these terms is to emphasize a purely formal idea of the latter and neglect the problem of the motivations that inspire the demand for justice, namely, *affective* motivations, which originate in certain passions and therefore do not exclusively belong, I argue, to the care perspective.

It is precisely in this direction that, for example, Martha Nussbaum's reflections seem to be oriented when she attributes an important role to moral sentiments—and, in particular, to compassion on the part of those who witness unjust situations—in making up for the shortcomings of the contractualist model of justice, which is based on the sole criterion of mutual benefit.[7] However, as we shall see, Nussbaum's limit is that she proposes a vision of care that is not autonomous but is actually incorporated in, and subordinated to, the paradigm of justice.

Taking the *passions for justice* seriously also means changing, even more radically, the perspective from which the problem is addressed. It means renouncing, as Amartya Sen proposes, an ideal and perfect model of justice, such as that which inspires the Rawlsian paradigm, and starting instead from the concrete claims of individuals and groups that arise from the perception of injustice.[8] In other words, we must start from injustice and our desire to fight it, and mobilize those feelings, such as humanity and generosity, righteousness and indignation, which characterize us as human beings.

This is undoubtedly true for those who witness unfair situations, practices, and behaviors. Yet, it also applies to those who suffer these situations personally and fight for the defense of their rights and dignity insofar as these struggles contain an emancipatory and normative potential that crosses the boundaries of pure individual interest and involves an entire social structure and the interest for the common good. The "experience of injustice," as Emmanuel Renault calls it,[9] is in fact what gives rise, through the sharing of a "feeling of injustice" on the part of victims, to the claims and struggles of the various social movements, in which we can recognize a normative model of society that is an alternative to the existing one. In this regard, it is useful to recall some protest movements that have become the bearers of emancipatory action. Among them are the movements of revolt fueled by a just anger that, a few years ago, motivated the Arab world with legitimate demands for democracy, so much so that we speak of an "Arab spring"; the global movement of the Indignados that, starting from Spain, has spread to the entire Western world; the various Occupy movements that are multiplying around the planet; the unprecedented growth of gender-oriented petitions such as those of MeToo and the LGTBQIA associations; and the anger of the gilets jaunes, despite their undeniable ambiguity.

To address the problem of the aforementioned negative aspects, however, we must not underestimate the fact that, today as always, there are movements and revolts that hold up regressive claims and destructive objectives (such as the various fundamentalisms and racisms, whose extreme fringes form the breeding ground for violent identity conflicts and drifts into terrorism). Recognizing the different nature of the affective impulses underlying social movements and collective struggles gives us a precious tool to distinguish between legitimate and illegitimate claims. I show how this is possible by dwelling, as a significant example, on the link between two passions that are not always easily distinguishable, namely, indignation and envy.

In short, focusing attention on the emotions allows us to think of a different idea of justice. But this is not all. It also allows us to understand better the motivations that inspire the disposition to care, which is often defined through an all too general and hasty equation with the affective dimension. In other words, it is necessary to question ourselves more deeply about the nature of the passions and feelings that are at the origin of the ethics of care. This necessity is due to at least three fundamental reasons: first, to remove care from a purely altruistic and self-sacrificing vision and instead bring it back to the condition of human *vulnerability*; second, to highlight the extent and differentiation of the contexts in which it is able to operate, be it in the private, professional, or social sphere, in which care is anything but free from negative feelings such as resentment and disgust (which is, unfortunately, quite common in the field of care and assistance for those in need); third, to enhance the aspects that distinguish it from the ethics of justice. In fact, if the motivations and objectives of justice remain inscribed in what, with Paul Ricoeur, we can call a "logic of equivalence," by mobilizing feelings such as attention, generosity, and love, care prompts a "logic of superabundance"[10] that, in my opinion, has its roots in the awareness of the reciprocity of *debt* and the circularity of the gift.

It is therefore a matter not of opposing the two ethical perspectives in a mutually exclusive way, but of proposing a desirable integration between the two, which translates into a sort of productive division of labor. In this division, the ethics of justice continually seeks to restore equality and symmetry through fights against injustice, impartial defense of rights, and fair distribution of resources, whereas the ethics of care tends to affirm what I would like to call the value of bonds and relationships by recovering gratuitousness and the gift-giving dimension inspired by the awareness of (one's own and the other's) vulnerability and free from resentful impulses. In other words, whereas, in the case of justice, the emphasis on emotions allows us to distinguish or, at least, to orient ourselves between *legitimate* and *illegitimate* claims, in the case of care it allows us to distinguish between *good* and *bad* care.

This division of labor arises again, as we shall see, in the face of that unprecedented challenge of our time—one on which I have placed particular attention—and that I propose to summarize in the figure of the *distant other*, who can be either distant *in space* or distant *in time*. A figure peculiar to the global age, the distant other strongly tests both ethical perspectives and poses even more questions on the possible emotional and motivational foundations of just, attentive, and supportive action toward someone who lives in far-off places and is forced by increasingly extreme causes to cross our borders (the example of migrants is all too obvious) or toward some, like future generations, with whom we apparently have no ties, as they are suspended in the dimension of the "not yet."

Suggesting the need for integration between the two different ethical perspectives is therefore equivalent to challenging Aristotle's well-known statement in the *Nicomachean Ethics*: if there is friendship, there is no need for justice, whereas, if there is justice, we still need friendship.[11] The fact is that, on the contrary, we always need both.

While all this obviously presupposes that an *ethical* function can be attributed to emotions, the paths and strategies to be adopted for this function to take shape and operate effectively are less clear. If, on the one hand, there seems to be increasing agreement over recognizing the cognitive and communicative function of emotions, which various disciplines have by now long released from obsolete and erroneous accusations of irrationality or from the myth of unchangeability, the task of recognizing and showing their ethical potential seems to be more difficult. The difficulty comes from the fact that this task presupposes a subject capable of assuming a critical and reflective stance with respect to its own inner "upheavals"—an individual capable of knowing how to find its way in the complexity and ambivalence of emotions, of dwelling in their unpredictability, of knowing how to welcome the new that comes from them, and of fostering or generating the best.

To this end, then, it is necessary, as I propose in the final chapter of this work, to engage in a sort of *paideia* of the emotions that promotes, together with their ethical quality, their ability to produce the *metamorphosis* of the subject. It is true that today it has become more imperative than ever, as Peter Sloterdijk reminds us, to radically change our lives, our relationship with others, ourselves, and the world.[12] However, it is my belief that this change must be the work not of a sovereign and isolated subject, a *maître de soi*, who is capable of ascetic and rational self-control, but of a subject who perceives itself as constitutionally related, that is, a subject who transforms and re-generates itself through the provocation prompted by the emotional relationship and the adherence to emotion's unpredictability—a subject who responds to the appeal, whether silent or loud, provocatively made by the other in his, her, their, or its infinite forms and epiphanies.

One

Beyond *Homo Oeconomicus*

Empathy and Moral Sentiments

Is There an Ethical Role for the Passions?

For the past few decades, there has seemed to be no doubt regarding the cognitive function of the passions and the need to overcome the traditional dualism between the passions and reason. The passions are no longer considered blind and irrational powers. They are not, in Jon Elster's words, "sand in the machinery" of rationality but, rather, motivational forces that presuppose beliefs and judgments and orient our actions and choices at individual and social levels.[1] In this regard, Martha Nussbaum's definition of emotions as "upheavals of thought," endowed with their own particular intelligence, seems especially convincing.[2] Without subscribing to an "Apollonian" conception of emotions, whose intrinsic dynamism and unsettling character she acknowledges, Nussbaum advances a cognitive-evaluative conception of emotions: she sees them as forms of judgment that attribute great importance and value for our well-being to specific things and people.[3]

This more correct viewpoint, which frees passions from a centuries-long devaluing gaze and which, for a while now, has brought together various disciplines (from psychology to sociology and the neurosciences), is not matched, however, with a lexicon of emotional life that is sufficiently clear and adequate, and that reflects their overall complexity.[4] I would like to offer at least two examples that I consider particularly meaningful for the purpose of my arguments.

The first example concerns the increasingly common semantic slip toward the word *emotions* that, as has been correctly noted, finds its root in the nineteenth-century positivistic turn and tends to obliterate the distinction, which we have received from philosophical thought since the eighteenth century (from Kant and Hume), between emotions and passions.[5] Here, emotion indicates a temporary and transient emotional dimension that originates from a sudden and contingent event, such as the fear of a noise at night or the joy of seeing a friend again. Passion instead corresponds to an intense and long-lasting affective energy that pervades the entire personality of the self and, eventually, leads to an overwhelming of the self and damaging its will, much like the love passion that has so deeply pervaded the Western and modern imaginary. Thus, let us indeed call them "emotions" and use the two terms interchangeably, as I myself intend to do. In truth, though, it is the passions that remarkably affect our cognitive processes, our relationships, and our choices of behavior and life.

The second example concerns the notion of *sentiment*, especially when the adjective "moral" is added to it. In this case, its difference from emotions and/or passions is quite sharp. Whereas the latter two indicate an affective dimension that is ambivalent insofar as it may have a positive as well as negative meaning, moral sentiment—when we follow the tradition of moral sentimentalism starting with the seventeenth- and eighteenth-century reflections by Shaftesbury and Hutcheson up to its contemporary representatives—always presupposes, as we shall see, a positive aspect that describes its relational, ethically oriented structure. It is true, however, that, as one can already deduce from Adam Smith and his *Theory of Moral Sentiments*, one can define as "moral sentiment" the same passion or, better, any passion that is intrinsically or potentially endowed with an ethical connotation (for example, compassion or love).[6]

The last move, which is not at all natural or automatic, becomes crucial within the context of a reflection on the passions as social resource. Whereas it is true that passions always entail an evaluation, understanding whether and to what extent they enable a *good* evaluation—that is, understanding what their role or contribution may be within an ethical perspective—is more difficult, as Nussbaum remarks.[7] In other words, can we say that emotions drive us to act ethically? And if so, which emotions?

Modern philosophical and liberal thought has handed down to us a model of possessive individualism and the hegemony of *homo oeconomicus*.[8] This is the figure of an individual who is autonomous and project-oriented, instrumental and calculative while rationally pursuing his own self-interest. Now, without necessarily evoking Amartya Sen's sarcasm, which exposes the partiality of this view and its "foolish" lack of realism,[9] we can still advance two fundamental objections to this model. The first is its claim of rationality. A careful look at early modern philosophers suffices to make us realize that, prior to the rational pursuit of utility, one finds the mobilization of the passions and emotional dynamics, which, among other matters, also explain the power and persistence of this model so seemingly disconcerting to Sen. Homo oeconomicus is not a dispassionate individual but, rather, one who is animated by essentially egoistic passions—whether they are acquisitive and geared toward gaining material goods or identitarian, that is, geared toward self-affirmation and the acquisition of prestige and social status.[10] Homo oeconomicus establishes the relationship with the other in essentially instrumental forms, geared toward domination at worst (Hobbes) and toward antagonism and competition at best (Smith). Briefly, starting with Hobbes, the modern liberal tradition has handed down to us the idea that individuals are motivated essentially by self-interest and egoistic passions (such as Adam Smith's self-love) that have negative effects on common life and find a solution only through self-regulative strategies (the market) or rational norms and artificial institutions (the State) capable of establishing some sustainable social coexistence.

The second objection (to the paradigm of possessive individualism) concerns exactly this presumption of unilateral egoism as the only motivation of human action.[11] Homo oeconomicus is, seemingly, completely identified with egoism and individualism, and is void of all other motivations that are not reducible to the unlimited desire for wealth and/or lust for power and prestige. This reflects a unilateral, miserable, and mutilated image of the individual, which nevertheless has imposed itself on us with great force up to today: it has been made to represent the only possible truth and the only one with which we must come to terms.[12] Due also to the cyclical and recurrent crisis of such a model, this has not prevented the continuous reemergence of other perspectives, which contest its truthfulness and adopt different logics and viewpoints. Without denying the truth of egoism as an ontological feature of the human being, these logics nevertheless contest its unilaterality and affirm the existence of other trends, qualities, and expectations, which have been removed and sacrificed by the totalizing hegemony of possessive individualism and its economicist vocation.

By pursuing this path, we come to the revaluation of a different trend of thought, that is, "moral sentimentalism," which expounds the reflections of David Hume, Adam Smith's *Theory of Moral Sentiments*, and Max Scheler and affirms the existence of precisely other and different motivations for action beside interest. These motivations are inspired by moral sentiments such as benevolence and generosity, compassion and sympathy, trust and love.[13] According to this perspective, which is oriented toward a criticism of moral rationalism,[14] it is on the basis of our moral sentiments as constitutive part of human nature that we can formulate judgments on what is good and just and, consequently, we can act ethically. This position is currently reproposed by authors such as Amartya Sen and Martha Nussbaum,[15] who are engaged in correcting some of the tenets of liberal thinking, and it finds additional confirmation in the scientific research of psychologists and biologists, and in the discoveries of the neurosciences. Antonio Damasio is to be credited with the anti-Cartesian revaluation of emotions that, far from being "intruders in the bastion of reason," play an active role in our cognitive and moral processes.[16] To theorists of moral psychology such as Jonathan Haidt we owe the recognition that emotions are the sources of our immediate moral intuitions ahead of any rational reasoning or evaluation.[17] It is especially from the neurosciences, starting with Giacomo Rizzolatti's famous discovery of mirror neurons, that we derive the valorization of the peculiar emotive disposition of empathy, that is, the intrinsic and natural capability of sharing others' emotions.[18] This confirms not only the cognitive function of emotions but also their potentially ethical function.

A "nomadic" concept, as it has been defined,[19] insofar as it can migrate across multiple disciplinary fields (from ethics to aesthetics, from psychology to philosophy and the neurosciences), empathy opens a greatly interesting perspective on the anthropological-emotional structure of the subject, as it reveals the subject's irreducibility to purely egoistic passions as well as its constitutive tendency to prosocial behavior. This perspective is therefore destined to become indispensable, if we wish to account for the emotional foundations of ethics and confirm the very intuitionist vision of moral psychology. I maintain that this can be the case, though, only if we pay attention to the risk of falling prey to naturalistic simplifications. Before we test the fecund implications of this perspective for the nexus of care and justice, it is appropriate to introduce some clarifications and mediations without the pretense of claiming a complete, absolute answer. We need to do so not only out of love for conceptual clarity, which, in the case of empathy, is absolutely necessary, but also and moreover in order to cast light on the far from automatic path, as we shall soon see, from empathy to moral sentiments and from moral sentiments to an ethically oriented social acting.

Rediscovering Empathy: The Force of Imagination

Let us begin by asking, What exactly is empathy? There is no doubt that the great rediscovery of this concept by multiple disciplines is not currently matched by the same number of clear and unanimous descriptions of its meaning and function. A term introduced at the beginning of the twentieth century through the English translation of the German term *Einfühlung*,[20] empathy is what, according to a recent synthetic and effective definition, allows us "to take part in the other's affective situation, and adopt the other's perspective."[21] Empathy enables us to participate, albeit vicariously, in the other's emotions and experience.[22]

We find a suggestive echo of these definitions in the early twentieth-century phenomenological reflection, which first renewed interest in empathy. It will suffice for now to recall the reflections of Edith Stein, who, in her seminal text, defines empathy as the ability "to feel the other," to become aware of their emotions and lived experiences.[23] In other words, it implies the "discovery of the other," the recognition of the other's existence, of the fact that the other is a constitutive part of the world in which we live.[24] Even though eloquent, this definition simultaneously opens a set of questions that, not by accident, currently appear in various disciplinary approaches to this theme. What does it mean to partake in the emotions and experiences of the other? Is this an emotional or cognitive process? Where does the boundary between the I and the other lie? Who is properly the other in the empathic relationship: is it the neighbor, the familiar, or the distant one? Moreover, does empathy have an ethical and social role? And what is it?

Trying to answer these questions requires, first, that we step back and return to the originary conceptual source of empathy, namely, the eighteenth-century theory of sympathy as formulated especially by David Hume and Adam Smith. As is widely acknowledged and remarked, Hume's and Smith's concept of sympathy has less to do with the current use of the term (to which I will return) than with the actual theories of empathy.[25] In his 1739 *Treatise on Human Nature*, Hume writes, "No quality of human nature is more remarkable, both in itself and in its consequences, than that propensity we have to sympathize with others, and to receive by communication their inclinations and sentiments, however different from, or even contrary to our own."[26] As is already clear from the claims above, Hume's reflection on sympathy is directly tied to his clearly anti-Hobbesian vision of the human being as an eminently social being,[27] as "the creature of the universe, who has the most ardent desire of society." It is not difficult to notice, he adds, that all pleasures are enhanced and all sorrows are lessened if we share them. From this, we can conclude that "a perfect solitude is, perhaps, the greatest punishment we can suffer."[28] As animating principle of all passions, sympathy draws its strength from the social nature of the human being, from the human constitutive tendency to relationships and sharing.[29] Introducing a partly problematic aspect on which I will return later, Hume claims that this tendency is due to the general "similarity" of human beings. Moving from this resemblance characterizing human nature, we are able to understand the other's similar passions, which we grasp through their expressive gestures, transforming them into a vivid experience of our own thanks to the force of the imagination.[30]

Hume's analyses are echoed by Adam Smith's reflections on sympathy as the sentiment of partaking in the other's experience and affections. Explicitly contesting the presuppositions of possessive individualism, Smith claims that the human being is not simply an egoist but also an individual who possesses natural principles "which interest him in the fortune of others, and render their happiness necessary to him."[31] This is undoubtedly a radical claim, which finds its origin in the initial observation of some kind of instinctive tendency to put ourselves in someone else's shoes. This is what, for example, happens to the crowd that, while apprehensively following the movements of "the dancer on the slack rope," is automatically pushed to twist and balance with that individual.[32] For Smith, too, this identification occurs thanks to the faculty of imagination through which we come to feel, even though with a weaker intensity, the same emotions of the other, be they emotions of joy or of sadness.[33] Briefly, sympathy may "be made use of to denote our fellow-feeling with any passion whatever."[34]

Yet this claim, for which we find evident similarities in Hume, cautions us against presupposing an automatic connection between sympathy and the moral dimension. In other words, sympathy is evidently a social sentiment or, as contemporary theorists of empathy claim, a "fundamentally social capacity"[35] that, in Hoffman's words, acts as "the spark of human concern for others, the glue that makes social life possible."[36] Can one also assert, though, that sympathy tout court gives birth to moral actions? Both Hume and Smith do not hesitate to answer this question positively. For Hume, the origin of morality undoubtedly resides in sympathy as it pushes us *naturally* to approve, insofar as we derive pleasure out of them, those features that are oriented toward the good of society, namely, the various and multiple virtues, be they natural, such as meekness, charity, generosity, equity, or artificial such as justice.[37] As he writes, "We have no such extensive concern for society but from sympathy; and consequently 'tis that principle, which takes us so far out of ourselves, as to give us the same pleasure or uneasiness in the characters of others, as if they had a tendency to our own advantage or loss."[38] For Smith, to sympathize means to approve of others' emotions and behaviors, and derive pleasure from this correspondence of sentiments: "To approve of the passions of another, therefore, as suitable to their objects, is the same thing as to observe that we entirely sympathize with them; and not to approve of them as such, is the same thing as to observe that we do not entirely sympathize with them."[39] To be entirely moral, however, this approbation must be founded on an impartial evaluation and judgment, which can be guaranteed not by an automatic and immediate sympathy but only by an indirect sympathy, endowed with a reflective dimension. This presupposes a subject that is capable of reflecting on its own tendencies, choices, and orientations. Despite their different strategies, Hume and Smith agree, as some contemporary interpreters aptly remark, on proposing the idea of a "reflective sentimentalism" that finds its core precisely in the ethics of sympathy.[40]

As is well known, Smith relies on the figure of the "impartial spectator." We sympathize with the other's passions and behaviors only after we have, through imagination, evaluated them by assuming the parameters of a spectator who—this needs to be emphasized—can verify the appropriateness of a certain passion (that is, its adequacy to the situation) insofar as the spectator is the representative of a medium degree of passions.[41] This means, among other things, that whereas we have a tendency potentially to sympathize with "any passion," it is also true that, as Smith details through careful distinctions, we orient ourselves toward those passions that would be approved by an impartial spectator. First, we sympathize mostly with small joys and great sorrows.[42] Second, we are inclined to approve: almost always of *social* and benevolent passions (generosity, humanity, and so on); often of *egoistic* passions, especially when caused in the other by a painful experience; and only conditionally of *asocial* passions (such as resentment).[43]

A particularly interesting aspect of Smith's strategy lies in what we could call the *reciprocity* of sympathy, as it implies that the evaluative process concerns not only the other's passions but also one's own. There is, in other words, reciprocal adaptation thanks to which, on the one hand, the spectator will try to put themselves in the place of the affected persons in order to understand and perceive their emotions and circumstances. On the other, the person who is directly affected will try in turn to tone down the violence of their sentiment in order to obtain the spectator's approbation so that the "reflected passion" that ensues, which is weaker than the original one, may allow for an impartial look upon oneself.[44] Briefly, the dynamics of sympathy becomes an instrument for the moral evaluation of emotions and behaviors—those of both the other and oneself.

In Hume, the distinction between direct and indirect sympathy is even more explicit, so much so that to indicate the former Hume uses terms such as "contagion," which we will find in Max Scheler's diagnosis as well as in the contemporary reflection on empathy.[45] In contagion as a fundamentally fusional dynamic, what is lacking is the ability to distinguish between oneself and the other. This ability is, on the contrary, fundamental for the moral dimension of sympathy and pertains only to reflective sympathy.[46] Through it, we can correct the partiality of our passions and adapt ourselves to those "general principles" that are always valid and authoritatively guide, under all circumstances, our judgments and our opinions.[47] It is mainly the faculty of imagination that enables this correction,[48] as the "imagination adheres to the *general* views of things, and distinguishes the feelings they produce, from those which arise from our particular and momentary situation."[49] It is imagination, in fact, that enables us to appreciate, always and anyway, a character that we consider virtuous (insofar as such a person tends toward the good of society) even when fortuitous and contingent circumstances partly impede its action and effectiveness.[50] According to virtue ethics, to which we will return later,[51] moral approbation concerns not singular aspects or actions, but rather permanent character traits.[52]

Briefly, the moral sense undoubtedly derives not from reason, but from "a general sympathy with humankind." Nevertheless, it is stronger when it is reflective. "A sense of morals is a principle inherent in the soul, and one of the most powerful that enters into the composition. But this sense must certainly acquire new force, when *reflecting on itself*, it approves of those principles, from whence it is deriv'd, and finds nothing but what is great and good in its rise and origin."⁵³ Additionally, the reflective feature of sympathy allows us to approve or disapprove, through imagination, of that which does not concern us personally or closely. As Hume often repeats, it is true that, due to similarity, we tend to sympathize more with those who are close, known, and familiar; and we would never be able to feel for someone who lived in ancient Greece, for example, what we feel toward a fellow citizen.⁵⁴ It is precisely for this reason that, through reflection, we establish "steady and general" principles that will hold true whether in proximity or at a distance, thereby correcting the partiality and limits of our feeling.⁵⁵ In other words, we are capable of widening the circles of inclusion of sympathy⁵⁶ and extending it potentially to ever new individuals also by virtue of the fact that our situation is changing and fluctuating, "and a man, that lies at a distance from us, may, in a little time, become a familiar acquaintance."⁵⁷ We will see how this feature becomes particularly relevant with respect to the unprecedented and exquisitely contemporary recipient of the ethics of care and justice, namely, the *distant other*.⁵⁸

Without explicitly addressing this point, Smith too provides us with arguments to expand the circles of sympathy when he insists on the great power of imagination. Not only does he underline, as we already mentioned, that we feel specific sentiments for subjects that are themselves unaware of them (such as shame for the impudence of another, anxiety for the unconscious unhappiness of the fool, or the mother's suffering for the newborn's sickness), but we also feel sympathy even toward the dead, and we are paradoxically distraught by that which, in truth, can in no way affect them, such as being deprived of sunlight or of the company of others.⁵⁹ As these sentiments arise out of our simply imagining ourselves in the place of others, we can deduce that the extension of our abilities for imaginary identification may be more or less unlimited.

It is this reflective and "extensive" sympathy⁶⁰ that properly becomes, as Hume claims, "the principal source of moral distinctions" as it loses that neutrality characterizing it as participation in any passion and pushes us to choose those passions and behaviors that tend toward the good of humanity. In other words, it opens the space for the genesis of moral sentiments insofar as it enables us, as it were, to recognize (and choose), within the multiplicity of passions, those that are ethically oriented. As Hume continues, there is no doubt that "moral good and evil are certainly distinguish'd by our *sentiments*, not by *reason*." These sentiments, however, "may arise either from the mere species or appearance of characters and passions, or from reflexions on their tendency to the happiness of mankind, and of particular persons."[61]

The ethics of sympathy reaches here a neuralgic and partly controversial point, which we find again in the contemporary reflection on empathy. Many authors in fact claim that empathy is, in general, a neutral state that implies the nonevaluative identification with the other's sentiments and condition.[62] It can even take up negative twists.[63] One can, in fact, sympathize with one who is bad or with the criminal, or feel resentment and envy toward those whose passions one nevertheless understands; one can exploit one's ability to understand the other's emotions to manipulate such a person (for example, the psychopath with the victim) or to eliminate that person from competition (such as in business).[64] An interesting precursor of this position within philosophy is Max Scheler who, in his rich and insightful review of the forms of sympathy/empathy, denies that they have any moral connotations.[65] More precisely, Scheler proposes a subtle and important distinction between the fusional forms of sympathy/empathy (contagion, unipathy), which are grounded on affective identification, and "co-feeling," which is instead grounded on the capacity of the I to distinguish between self and other and to participate in the lived experiences of the other.[66] Nevertheless, Scheler claims that access to values can only be provided through the move from sympathy to moral sentiments (especially love). The neutrality of empathy is stressed, among others, also by Martha Nussbaum, who distinguishes empathy from moral sentiments and, especially, from compassion, claiming, as we will see, that it is only compassion that presupposes moral judgment and evaluation.[67] Other authors—among them Martin Hoffman, Michael Slote, and Frans de Waal—assert, on the contrary, the intrinsically moral connotation of empathy.[68]

The eighteenth-century ethics of sympathy would be, most likely, able to bridge these two positions by suggesting, as we have seen, the distinction between two levels—or qualities—of sympathy. Some contemporary theories too seem to move in the same direction of this perspective. Examples here include theories that propose a distinction between a "basic" and a "reenactive" empathy;[69] or those that claim that empathy is indeed an automatic mechanism but is also a mental state, which we can control and reflect on;[70] or, even, the theories that speak of "genuine empathy," thereby presupposing also, evidently, a nongenuine and nonauthentic connotation of it.[71]

Briefly, similar to Hume's and Smith's reflective sympathy, authentic empathy is that which, unlike contagion and the immediate forms of identification, implies, together with the distinction between oneself and the other,[72] the impartial evaluation of sentiments, whether ours or another's, thereby enabling access to ethics.

As is well known, the theme of reflectivity is currently the core of a broad debate on moral agency among philosophers of various lineages. From Harry Frankfurt's "wholehearted identification" to Christine Korsgaard's "reflective endorsement," from Peter Singer's works to some theoreticians of sentimentalism mentioned above, what clearly emerges is the shared idea of the necessarily reflective character of morality (and of altruism).[73] I cannot address, here, the complexity of this debate. Nevertheless, I argue that what interestingly differentiates the ethics of sympathy from the abovementioned proposals consists in what I would like to define as the relational character of reflectivity and, therefore, the relational origin of normativity. This means that reflectivity is capable of providing us not only with a normative parameter but also with the indication of a process and a possible strategy we may want to adopt, that is, the idea that the moral agent constitutes itself reflectively through a dynamics that is sympathetic with the other and within the social context.[74]

From Empathy to Moral Sentiments, from Sentiments to Engagement

I want to emphasize, however, that empathy is not itself a moral sentiment. This is a point of agreement not only for philosophers who come from different perspectives but also for contemporary studies that distinguish it from two usually associated sentiments, namely, compassion and sympathy. In other words, empathy is not compassion because compassion, according to a synthetic and effective definition, is a sentiment that "arises in witnessing another's suffering and that motivates a subsequent desire to help";[75] therefore, compassion is an emotional response that is activated only in the presence of the other's suffering. Nor is empathy sympathy, understood in the current sense of the term, which implies a certain interest in the well-being of the other,[76] so much so that it is defined as a "feeling for (the other)" in order to distinguish it from empathy, which is rather a "feeling as (the other)."[77] We could say, then, that empathy is a source of morality—and of a prosocial behavior—when, through a reflective process that uses imagination, it corrects its automatisms and partialities and is a prelude to the birth of moral sentiments, which act as the truly ethically motivating forces.

What are, and which are, properly, moral sentiments? As Hume clearly claims, they tend toward the good of society and humanity or, to evoke Smith's even more radical terminology, they induce the human being to "interest him in the fortune of others, and render their happiness necessary to him." Briefly, they are virtuous and disinterested sentiments or, better, they are virtuous insofar as they are disinterested. Thus, they must be distinguished, as already mentioned, from the passions (or emotions) generally understood, which also include destructive, selfish, or at least ambivalent aspects. It is not by accident that the two contemporary authors who explicitly draw from the tradition of moral sentimentalism emphasize the disinterested feature of moral sentiments. For Martha Nussbaum, they are "ubiquitous in the lives of real people"[78] and testify to the fact that human beings not only act in view of mutual benefit but they also have "deep and motivationally powerful ties with others."[79] These sentiments lead us to evaluate the welfare of others as a constitutive part of our own welfare and, consequently, inspire actions, behaviors, and choices from which we do not gain anything. For Amartya Sen, it is a matter of motivations, such as commitment and sympathy, generosity and public spirit,[80] which do not directly tend toward the maximization of our self-interest, but rather go beyond the quest for our personal gain. Nonetheless, he strongly argues, they cannot be considered irrational as, on the contrary, they "may even be very productive for society."[81]

Briefly, moral sentiments represent the most eloquent manifestation of the fact that the paradigm of homo oeconomicus, on which modernity has built the anthropology of egoism and utilitarianism, is to be regarded at least as partial and unilateral. This does not mean falling prey, on the contrary, to the rhetoric of altruism. The latter can, in my view, be warded off through some important clarifications whose implications for the ethics of care and justice will be addressed later.

First, moral sentiments are not only the "positive" sentiments (including compassion, sympathy, and love), as claimed by the tradition of moral sentimentalism; rather, they can also include the passions that are traditionally considered "negative" or conflictual. One can simply think of *indignation* and *rage*, which, as Peter Sloterdijk reminds us, have often functioned as sources of inspiration for emancipatory social movements.[82] One can also think of *shame* insofar as it implies the will to self-correction on the side of the self so as not to incur the other's judgment;[83] or one can think of the *sense of guilt*, which psychology has always described as the potential source of moral conscience[84] (it is not by accident that guilt and shame have been defined as "self-conscious emotions" or, more precisely, as the voice of moral conscience).[85] One could even think of *fear* when it becomes *fear for*, such as fear for the other's destiny, as has been suggested by Hans Jonas in his proposal for an ethics of responsibility.[86]

Secondly, the very same sentiments that are considered "positive" are not exempt from problematic aspects, ambiguities, or excesses. Exemplary is the case of *compassion*, which has often been the target of criticism by philosophers (from Friedrich Nietzsche to Hannah Arendt)[87] who denounce complacency or hidden hypocrisy while opposing a pain-based ethics that needs the other's suffering for its own activation.[88] One could say the same of love, generosity, or gratitude, whose ambivalences and dark sides have always been highlighted by literature and psychoanalysis.

Thirdly, moral sentiments are not a natural and spontaneous given; rather, they are emotional structures steeped in history and in specific social and cultural contexts. What applies to all sentiments and passions is also true for moral sentiments: they are always subjected to transformations, regressions, and evolutionary processes insofar as they are linked, time and again, to specific worldviews. Briefly, as suggested by Freud's classical theory of drives, emotions and sentiments are characterized by elasticity, dynamics, and plasticity that make them open to change and correction. This means that we can educate them or, in Nussbaum's words, cultivate them.[89] Or, better, as I will try to argue later, we can take care of them, orienting them in an emancipatory direction capable of keeping in mind, together with our own well-being, what Hume calls "humanity's well-being," thereby contributing to the formation of a decent society.[90]

It is important to add, however, that not even moral sentiments suffice to access the ethical dimension. It is true that, unlike simple empathy, they produce the motivational push toward moral and prosocial action; nevertheless, they potentially imply the risk of stopping at pure feeling, without its transformation into concrete and effective action. In other words, we may feel a shared and suffering compassion when confronted with the consequences of a war or an ecological disaster on people, yet this does not automatically translate into an active mobilization in favor of the victims. We may feel lively sympathy for a friend who is having financial troubles, but no action of solidarity with such a person may ensue. We may feel indignation in front of the display of exploitation and humiliation, yet we do not necessarily decide personally to fight and resist such a situation.

In other words, the move to ethics requires an additional element that compels us to go beyond the proposals of moral sentimentalism; that is, it requires the element of action and engagement. The notion of engagement is, in some way, elusive; it has been often evoked, yet it has never been the object of systematic treatment. It has recently returned to the attention of some ambitious theoretical proposals that turn it into the core of the very constitution of the I or the new foundation of a theory of ethical subjectivity.[91] Here, though, I propose that we take it up in a more sober way in the sense of action, of concrete practice. This meaning of the term we can undoubtedly find, albeit without full identification, in some major twentieth-century thinkers such as Hannah Arendt, Simone Weil, or Jean-Paul Sartre.[92] To my mind, "engagement" alludes, in fact, not only to our ability to recognize the importance and priority of action but also to our ability to translate feeling into acting, to subject our emotions to a reality check, to risk oneself in and through action, and to attest to the consistency between our emotional life and our active life.

In this regard, the work of care theorists who share the vision of care as "practice" is significant.[93] Virginia Held, in particular, emphasizes this aspect, considering it one of the differences of care ethics as opposed to virtue ethics and the tradition of moral sentimentalism.[94] Despite their affinities, according to Held, the two ethical approaches differ on an essential point: whereas the former stops at the subject's motivations and character dispositions, the latter stresses relations and practices that develop within the relation of care. She concludes that "a caring person not only has the appropriate motivations in responding to others or in providing care but also participates adeptly in effective practices of care."[95] In short, the ethics of care is not content with ascertaining the presence of a virtuous motivation or a character disposed to moral action; rather, it is concerned with verifying its effectiveness through the activation of concrete engagement, because "caring is not only a question of motive or attitude or virtue" but rather, more precisely, a social practice geared toward attaining results.[96]

We will see how the insistence on this point is fundamental for delineating the notion of good care. Here, however, I would like to underscore that what holds true for care also holds true for justice, albeit in different forms. If it aims at attaining answers, the demand for justice cannot be limited to an emotional reaction (even when such a reaction is its irreplaceable motive) or to a passionate denunciation; rather, it must include engagement, which, in this case, is to be understood as struggle and willingness to engage in conflicts. Translating feeling into ability to act means fighting for justice, personally exposing oneself, putting oneself at risk through collective practices of solidarity.

Two

Care *versus* Justice or Care and Justice?

Toward a Reciprocal Integration

Turning to the theme of motivations, we ask: What is the precise role of emotions in grounding an ethics of justice and care? If it is true that both justice and care presuppose a capacity for empathy, which emotions motivate us to justice and which motivate us to care? If we can legitimately affirm that, on the ground of empathy/sympathy, we can cultivate alternative feelings that prelude to different ethical comportments, let us now show that the foregoing distinction allows, on the one hand, for the development of a different idea of justice and, on the other hand, for the restoration of the complexity of affective motivations that lie at the foundation of the ethics of care.

As mentioned earlier, the care model was introduced—largely by feminist thought—in close relation to the liberal paradigm of justice.[1] Carol Gilligan approaches the problem by reflecting on the criteria of moral choice, ultimately criticizing mainline developmental psychology (in particular, Kohlberg's theory)[2] for presenting a generalized model that, in fact, is based on the male subject: a model founded on abstract criteria of autonomy, impartiality, and the formal respect for rights. This move results in the devaluation of a different moral perspective, namely, the feminine, which is based, as Gilligan has shown through her empirical studies on young women, on concrete and contextual criteria[3] that safeguard the affective dimensions of relationships[4] and that are mindful of the specificity of singular situations.

In her revaluation of women's moral perspective, Gilligan demonstrates the insufficiency or, more precisely, the unilateralism, of the hegemonic paradigm of rights and justice that seeks to impose itself as the only and universal model of ethics. She proposes a twofold scheme that sees, on one hand, the (male) morality of rights and justice and, on the other hand, the (feminine) ethics of responsibility and care. Her goal is not—and we should reject this claim from the start—to theorize an opposition or, even less, a mutual exclusion; rather, she seeks to integrate two different approaches to morality that derive from two different ways of thinking. Gilligan warns against the opposite and mirroring risk that is intrinsic in each ethical perspective, namely, the risk of egocentrism that is particular to an ethics of justice and the risk of self-forgetfulness that is peculiar to the ethics of care.[5]

In other words, in no way does the ethics of care exclude the necessity of an ethics of justice, insofar as it presupposes that each ethics responds to problems and challenges that are different, yet unavoidable. However, the ethics of care enables us to adopt, as many care ethicists claim, a critical perspective on, and underscore the limitations of, the aforementioned model of justice that is still decisively dominant in contemporary social and political thought. Thus, it posits the premises for thinking, even at the global level, of a more efficient integration of the two ethical perspectives.

Starting from a theory of the emotions will enable us, as we shall see, to reach some conclusions relevant for rethinking not only the idea of care and justice but also the possible forms of their reciprocal relation. It will allow us, first, to think of an idea of justice different from the one that grounds the traditional rationalistic model, ultimately allowing us to distinguish between emancipatory claims and pathological instances, that is, between legitimate demands and illegitimate claims for justice.[6] Second, concerning care, a theory of emotions will enable us to remove care from an exclusively altruistic interpretation. For example, Virginia Held affirms that care is not to be understood as altruism; rather, it is a collaborative activity in which the interests of the caregiver and the receiver are seen as interdependent.[7] Here, the theory of emotions will also enable us to highlight possibly negative twists of care, such as domination by the other and resentment. Third, the theory of emotions will allow us to reaffirm, even though in their respective differences, the necessary complementarity of the two models of ethics.

If it is true, as Luc Boltanski claims with great clarity, that the social is constituted by different models of interactions and that different "regimes of action"[8] coexist in it, then we must understand what the demands are that each of these models responds to and how they intertwine to tackle, time and again, the new challenges faced by individuals. In terms of my own proposal, this means that, whereas responsibility responds to the necessity of taking charge of the future and solidarity must be mobilized to cope with the problem of the coexistence of differences, justice, understood essentially as social justice, calls for the introduction of the criterion of equity. This criterion is the more necessary today the more injustice and inequality grow and expand at the planetary level—a fundamental criterion that we must see as primary and as standing before all other criteria. It seems almost trivial to have to restate the inevitability, for a "decent society,"[9] of the presuppositions of any theory of justice, namely, equality of rights and of opportunities to access goods as well as the impartiality of ethical judgment.

As Gilligan and other philosophers of care show, including Joan Tronto, Virginia Held, Eva Kittay, and Martha Nussbaum,[10] the issue consists in showing the insufficiency of the justice paradigm when it presents itself as exclusive or paramount. In this case, its premises of equality, rationality, and independence end up obscuring and neglecting other premises equally necessary for achieving a more just world.

I think it is legitimate to summarize these other premises, beyond the differences among the various analyses and proposals, which we will see shortly, as consisting of two fundamental aspects: first, the dependence and vulnerability of human beings[11] and, second, the importance, in ethical choices, of the affective dimension. The limitations of traditional theories of justice consist in ignoring these aspects, which the care perspective assumes as indispensable values: the former, namely, dependence and vulnerability, as they emphasize what we could consider the ontological truth of the human, and the latter, namely, the affective dimension, as it underscores the problem of the motivations for action and the relevance of emotions even in ethical choices.

Even if not fully articulated, the foregoing issues are already present in Gilligan's work. The author of *In a Different Voice* maintains that women's moral perspective, which is oriented toward care, is not at all deficient when compared to men's view; rather, it is simply "different" as it is informed by a different image of the self; it also is a resource that allows us to bring forward a wider and more complete vision of moral development.[12]

It is, therefore, neither a question of challenging the legitimacy of the (male) criterion of equity nor of replacing it with (the female) one of responsibility; rather, the matter is to show the one-sidedness of the male one. Although Gilligan does not fully engage the paradigm of justice, limiting herself instead to a general definition, she does recognize its importance, even offering some reflections on its specific function in later works: "Since all relationships can be characterized both in terms of equality and in terms of attachment or connection, all relationships— public and private—can be seen in two ways and spoken of in two sets of terms. By adopting one or another moral voice or standpoint, people can highlight problems that are associated with different kinds of vulnerability—to oppression or to abandonment—and focus attention on different types of concern."[13] Whereas the ethics of justice is concerned with the problem of the defense of equality (against oppression and inequality), the ethics of care is concerned with the protection of relationships (against abandonment and the resulting damage to the person). In short, these are two different "regimes of action," to borrow once again Boltanski's words; yet, they both have equal dignity and effectiveness.

We entirely agree with the fact that the emphasis of feminist thought falls necessarily on the second, that is, the dimension of relationships, as it is a dimension that is completely devalued by, if not entirely removed from, Western and modern thought. The issue is then to compensate for the procedural abstractness of the ethics of justice, guided by a criterion of pure respect for the rights of others, of formal adherence to principles, and of noninterference, by highlighting the concreteness of the ethics of care, supported by emotional involvement, attention to the single case, and concern for the consequences that a choice can have on the network of relationships.

Gilligan seems clearly to propose here the complementarity of the two moral visions, so much so that she claims that, for both sexes, moral development ought to entail the integration of rights and responsibilities.[14] Thus, she raises a problem that lies at the center of later reflections on care and social justice already mentioned above. On the forms and modalities of this integration, however, Gilligan's proposal appears unsatisfactory, not because it is limited to its exquisitely psychological focus without addressing the problem of its translatability on a social level; rather, because the care perspective remains confined to the restricted dimension of private life.

On this point, the most convincing criticism is undoubtedly that by Joan Tronto, who maintains that Gilligan's proposal ends up reconfirming those "moral boundaries" in which the care perspective has traditionally been confined.[15] Therefore, it is not only necessary to liberate care from an identification with feminine morality, which, to be fair, Gilligan does not fail to suggest, but it is also necessary to blur the lines between private and public, endowing care with a unique political value that enhances its effectiveness. Extending care to the public sphere is tantamount to recognizing it as a universal aspect of human life, removing it from its secular marginalization and devaluation. The merit of Tronto's work also consists in explaining the reasons for this devaluation. These reasons reside in the fear on the part of the modern subject—built on the values of autonomy and rationality—of recognizing the importance of emotions and needs and of admitting its own constitutive dependency. First, care is devalued, says Tronto, "conceptually through a connection with privacy, with emotion, and with the needy. Since our society treats public accomplishment, rationality, and autonomy as worthy qualities, care is devalued insofar as it embodies their opposites. . . . [Second,] caring is by its very nature a challenge to the notion that individuals are entirely autonomous and self-supporting. To be in a situation where one needs care is to be in a position of some vulnerability."[16] Here emerge clearly those foundations of the ethics of care that I propose to sum up in the recognition of the importance of the emotional dimension and human vulnerability. Tronto warns us of a danger that lies in the first aforementioned aspect: the connection with emotions harbors the risk of reducing care to a purely sentimental disposition, unless one views care as a "practice" that is effective and operative on the social and political level.[17] But this is precisely the crucial issue whose different perspectives we will examine later. What I wish to underscore here is an important insight of Tronto's that, with respect to Gilligan, allows us to clarify more precisely the link between care and justice by highlighting the specific configuration of their respective roles. The division between the two ethics, Tronto affirms, is contrived in that each moral theory is "better able to address some moral questions than others," primarily because "[d]ifferent questions will seem more pressing at some times and in some circumstances than at other times."[18] In other words, verifying the adequacy of a moral theory requires its contextualization, pondering which specific problems, challenges, and urgencies it is able to address time and again. This means that, although the role of the theory of justice is always essential as a bulwark for the defense of autonomy and equality and as the guarantee of democratic speech, its universalistic version of Kantian descent, which finds its historical

origin in the late eighteenth century, currently reveals its limitations as
"[i]t maintains that our moral principles can be established and defended
regardless of context."[19] With clear reference to the theories of Rawls
and Habermas, on which it is no coincidence that Kohlberg's model
had a significant influence,[20] and without going into the details of the
argument, Tronto criticizes the abstractness of assumptions that renders
such theories inadequate to face the complexity of the present. In her
hints to the epochal transformations that are taking place, including
the global extension of capitalism, the collapse of the colonial system,
the end of the separation between the domestic and economic spheres,
and the emergence of a society that is more and more diverse, Tronto
essentially emphasizes the issue of alterity and differences as a central
moral problem. And, from it, she infers the need for a different ethical
approach grounded on the awareness that human beings are not only
autonomous and equal but also dependent, interdependent, and in need
of care. In short, "[t]he twentieth century has made the importance of
care more visible and public,"[21] has disclosed the limits of a universalist
morality as too "relentlessly abstract" to address "many of the originating
sources of injustice,"[22] and has made urgent the integration of a moral
perspective that is up to date, concrete, and contextual, as is the case
with the ethics of care.

In full agreement with Tronto's observations, I believe this urgency
becomes even more evident in the face of the unprecedented challenges
of the global age (from climate change to nuclear risk that threaten the
very life of the planet and of future generations, from mass migration to
planetary conflicts, from the depletion of resources to increasing poverty and inequality), which demand that we avoid sterile metaethical
arguments and, rather, measure ethics against the destinies of the world.

A further conceptualization of the care-justice nexus, which introduces a broader and more systematic definition of both terms and which
also pays attention to the global dimension, is proposed by Virginia Held.
In *The Ethics of Care*,[23] Held reiterates the two fundamental aspects
that characterize the ethics of care, namely, the recognition of human
beings' constitutive dependency and the valorization of emotions. She
clarifies the presuppositions of the ethics of care through a directly critical confrontation with the foundations of the liberal tradition. At the
base of the dominant moral theories of this tradition, especially those of
Kantian descent, we find the idea of an independent and self-sufficient
individual that is driven by selfish passions; to such passions, one must

necessarily respond with rational, universalistic, and abstract moral rules that neutralize conflict while restoring impartiality. Care ethics, on the contrary, which Held is concerned to characterize as a feminist ethics to protect it from the danger of reproposing a devalued image of women,[24] radically disputes this view of the individual and morality. It opposes it, first, with the relational vision of the person as involved in a set of bonds that constitutively determine the person's actions and choices and, second, with a different evaluation of the nature and role of emotions. Against the hegemony of liberal individualism, it is necessary to recognize the constitutive dependence and interdependence of individuals as well as the fact that they are motivated not only by self-interest and selfish passions but also by "moral emotions" (from empathy to sensitivity/receptivity/responsiveness) that can play an essential positive role in the care of the other.[25] Without entering into a discussion of specific emotions, Held emphasizes their importance for care ethics, and she briefly suggests a possible expansion of the ethics of care in correspondence with the expansion of the figure of the other within the global context. The other, she specifies against any temptation to reduce care to a matter of private care, is currently not exhausted by the figure of the neighbor and the family; rather, in a world that is increasingly interdependent, it extends to the distant other, to the whole society, to the environment.[26] All this does not mean denying the role of theories of justice that are based on the liberal assumptions of impartiality and equal rights. Yet, in line with the positions of Gilligan and Tronto, it means criticizing their rationalistic assumptions (shared by Kantian ethics, including its Rawlsian formulation, and by utilitarian moral theories)[27] and dethroning them from their position as the only possible moral theories. This same position is shared by Annette Baier who, in her article "The Need for More than Justice,"[28] specifies with great clarity, from a Humean perspective, that the matter is not rejecting the relevance of justice for morality; rather, what we need to reject is the peculiar claim of liberalism and the Kantian tradition of making justice the exclusive foundation of morality.

Here too, the goal is to wish for and promote the integration of the two perspectives. Held pauses, however, to consider more deeply the forms of this integration, underscoring its problematic nature. One must not conceive of the two ethics as possible alternative responses to the same moral dilemma, as Gilligan actually proposes, for this does not clarify *why* we should choose one answer over another in the same circumstances.[29] And it is not even a question, as some propose, of reducing justice to care, making the latter the exclusive or dominant moral concept.[30]

The ethics of care cannot do without the respect for rights. It is no coincidence that many voices of feminist thought have reiterated the importance of the legal dimension and the defense of rights, for example, the rights of the minorities, or of women against sexual harassment, abuses, and domestic violence or in favor of reproductive freedom.[31] Rights guarantee a series of indispensable conditions for the conquest, by women and other socially marginalized subjects, of a statute of equality and freedom protected by law. However, although necessary for certain objectives and contexts, the rights approach reveals itself as unsuitable in other contexts in which it is more a matter of protecting relationships, satisfying needs, and acting in solidarity: "Whereas justice protects equality and freedom, care fosters social bonds and cooperation."[32]

Held then proposes an integration of rights and care that also maintains the differences between the two approaches: "In the dominant moral theories of the ethics of justice, the values of equality, impartiality, fair distribution, and noninterference have priority; in practices of justice, individual rights are protected, impartial judgments are arrived at, punishments are deserved, and equal treatment is sought. In contrast, in the ethics of care, the values of trust, solidarity, mutual concern, and empathetic responsiveness have priority; in practices of care, relationships are cultivated, needs are responded to, and sensitivity is demonstrated."[33] Of course, the aforementioned task is still to be achieved and it requires the ability to think and create new images that avoid any form of reductionism.[34] A clear definition of the differences between the two models of ethics serves to outline priority areas for each paradigm while also remaining open to each other's enriching contributions. In the legal and political spheres, for example, justice should have priority when guaranteeing rights even in the presence of considerations of care. Conversely, for example, in the sphere of the family, priority should be given to care, even though principles of justice relating to the protection of the autonomy of individual family members remain necessary.[35]

It is therefore necessary to reject all visions that oppose the two ethical perspectives, especially avoiding the reduction of the former to the public sphere and the latter to the private one:

> Justice is badly needed in the family as well as in the state: in
> a more equitable division of labor between women and men in

the household, in the protection of vulnerable family members from domestic violence and abuse, in recognizing the rights of family members to respect for their individuality. . . . At the same time, we can see that care is badly needed in the public domain. . . . Care is needed by everyone when they are children, ill, or very old, and it is needed by some most of their lives. Assuring that care is available to those who need it should be a central political concern, not one imagined to be a solely private responsibility of families and charities.[36]

Even though reciprocal integration is proposed, Held maintains that care is the base moral value, a "wider moral framework"[37] that secures the protection of the social fabric and guarantees relationships of trust and community attention to the others and their needs—relations within which the value of autonomy can be itself more effectively promoted and sustained. This claim, Held argues, holds also for the international sphere. Here, it is not sufficient to posit a fair distribution of resources as the end goal, as do many Rawlsian-inspired theories of justice, from Charles Beitz to Thomas Pogge;[38] rather, it is necessary to promote social relations and cooperation understood in a fuller sense than in Rawls's perspective. This can be done both through a positive involvement in the life of those who are distant from our own lives[39] and through attention to ever-expanding social, ethnic, and cultural differences, which create situations of domination and conflict. With its attention to relationships and contexts, its sensitivity toward the particularities of the other, its valuing of moral emotions like empathy, sensibility, and trust, and, above all, with its fundamental presupposition of reciprocal interdependence, the ethics of care appears more capable of dealing with the challenges of a global society. It also seems potentially compatible with certain contemporary tendencies in which we can see the seeds of a "global civic society,"[40] for example, the growing influence of nongovernmental organizations, civic and volunteer associations, the development of transnational social movements that promote "globalization from below," and more recent global movements like Fridays for Future.

We could therefore reiterate, as I have already suggested, that what is being proposed more and more clearly, from Gilligan to Held, is a kind of division of labor between care and justice, as both are equally indispensable for the balance of society and the self-realization of individuals, but each has its own specific tasks and functions. Integration consists in being able to discern the challenges and priorities that emerge in the social sphere now and again, and to understand which of the two ethics allows us to put forward the best suitable response, and to which problems. Through affective criteria and the awareness of the frailty of humans, care will act as a perspective necessary for social cohesion, the protection of relationships, and attention to others in their multiple figurations. Justice will take care of guaranteeing, through objective and rational criteria, the protection of rights, access to citizenship, and equity in resource distribution.

Another Idea of Justice

I believe that the foregoing proposal is largely acceptable, not only because it strongly affirms the pressing importance of a removed or, at least, marginalized value, namely, care,[41] but also because it refuses all binary perspectives by reaffirming the importance of the value of justice. Yet justice must be dethroned from its dominant and exclusive position, and one must disclose its insufficiency in areas and contexts that require more adequate responses.

This division of labor, however, ends up obscuring an aspect that, in my view, is fundamental both for the definition of justice tout court and for thinking differently about it, especially with respect to the image consolidated by dominant theories. I refer here to the possibility of thinking of a concept of justice that critically reconsiders its image as a purely abstract, rational, and formal ideal and includes, within it, the presence of an emotive element. In other words, is it legitimate to hypothesize a connection between justice and emotions, without considering emotions as exclusively belonging to the ethics of care? And, if the answer is affirmative, what are the passions of justice?[42]

We find a first response to the foregoing questions in Martha Nussbaum's *Frontiers of Justice: Disability, Nationality, Species Membership*.[43] In her discussion of Rawls, she emphasizes the need to highlight the affective dimension of justice. Nussbaum's description of justice is clearer than those of Gilligan and Held, and it allows us to focus further on its insufficiencies. Let us briefly examine the arguments given by Nussbaum to highlight the importance of the affective dimension as a motivation to justice.

While recognizing the indisputable validity of the Rawlsian and, in general, of the liberal model, Nussbaum proposes its necessary correction and integration in light of a confrontation with what she considers the current problems left unresolved by the principles that ground that very model. Three seemingly very different problems emerge: the treatment we owe to the disabled; fairness toward all the inhabitants of the planet, regardless of their national affiliation; and the defense of the dignity of animals. These problems share an essential aspect concerning the asymmetries of power and the different capacities of living beings and the need to take charge of this.

The liberal and contractualist model is unable to provide satisfactory solutions to these problems insofar as justice here is viewed solely as the outcome of a contract among free, equal, and independent people that is mutually beneficial to all parties. Nussbaum develops her critique of these assumptions, inspired by a strong rationalism, by starting from her well-known position framed within a capabilities model.[44] She defines capability as "what people are actually able to do and to be—in a way informed by an intuitive idea of a life that is worthy of the dignity of the human being."[45] Far beyond the Rawlsian model, the capabilities approach allows for a minimal denominator of basic respect for human dignity. Therefore, in relation to the first presupposition of contract theory, namely, the vision of individuals as free, equal, and independent, Nussbaum's capabilities approach, which presupposes the liberal theory of rights while amplifying it, obviously does not intend to put into question the universal rights of freedom and equality. Rather, she argues for the need to recognize *also* the reality of dependence and need. This requires that those who find themselves in this position be included in the concerns that found the principles of justice so that they may be guaranteed the dignity and flourishing that are the inalienable right of any living being.

On this point, one finds an indisputable agreement with care theorists. Among them, Nussbaum seems to privilege, as is also apparent from other texts, Eva Kittay's reflections, which allow Nussabum to deal with the first of the three unsolved problems mentioned above. In *Love's Labor: Essays on Women, Equality and Dependency*, Kittay forcefully criticizes the contractualist theory of justice up to Rawls. As it is founded on the premise of the self-sufficiency and equality of people, according to Kittay, this theory omits a fundamental aspect of the human experience, which consists precisely in relationships of dependence. Thus, it ends up endorsing an elusive concept of equality that excludes significant parts of our lives and broad strata of the population.[46] Starting from emblematic situations of extreme dependence (such as disability, both physical and mental), Kittay emphasizes the unavoidability of the condition of need and vulnerability in order to unmask the "fiction" of our independence and, instead, valorize our interdependence.[47] This implies recognizing the necessity of care, understood in its dual aspect of need and performance. In other words, this means restoring dignity not only to those in need of care but also to those who take care (the dependency workers). And this, says Kittay, is precisely a matter of justice: "How a social order organizes care of these needs is a matter of social justice."[48]

Reaffirming the relational vision of the human being of Aristotelian-Marxian matrix, which is foundational for the capabilities approach, Nussbaum claims to share the foregoing position, both the importance of the recognition of dependence and the need to valorize care, which must be introduced into the Rawlsian list of primary goods. She insists that primary goods cannot be limited solely to material resources (income and wealth) but include precisely the attention to the fabric of reciprocal relations without which there can be no personal dignity. There is no need, she specifies, to renounce liberal theory, as Kittay's radical critique seems to suggest; it is sufficient, says Nussbaum, to propose integrations aimed precisely at expanding the presuppositions of the theory of justice while drawing a richer picture of social cooperation.

This is the direction that also orients the criticism of the second presupposition of the contractualist model, namely, the critique of the idea that the goal of the contract and cooperation among individuals is the mutual benefit of the involved parties.[49] This point is particularly relevant as it addresses what, in my view, is most important, namely, the problem of the *motivations* that lead individuals to search for justice. Nussbaum's criticism here is even more severe and decisive, for it tends to strike at the crucial premise of social contract theories, namely, the assumption that the sole motivation is the pursuit of personal interest and mutual advantages. This assumption is contested both on the factual and theoretical levels. On the factual level, it is not true that we always benefit from cooperation because, in the case of the three unsolved problems (disability, poverty, and dignity of animals), one could claim that there is nothing to be gained, in terms of material resources, from caring for people with disabilities and from fair treatment of nonhuman animals or the world's poor. On the theoretical level, the theory of mutual benefit excludes or obscures another type of motivations, which we can intuitively grasp on the base of the presupposition of human beings' sociability and which consists in the universal existence of moral feelings in the life of real people.[50]

The contractualist tradition (with the exception of Rousseau) is largely skeptical of moral or benevolent sentiments, as they are deemed ineffective or insufficient for the purposes of fostering cooperation and guaranteeing the stability of political society. This tradition emphasizes the presence of selfish feelings "without assuming that human beings have deep and motivationally powerful ties to others."[51] It is true, adds Nussbaum, that Rawls's position is more complex, not only because the presence of moral feelings is, in fact, implicit in the impartiality of the "veil of ignorance," but also because he maintains that a well-ordered society has to pay attention to the education of people with respect to these sentiments in order to ensure the stability of the principles of justice.[52] However, the capabilities approach presupposes something more: starting from the idea of sociability, it includes moral sentiments "right from the start," viewing them as capable of pushing people to conceive of shared ends as being a constituent part of the goals of individuals. Starting from the premise that a fundamental aspect of a dignified existence is a shared life respectful of equal dignity, the capabilities approach is, therefore "very demanding" of people, for it asks them to activate and cultivate those feelings that are omnipresent "in the life of real people."[53]

We will see later how Nussbaum assigns a privileged role to compassion among all moral sentiments, so much so that she visibly inserts it in the list of capabilities without which there is no chance of a life with dignity, as compassion implies valuing the others' good as part of one's own. I wish to emphasize here what I have premised at the beginning of this chapter, that is, the recognition by Nussbaum of an affective dimension of justice, which individuals pursue as a value in itself on the ground of the deep bonds tying them to one another and the desire to live in a decent society that safeguards their dignity: "Justice is about justice, and justice is one thing that human beings love and pursue."[54]

This is even truer at the global level. Nussbaum appreciates the proposals of Rawls-inspired contractualists such as Charles R. Beitz and Thomas W. Pogge, which are founded on the lengthening of the list of human rights and on the consideration of all human beings as morally equal. Nevertheless, she points out their limitations in detail, concluding that mutual benefit is not sufficient to explain international cooperation, if only for the fact that the agreements we must make to ensure justice for developing countries can be very onerous: "We live in a world in which it is simply not true that cooperating with others on fair terms will be advantageous to all. Giving all human beings the basic opportunities on which we have focused will surely require sacrifice from richer individuals and nations."[55] We must therefore adopt a broader vision of human cooperation that includes the capability of individuals and peoples endowed with better living conditions to accept the sacrifice necessary to help those who are most disadvantaged. This is possible, we can conclude, only if we recognize that there is a love of justice that is supported by the idea of sociability and the existence of moral feelings:

> If our world is to be a decent world in the future, we must acknowledge right now that we are citizens of one interdependent world, held together by mutual fellowship as well as the pursuit of mutual advantage, by compassion as well as by self-interest, by a love of human dignity in all people, even when there is nothing we have to gain from cooperating with them. Or rather, even when what we have to gain is the biggest thing of all: participation in a just and morally decent world.[56]

Nussbaum's merit consists not only in having proposed the integration of justice and care, but also in having enriched the paradigm of justice with an affective component, removing it from the abstraction of a purely rationalistic and formal ideal. Her view, however, opens up two problems, namely, the role of care and the nature or quality of the feelings that are the foundation of justice.

With respect to the first problem, in my opinion, the question lies in the fact that, in comparison with earlier theories of care, in Nussbaum care loses any autonomous status, becoming a sort of appendix, albeit important and desirable, of justice. Furthermore, care remains limited to extreme situations (disability), and it is clearly not elevated to a universal value. It is true that here Nussbaum adopts Kittay's proposal as her own, but Kittay also specifies that the choice to focus on situations of extreme dependence aims to underscore, in an exemplary way, the constitutive condition of interdependence that characterizes the human condition.[57] This means that we take up dependence and interdependence as universal dimensions that affect us all insofar as "we are all—equally—some mother's child," as Kittay eloquently puts it.[58] The source of everyone's right to equality resides precisely in recognizing oneself as "a mother's child," that is to say, in recognizing our own mutual dependence, Kittay specifies in contrast to liberal theories: "And herein lies a claim of equality, one that is an alternative to conceptions which dominate the discourse in liberal political theory."[59]

While Kittay seems to consider care as an ontological dimension of the human, Nussbaum, though emphasizing the need to inscribe it in the Rawlsian list of primary goods, seems to limit it to specific needs and to certain periods of life. Furthermore, it is not even entirely clear whether care must be fully included in the list of core human capabilities, because although it may be implicitly contained in the capability of "belonging" or in having feelings for and attachment to people, it is not actually explicitly named.[60] Care remains an appendage of justice that liberal theories must integrate into their accounts to respond to the specific problem constituted by physical and mental disability and thereby extend the notion of dignity. I shall return to this point later, but I wish to affirm here, in line with care theorists, the necessity of recognizing the autonomy and universality of care as that which is to be applied to circumstances not limited to extreme dependency situations.

A position that contrasts with and mirrors Nussbaum's view insofar as it includes justice in the ethics of care is that of Michael Slote.[61] Slote, who is an important figure in the tradition of moral sentimentalism, regards empathy, which, he points out, Hume calls sympathy, as the source of moral actions.[62] If we adopt a broad care ethics perspective, Slote maintains, criticizing, in part, both Gilligan's and Held's approaches, we can say that justice itself is grounded not only on rational foundations (autonomy, rights) but also on sentiment and empathy. In other words, empathy grounds not only our morally good deeds but also the formation of moral judgments, for it prompts us to think that "we should" be concerned about the suffering of the other. Slote's position is partly acceptable, in my view, as he restores, albeit fleetingly, an affective foundation to justice. Yet he ends up entirely incorporating justice within the dimension of care, thereby forfeiting the possibility of distinguishing between the two moral perspectives and of recognizing their autonomous value within the context of a reciprocal division of labor.

Three

The Passions of Justice

Not Only Compassion

Empathy and Compassion

Let us address the second problem, which, as I mentioned earlier, concerns the nature and quality of the sentiments motivating us toward justice. As we have seen, Nussbaum presupposes a love for justice that originates from moral sentiments, which are activated thanks to human sociability when we witness a violation of the person's dignity, the loss of their abilities, and/or the infringement of their rights. In other words, when we are confronted with situations of injustice that humiliate individuals, we are capable of feeling benevolence and compassion as we understand their well-being to be a constitutive part of our own well-being and ends, namely, living in a decent society, respectful of the dignity of all.

Nussbaum especially highlights compassion (which she prefers over the term pity) as the moral sentiment par excellence that leads to the demand for justice. She does so while reiterating some of the fundamental characteristics of compassion that she had already highlighted, within the context of her cognitive-evaluative conception of emotions, in *Upheaval of Thought*. Here, compassion is defined as "a painful emotion occasioned by the awareness of another person's undeserved misfortune" and is included in those emotions (such as love) that, unlike others (such as disgust and shame), have the ability to "expand the Self" to such a point that compassion is explicitly mentioned in the list of human capabilities.[1]

39

Drawing accurate terminological distinctions, Nussbaum asserts the equivalence of sympathy and compassion insofar as sympathy entails the judgment that the other person's distress is bad. She takes great care to distinguish, instead, compassion from empathy. Even though empathy is a mental ability that is important for compassion—insofar as it promotes the expansion of the Self—empathy is nevertheless morally neutral as it is "an imaginative reconstruction of another person's experience."[2] This means that we can be empathic indifferently, toward joyful as well as sad experience, or that we can have great understanding for someone who is suffering without feeling any real compassion.[3]

For there to be compassion, one must certainly presuppose that, on the observer's side, there be three fundamental, cognitive requisites: a judgment of *seriousness* regarding the other's suffering and misfortune; the evaluation of the *undeserved* nature of such suffering; and, above all, what Nussbaum defines as *the eudaimonistic judgment*, which we already mentioned earlier. According to this criterion, the observer is at a distance from the other as the observer is aware of the distinction between his, her, or their own life and the life of the sufferer; nevertheless, the observer recognizes the sufferer as an important part in the ensemble of his, her, or their own interests and goals. That is, as part of his, her, or their own "circle of concern."[4] This implies, in turn, the recognition of shared vulnerability and neediness,[5] which is where the strongest antidote to pathological narcissism lies—narcissism being one of the most serious obstacles to compassion and the realization of a good society.[6] "In short, implicit [in compassion] is a conception of human flourishing and the major predicament of human life, the best one the onlooker is able to form."[7]

Nussbaum's conclusion is that, for this reason, even in a just society, we need compassion, as this emotion is capable of sustaining and stabilizing the principles of justice. The best outcome we can expect and to which we must commit is reciprocal interaction insofar as individuals capable of compassion establish just institutions and, vice versa, just institutions favor and teach compassion.[8]

Despite these lines of thought, Nussbaum is perfectly aware of the controversial character of compassion and the devaluation that has often affected it, from the Stoics to Nietzsche. She herself notices its limits, which lie in the danger that this passion stops at the pure complacency on the part of the observer, without transformation into real and concrete engagement.[9]

Let us dwell then, albeit briefly, on the limits of compassion, which are highlighted by a substantial list of authors. We can start with the disenchanted analysis by Bernard Mandeville at the onset of modernity. Mandeville considers compassion, understood as "a fellow-feeling and condolence for the misfortunes and calamities of others,"[10] as nothing else than the egoistic desire to free oneself of the sense of uneasiness that comes from the vision of suffering. Hypocritically, though, this desire masks itself as a pure and disinterested sentiment and is mistaken for the virtue of charity. We can also evoke the equally severe criticism of Nietzsche who, against Schopenhauer, wishes for the absence of compassion, because, as participation in the other's suffering, compassion disempowers us, thereby harming our ability to adhere to life.[11] We can also draw attention to Simone Weil, who, even though she praises compassion as a divine sentiment, nevertheless is careful to distinguish it from *pity*,[12] as pity always implies a fusional and asymmetric relation that may create, in the one who receives it, feelings of bitterness or even hatred.[13] It is worthwhile to dwell, though, on the particularly meaningful critical diagnosis proposed by Hannah Arendt in *On Revolution*.[14]

In truth, Arendt is not opposed to this passion, which she credits with the ability to induce an understanding of the other and a sense of potentially universal community among human beings in their nakedness and the animal "givenness" of their existences. So long as compassion remains silent and circumscribed to a prepolitical space, its inability to introduce a distance between self and other is compensated by its ability to address the singularity of the other. The problem emerges, however, when compassion claims to enter the public sphere and becomes (as it happened during the French Revolution) a *politics of pity*, which is responsible for the sentimentalist drift that is most alien to the public and worldly dimension for at least two fundamental reasons: even though it reintroduces distance, the sentiment of pity is insensitive to differences, transforming the other, its recipient, into an indistinct and faceless ensemble (the unhappy one, the people); furthermore, pity risks paradoxically glorifying the very suffering it aims to abolish. Arendt writes, "Without the presence of misfortune, pity could not exist, and it therefore has just as much vested interest in the existence of the unhappy as thirst for power has a vested interest in the existence of the weak. Moreover, by virtue of being a sentiment, pity can be enjoyed for its own sake, and this will almost automatically lead to a glorification of its cause, which is the suffering of others."[15] In short, pity needs the suffering of the other to be activated and manifest itself. For this reason, Arendt contrasts it with solidarity, which is not a sentiment, but rather "a principle that can inspire and guide action." Solidarity needs no unhappy individuals to transform itself into engagement and political praxis; it possesses an ability to generalize that enables it to understand the whole of humankind: "It is out of pity that men are 'attracted toward *les hommes faibles*,' but it is out of solidarity that they establish deliberately and, as it were, dispassionately, a community of interest with the oppressed and exploited."[16] Arendt's criticism is acceptable, to my mind, as it highlights a decisive aspect pertaining to the limits of compassion (or, better, of pity), namely, its being tied to the very existence of suffering. It becomes less convincing, however, when it yields to a generalized suspiciousness toward passions and sentiments, and to the negation of any possible role that they may play within the public sphere. As I will argue later, we must undoubtedly subject emotions to critical scrutiny capable of differentiating between emancipatory and destructive, pathological and simply ineffective aspects. Yet, this does not amount to denying a priori their social and political value.

In this sense, Nussbaum's approach is more convincing than Arendt's. Nussbaum proposes an "education to compassion" and suggests to use all available tools (from institutional to media-based) to stimulate, in the most adequate manner, the capability to imagine and empathize that is foundational to compassion.[17] This invitation to think of "compassion within the limits or reason,"[18] however, presupposes, unlike in Arendt, the recognition of the important emotive contribution that compassion brings to morality and public life insofar as it "supplies an essential life and connectedness to morality, without which it is dangerously empty and rootless."[19] In short, Nussbaum seems to identify compassion as a fundamental dimension that fills in, in one case from the inside and in the other from the outside, the insufficiencies of the paradigm of justice through the integration of the emotive factor.[20] In turn, a revaluation of compassion seems to be especially pressing, as we shall see, as we face the unprecedented challenges of the global age and the contradictions it produces.[21]

At this point, even without sharing Arendt's suspiciousness of compassion, we may legitimately ask, as Susan Sontag suggests, whether this passion *alone* ought to be the emotive answer to situations of suffering, given that one of its intrinsic limitations is that it exonerates us from engagement.[22] What, in other words, I would like to suggest is that, especially when it seems clear that the suffering, misery, and unhappiness being witnessed are due to injustice, one could think of mobilizing other and different passions; among them, as a meaningful example, one could have the "thymotic passions," on which Peter Sloterdijk recently directed our attention.[23] One could think, that is, of the insurgence of a right indignation in the face of intolerable situations.

I will return soon to the distinctions among the passions of justice or, better, the passions that inspire a demand for justice. What is certain, though, is that, when we start from the passions, we advance an approach to justice that is different from the contractualist or Rawlsian approaches and we recognize the *perception of injustice* as the foundational motivation, the emotive spark, as it were, from which the demand for justice emerges.

The Sentiment of Injustice

The invitation to start with concrete reality and situations of injustice rather than with the definition of an ideal model of justice comes, above all, from Amartya Sen's *The Idea of Justice.*[24] Critical of the tradition that he defines as "transcendental institutionalism" (and which includes Rawls), Sen proposes, in the concluding pages of the book, to proceed by "focusing questions of justice, first, on assessments of social realizations, that is, on what actually happens (rather than merely on the appraisal of institutions and arrangements); and second, on comparative issues of enhancement of justice (rather than trying to identify perfectly just arrangements)."[25] Distancing himself, like Nussbaum, from the contractualist tradition while valuing that line of European Enlightenment inaugurated by Adam Smith, Sen thinks it necessary to pay attention not only to the possibility of producing just institutions but also to individuals' actual behavior. This ought to be done within a comparative viewpoint that, even while respecting the criterion of impartiality, takes into account the possible plurality of reasons and choices. Sen acknowledges Rawls's merits without hesitations.[26] Yet, Rawls's limitation lies in theorizing a single system of justice geared toward building, according to the presuppositions of transcendentalism, a model of perfect justice that is universally valid. According to Sen, however, the perfect solution is not sufficient on the grounds of social choice theory,[27] as there can be different evaluations as to what constitutes justice that are nevertheless rational and legitimate. Nor is the perfect solution necessary as even an incomplete and partial arrangement may prove to be useful and coherent in the absence of a perfect agreement among individuals' preferences.

We must then start from actual reality and admit the possibility of partial and imperfect solutions that are to be periodically explored, thereby abandoning claims to completeness and the logic of "either all or nothing"[28] while aiming at a justice founded on concrete and effective achievements.[29] We must ask not how we can obtain perfect justice and just institutions that cohere with abstract principles, but how we can concretely realize "*more* just societies."

The merit of this theoretical perspective is the adoption, unlike ideal theories of justice, of a more realistic and pragmatic approach that pays attention, first, to recognizing and confronting the injustices that exist here and now rather than identifying them on the basis of an abstract model of a perfectly just society. This perspective seems capable of supporting the attention to subjective motivations that I am proposing, which consists in acknowledging a cognitively and emotively active function to moral sentiments. Whereas, in ideal theories, sentiments of justice are configured as the outcome of the subjects' affective conforming to a model of a perfectly just society, the approach I propose aims to seriously consider the sentiments of injustice that are widespread in societies that are not yet, and will never be, wholly just. Together with the motivations for justice, we must seek contextually, even in unjust societies, the criteria that rectify situations of injustice while deciding which choices may be "less unjust" than others.[30]

The theory of justice must therefore start from injustice. According to Sen, this is what actually happens when we question the motivations that urge people to demand justice. "What moves us, reasonably enough, is not the realization that the world falls short of being completely just—which few of us expect—but that there are clearly remediable injustices around us which we want to eliminate."[31] What motivates us is the *perception* of injustice, whether it concerns us personally or others, whether they be more or less close to us. What motivates us is the fact of either personally experiencing, in the first-person, or witnessing manifest and concrete situations of prevarication and humiliation that strike us and make us want to eliminate them.

The function of *sentiments* and the emotive dimension become relevant here.[32] No one, not even the supporters of a transcendental theory of justice, can deny that, as human beings, we are joined together by a general aspiration to justice, for justice is rooted in our sympathetic nature, in our sensitivity to others' suffering, in the love for freedom and the interest in "goodness, rightness, and justness." Beyond the different answers each theory gives, none can deny that the demand for justice has to do with "the feelings, concerns and mental abilities that we share as human beings."[33] By questioning the hegemonic model of homo oeconomicus, Sen espouses Adam Smith's intuition that we are motivated not only by personal interest and self-love. Against the popular opinion that brings together the positions of traditional economic thought, we must recognize that human action has a plurality of motives; that self-love is simply one of these and may be contrasted with other sentiments that attest to the nature of the human being as a social animal; namely, sentiments such as humanity, goodness, generosity, and civic duty. Briefly, one can act in a socially correct way not only, as the theory of rational choice claims, because one is motivated by the quest for one's own interest and mutual benefit by limiting one's selfish claims, but also because one is capable of disinterested sentiments that stem from an empathic relationship with others.[34]

Thus, we must take seriously the role that emotions and sentiments play in the quest for justice, both because they are the expression and the manifest symptoms of situations of injustice and because they contain the initial spark, the first and concrete motive that "inflame[s] the minds"[35] and urges us to change the existent, to engage in remedying intolerable situations even though there is no claim to a perfectly just society. It may be a matter of compassion and solidarity or even, simply, of an "instinctive revulsion to cruelty";[36] and it may be the case of true and real thymotic passions, such as indignation and wrath generated by suffering and humiliation, whether one's own or of the other.[37]

We will see shortly how these passions, fleetingly referenced by Sen, can be relevant in the rebellion against injustice. What I would like to emphasize here is that Sen does not distinguish between the sentiments of those who witness injustice from the outside and those who undergo it personally;[38] he rather seems more sensitive to the former case insofar as he is interested in highlighting the presence of disinterested sentiments.[39]

Even when one starts properly from the direct victims of injustice, from the fight for the defense of one's rights and the recognition of one's dignity, the "sentiment" of injustice seems to imply an emancipatory and normative potential capable of involving and transforming the entire social structure. The reflection advanced by Emmanuel Renault through the notion of the *experience of injustice* is based on similar premises.[40] Even before Nussbaum and Sen, Renault promotes a critical approach to the abstraction and formalism of certain theories of justice (Rawls and Habermas)[41] as well as to the need for elaborating a *negative* theory of justice that takes seriously forms of injustice.[42] In this perspective, he inscribes his proposal within the *theory of recognition* formulated by Axel Honneth,[43] which enables him to provide a general overview of *all* forms of injustice—which cannot be limited, as in Rawls's perspective, to the unfair distribution of resources—concretely experienced by actors in the first person.[44] Following Honneth, Renault defines recognition as the condition for a positive self-relation (which he distinguishes in the three aspects of self-trust, self-respect, and self-confidence, which correspond to the spheres of love, rights, and society respectively). This relation is intersubjectively constituted and, therefore, always vulnerable and indissociable from the need for recognition on the part of others. This also means that recognition "is the origin of normativity," as recognition grounds "the whole of the ethical-moral life of the individuals on a set of normative expectations anchored in specific needs of the I."[45] Vice versa, the denial of recognition implies the nonsatisfaction of the normative expectations that are implied in the demand for recognition. This translates precisely into the experience of injustice, whose definition, however, implies, in comparison to Honneth's, the need of a broadening: that misrecognition be seen as the product of the functioning of social institutions[46] and be perceived essentially as an infringement of identity as identity is the content that always underlies the three forms of positive self-relation.[47]

By "experience of injustice," Renault therefore means "the manner in which [injustice] affects the lives of those who endure it and inaugurates dynamics that will develop demands [*dynamiques revendicatives*]."[48] He also adds that, to be able to speak of experience, injustice must be *perceived* and *recognized* as such by those who suffer it. There are, in fact, cases where this does not happen and where the "lived injustice" results into forms of social and psychic suffering that remain silent and invisible, as they do not translate into active claims.[49] It is only when the violation of normative expectations generates a feeling of injustice, a *sentiment d'injustice*, that we can properly speak of the "experience of injustice" insofar as this produces practical dynamics of transformation of the socially unjust situation.[50] This is what happens in the struggles for recognition by various social and political movements—struggles that "by negation" are bearers of an alternative model of society.

Taking charge of such struggles, giving voice and legitimacy to invisible suffering as well as to active claims, "taking stand" for both the *dominés*, those who are dominated, and the *démunis*, those who are destitute—this is the task of a theory that aims to be critical.[51] What emerges from Renault's proposal is that it is not sufficient to denounce, as Honneth does, the lack of recognition as social pathology; it is also necessary to legitimate the normative message that is implicit in the struggles for recognition, thereby drawing a bridge between theory and practice. Above all, to return to the theme I am most interested in emphasizing, we need to recognize the role of sentiments and the affective dimension in the fight against injustice as the sentiment of injustice possesses both a *cognitive* content that creates awareness of the injustices one has suffered and an *ethical* content consisting in the will to transform the existent situation.

Envy or Indignation?

We have to wonder, though: Is it always the way it is described above? Can we presuppose that social struggles against injustice always have an emancipatory value? Or, rather, does it depend on the peculiar nature of the sentiments that lie at the foundation of the demand for recognition and justice, especially when it comes from collective claims? If it may be true that we can identify compassion as one of the fundamental passions that lead individuals, as witnesses of injustice, to become promoters of a more just world, yet, which passions drive the direct victims of injustice?

I would like to preface that the foregoing question is most cogent as it is, above all, a targeted and in-depth investigation of sentiments that enables us to recognize and distinguish them from one another, thereby unveiling their respective opacity while simultaneously assessing their ambivalence[52] with the goal of acquiring an essential tool to differentiate between legitimate and illegitimate claims of justice.

Renault himself does not fail to raise the issue concerning the necessity of such a distinction. Certainly, all identities rightly demand not to be stigmatized and devalued according to a negative and "abolitionist" conception of justice; yet, we cannot presuppose that *any* identity is worthy of recognition. As the possibility exists that some claims and vindications are mistaken and unjustifiable, we must continuously question their legitimacy.[53]

This means, to my mind, that we must enact a critical analysis of the sentiments that underpin the struggles for recognition and justice. In this regard, I would like to linger on a meaningful example inspired by some events in the contemporary global world. One of the theoretical problems I consider unavoidable for those who investigate the affective motivations driving the demand for justice is the role played by two fundamental passions that may represent the source of collective claims, namely, *envy* and *indignation*. The reflective distinction between these two passions, the ability on the side of critical theory to recognize, in the one or in the other, the emotive drive inspiring specific social movements, is precisely a prelude to the possibility of distinguishing between a legitimate or illegitimate demand for justice.

Let us start with envy, then, which, albeit reluctantly, we cannot avoid acknowledging to be among the possible motives for some collective claims. This is so much the case that it has drawn specific attention from contemporary theory, but not only. On this topic, there are some who adopt bold and radical positions and maintain that, in truth, what lies hiding and masking itself behind apparently noble and emancipatory instances is envy with its emotive load of powerlessness and rancor, resentment and spirit of vengeance toward those who are considered responsible for one's own position of inferiority and marginalization. One could think, here, of the critique of resentment, which is a rancorous and long-lasting involution of envy, on which Nietzsche grounds his attack against Christianity and his peculiar vision of an epochal turn in the history of Western civilization.[54] Or one could think, more recently, of the bristling assessment of the economist Friedrich von Hayek who, as a strenuous supporter of the unlimited expansion of the free market, does not hesitate to define any claim to social justice as a mere "mirage." According to von Hayek, behind this claim there hides, in truth, a powerful envious passion on the side of those who, incapable of accepting the inevitable unbalance of a free society, would like to bridle the spontaneous dynamics of the market's "invisible hand," ultimately harming, through authoritarian equalizing interventions, the very freedom of individuals. This freedom can only be realized within the spontaneous and unregulated order of the market and competition.[55] Finally, one can mention the analysis by one of the most accredited scholars of envy, Helmut Schoeck, who does nothing but reiterate, with absolute obstinacy, that the workers' movements and the entire communist project are simply the outcome of envy and the resentment of the masses masked as utopian egalitarianism.[56]

Without entering the details of these various lines of thought, we can undoubtedly state that we are not ready to share the mostly ideological and unilateral nature of the foregoing positions, despite their differences. It is nevertheless true that envy is clearly a problem for justice. A confirmation of this insight comes from the fact that John Rawls, too, unexpectedly devotes some attention to envy, describing it through its worst attributes[57]—that is, as the passion capable of originating even self-damaging behavior insofar as it leads us to give up our own very advantages and worsen our situation in order not to grant benefits and privileges to others.[58] Rawls advances a line of argument, however, that does not help us recognize the motivations at the origin of the demand for justice. He presupposes that the principles of justice—the guarantee of basic freedoms and the "difference principle under conditions of fair equality of opportunities" in virtue of which the least advantaged would be willing to accept a moderate inequality, if this were to enable them to have more than what they would obtain in a situation of perfect equality—are chosen under a "veil of ignorance" by free, equal, and rational individuals, that is, free from passions and envy. It is true that, after excluding envy from the context of the "original position," Rawls takes care of reintroducing it as a possible outcome of the difference principle[59] insofar as the inequalities "sanctioned by the difference principle may be so great as to arouse envy to a socially dangerous extent."[60] Yet, Rawls concludes that a just society can succeed in containing and limiting the effects of envy, as such a society strengthens the self-esteem of the least advantaged and the respect for their rights, reduces inequality to a minimum, and avoids that the more fortunate show off their advantages, thereby humiliating the less fortunate.

Setting aside the multiple objections one could advance against Rawls's model, I would like to emphasize here that the problem I am trying to address is completely eluded by such a model.[61] The problem is that of the motivations leading individuals to demand justice or, better, to rebel against injustice. In other words, to respond to Rawls, we must acknowledge that envy, resentment, and vengeance may be the passions on which such motivations are grounded *ab origine*, from the origin, and despite us; and that we cannot escape these passions by presuming some alleged rationality. Only this acknowledgment gives us the tools not to mistake envious and reactive claims for just claims. Whereas vengeance and envy are aimed, as Nietzsche already acknowledges, to assert selfish and interested claims, "fastened exclusively to the viewpoint of the person injured,"[62] justice amounts instead—or, better, ought to amount, when we take up its ideal image—to an impartial evaluation of matters, void of egoisms and partialities, and oriented toward the common good.[63]

Concurrently, to reply to those who insist on seeing justice as a mere mask of envy, one can argue by drawing once again on Smith's presupposition, shared by Amartya Sen, of the plurality of the motives for acting. That is, one can object that it is possible to presuppose, besides envy, the existence of *other* passions and motivations that do not betray the fundamental criterion of impartiality. It is here that, as mentioned above, indignation enters the scene—the indignation that, as we shall see shortly, takes center stage in current social struggles against injustice.[64]

It is undeniable that the boundaries between the two passions— envy and indignation—may appear somewhat labile. Nevertheless, it is possible to articulate evaluative criteria that enable us to differentiate them, as confirmed above all by philosophical reflection. Helpful here is the distinction between resentment and indignation that Rawls, once again, advances in the work that precedes his *Theory of Justice*. He writes:

> Resentment and indignation are moral feelings. Resentment is our reaction to the injuries and harms which the wrongs of others inflict upon us, and indignation is our reaction to the injuries which the wrongs of others inflict on others. Both resentment and indignation require, then, an explanation which invokes a moral concept, say the concept of justice, and its associated principle(s) and so makes a reference to a right or a wrong. In order to experience resentment and indignation one must accept the principles which specify these rights and wrongs.[65]

This distinction is helpful and we can subscribe to it, but only in part, for at least two reasons. The first has to do with the fact that indignation is a reaction not only toward injustice experienced by others but also toward injustice suffered in the first person.[66] The second is that Rawls does not seem to grasp the negative and regressive aspect of this feeling, understood as a lasting and rancorous filiation of envy.[67]

As the emotive response particular to those who perceive themselves as lacking recognition, *resentment* is the reactive passion that, as emerges from Nietzsche's and Scheler's classical analyses, tries to compensate for powerlessness and the sense of inferiority through forms of retaliation and vengeance.[68] Max Scheler, who investigates the phenomenology of *ressentiment* and shows its multiple nuances more deeply than in Nietzsche's well-known analysis, defines it as a "self-poisoning of the mind."[69] Like envy, ressentiment too originates from a feeling of powerlessness of which the individual has, however, become conscious in a more explicit and, moreover, lasting manner. Ressentiment emerges when we know that, in principle, we could access the goods we want and the other possesses but, in actuality, we have no *chance* of obtaining them. Consequently, we react by brooding within ourselves and a rancor that drags along and sharpens with time develops, which ultimately poisons our entire personality with negative feelings such as vengeance, malice, and mean joy in others' misfortunes. Scheler writes, "*Ressentiment* can only arise if these emotions are particularly powerful and yet must be suppressed because they are coupled with the feeling that one is unable to act them out."[70]

Briefly, ressentiment is the reaction to an offense, attack, humiliation, or even simply a threat that may not even be real but is subjectively perceived as such. Consequently, as Scheler remarks with evident Nietzschean tones, it concerns especially the weak and powerless—those who, incapable of free and autonomous action and unable to respond aggressively in a direct and immediate way, are only able to react obliquely, passively, covertly.[71] Finally, it is a ferociously relational passion that, like envy, is nourished through comparison with the other—comparison that, however, in the case of ressentiment, is always failing and without possibility of redemption. The insufferable perception of one's own inferiority, due to the fact that we feel like we cannot access the same goods and qualities that the other possesses, results in a painful tension that finds a specific solution, be it self-harming or vindictive, in ressentiment.

I think it is more than legitimate, therefore, to cast some doubts on the moral quality of such a "sad" passion while distinguishing it sharply from indignation, which, on the contrary, possesses an indubitable moral charge. On this topic, Descartes's taxonomy of the passions appears more enlightening. In it, indignation is defined as "just envy," which arises "from seeing good coming to people one thinks are unworthy of it."[72] That is, it arises from rebellion against fortunes or misfortunes not based on merit. Descartes's proposed distinction seems evidently to evoke, in turn, the definition offered by Aristotle in the *Nicomachean Ethics*. Here, Aristotle claims that, whereas envy is always, "in all circumstances," pain in front of the success and fortunes of the other (or one's own failures and misfortunes), indignation (*nemesis*) arises where these successes clearly appear ungrounded and undeserved.[73] As mentioned above, indignation undoubtedly belongs to the constellation of passions that Peter Sloterdijk has called, using Platonic terminology, "thymotic passions." These passions find synthetic expression in rage (*menis*) and its multiple variations.[74] In the course of history, they have nourished emancipatory movements of rebellion against injustice, such as the class struggles between the nineteenth and the twentieth centuries. Currently, Sloterdijk adds, these passions seem to have undergone a radical weakening, and even a negative drift. Not only do they seem presently incapable of coagulating into politically effective and transformative "rage banks"—that is, into gathering centers able to lead to mobilization and action—but they have also fractured into a multiplicity of vengeful claims and resentful drives that, as shown by the exemplary case of Islamic fundamentalism, are void of any innovative and emancipatory spark of transformation of reality. This is so, I wish to emphasize, also because, rather than a degeneration of rage, as Sloterdijk would like to maintain, resentment shows deep affinities with that prime vice or "sad" passion—quite different from rage—that is envy and with the sense of frustration that it generates.[75]

What ultimately matters, then, is the ability to differentiate among the passions that act as motives for social action and be able to grasp their ethical potentialities together with their different emotive quality. In the specific instance, we find, on the one hand, the surging and explosive energy of rage, whose potentially transformative and regenerating function is underlined, in a Nietzschean mode, by Sloterdijk. On the other, we have the purely reactive quality of resentment, which spurs individuals not to fight for their own dignity and rights as much as to annihilate the other as the culprit of all evils.

Not even this distinction, however, is sufficient, to my mind, as rage itself may take up, in its excesses and unmeasurable aggression, a destructive connotation. We will therefore need to introduce the distinction between destructive and unjust rage (or wrath), which ends up simply producing ruins, and a just rage, which tends precisely toward restoring dignity and self-esteem to those who have suffered offenses and misrecognitions. As confirmed by a long tradition that finds its first systematic treatment, once again, in Aristotle, just rage amounts precisely to indignation.[76] In his *Rhetoric*, Aristotle writes, "Let us then define anger as a longing, accompanied by pain, for a real or apparent revenge for a real or apparent slight, affecting a man himself or one of his friends, when such a slight is undeserved."[77] Indignation is, in other words, a measured rage that takes up the virtuous aspect of *mesotés*, of the mean, and is capable of reacting with determination against an offense without falling prey to a sterile and destructive fury.[78] In agreement with Aristotle's diagnosis, Martha Nussbaum suggests a positive function of anger as "a major force for social justice and the defense of the oppressed," as long as it has an appropriate object deserving of blame and does not incur excesses of violence.[79] Under these conditions, it represents the fruitful manifestation of the *thymos* that spurs human beings to fight against injustice.

We can find clear and concrete testimony of the emancipatory function of anger and indignation in a series of contemporary social movements that have revamped the revolutionary power of these passions and have appeared a few years after Sloterdijk's aforementioned reflections. We can return to some of the examples already mentioned earlier, such as, first, the revolts that a few years ago (2010–11) swept through the Arab world, where from Tunisia to Egypt, from Libya to Syria, we witnessed forms of rebellion and protest, grounded on the citizens' claims to their rights and dignity, against dictatorial regimes. February 17, 2011, the date when the protest against Qaddafi began, was called precisely the "Day of Anger." It was an anger void of the envy and resentment toward the Western world that has instead inspired and inspires, for the most part, the fundamentalist movements, especially in their extremist fringes; this was so because this anger was born out of the desire to fight autonomously for rights, fundamental needs, and democratic freedoms. The Arab Spring, as it has been called, saw, among other things, the active engagement of young people alien to all lethal ideologies of the clashes of civilizations, as the image of the oppositional relation between the West and Islamic world had been configured for a long time. It also saw the participation of women, capable of reacting, finally, to forms of centuries-long oppression while openly manifesting their dissent (on social networks and even in the squares). These were not the only instances, though. "Indignation" was also the password that, inspired by a famous pamphlet by Stéphane Hessel, guided and coalesced at its outset the movement of the Indignados in the Western world.[80] This movement started in May 2011 in Spain on occasion of the administrative elections and rapidly took on a global dimension, as made evident in the slogans ("United for Global Change") that still accompany some manifestations such as those by the various Occupy movements. Here, claims to the right to work and participation emerge jointly with the fight against the strong economic and financial powers and the denunciation of the inefficacy of politics.[81]

The ability to recognize which passions are, now and again, at the origin of social movements and struggles and to distinguish between indignation and envy, anger and resentment, enables us to measure the distance between, on the one hand, mobilizations that are essentially produced by partisan and selfish interests or, even worse, by purely hostile and vindictive retaliations and, on the other, mobilizations that, on the contrary, are inspired by the desire for dignity and equality, sustained by impartial evaluations of the common good, and geared toward attaining democratic freedoms. Briefly, recognizing passions allows us to distinguish, as I proposed earlier, between legitimate and illegitimate demands for justice.

The operation of differentiation is, of course, far from simple and self-evident. This ought to lead us to a careful evaluation of those con-flict theories that emphasize the emancipatory potential of conflict by affirming the struggles for recognition as fights for freedom, as we have seen in Honneth;[82] or by opposing violent antagonism with the agonistic ability to "fight without killing," as advanced by Chantal Mouffe[83] with an evident allusion to an effective formulation proposed by Marcel Mauss in his The Gift;[84] or by going, as done by Miguel Benasayag, as far as to a "praise of conflict"[85] understood as the expression of collective passions capable of reintroducing, within the social reality, the necessary dynamism and innovative forces that, in our democracies, have been paralyzed by an implosion caused by "sad" passions.[86]

The fact remains, however, that we may come across ambivalent phenomena, such as the recent case of the gilets jaunes in France, where it is difficult to disentangle demonstrations of legitimate indignation and episodes of destructive fury. Or the rather enigmatic case of youth social movements characterized by what the sociologist Danilo Martuccelli has defined as a "participation with reservations" due to a sentiment of dis-illusionment with, and distrust of, collective action.[87] The ambivalence seems to disappear in phenomena that have an intrinsic ethico-political potentiality, as in the very recent phenomenon of the Fridays for Future. This movement is animated by young teenagers who, faced with an environmental crisis made ever more visible by the devastating effects of climate change, protest against an unprecedented generational egoism and fight for the defense of their future and the protection of the planet. It is a phenomenon, it is important to add, capable of contradicting the condition of weakness that, according to Alain Touraine's recent diagnosis,[88] characterizes current movements as void of an authentic ideal impulse.[89]

In sum, we could say that, starting with the very struggle for recognition, the quality of conflict and its emancipatory potentialities depend on the passions that animate it. Consequently, we must critically scrutinize the motivations that, now and again, inspire social struggles and movements. In this sense, Amartya Sen is right when he claims that both passions and reason concur in the evaluation of the forms of opposition against injustice. Reasoning, he claims, is needed to verify the trustworthiness of the feelings at stake and to decide whether the perception of injustice is more or less justified. This certainly holds true for indignation, which "can activate reflection rather than replace it." In other words, "Frustration and ire can help to motivate us, and yet ultimately we have to rely, for both assessment and for effectiveness, on reasoned scrutiny to obtain a plausible and sustainable understanding of the basis of those complaints."[90] An evaluation seems needed also with respect to those sentiments that appear tout court as positive, such as compassion or the revulsion to cruelty. "Even when we find something immediately upsetting, we can question that response and ask whether it is an appropriate reaction and whether we should really be guided by it."[91] Evoking Adam Smith's figure of the impartial spectator, Sen emphasizes the need for a critical scrutiny of sentiments that verifies their impartiality through reasoned comparison and public debate.[92]

Sen seems to say that, briefly, the more we take sentiments seriously and recognize their role in the demand for justice, the more we must rely on reasoning and public debate in order to act through objective criteria. As he amply argues, public debate must currently take into account an interdependent world and, thus, must extend itself, lest it fall into anachronistic parochialism, to the entire global sphere through the exercise of an "open impartiality."[93]

Four

The Passions of Care

For *Good* Care

What Passions Motivate Us to Care?

Taking feelings seriously presupposes, as we have seen, a different idea of justice, in which the evaluation of choices and principles takes into account the motivations that inspire them: both in those who witness situations of injustice (and react with compassion and/or indignation) and on the part of those who suffer them personally (and respond with anger and indignation).[1] It follows, then, that the opposition between justice and care—which is grounded on understanding the former as an abstract and rational ideal and the latter as an affective dimension and which is, in part, shared by certain theorists of care—comes to be challenged in its own assumptions. Both justice and care, in fact, mobilize passions, both have their origin in the affective involvement of individuals (and groups).

In short, the distinction between ethics of justice and ethics of care, which is necessary for a fruitful integration of the two ethical models, primarily concerns the *quality* of the sentiments that operate in both models. Consequently, the question I wish to raise is: If compassion, indignation, and anger can be recognized as the passions of justice, what are the passions of care?

It is worth reiterating that the first, fundamental premise of a caring attitude is the awareness of one's condition of vulnerability, to which both the self and the other are ontologically subjected and which they both experience in the care relationship. The second presupposition is, undoubtedly, the capacity for empathy. We have seen that empathy allows one to enter a relationship with the other right from the very discovery of the other's existence. Recalling the words of Edith Stein,[2] the empathic act coincides with an awareness of the other, of the other's experience and feelings, while nevertheless always maintaining an awareness of the difference between oneself and the other. Empathy becomes, according to a recent definition, the "unifying term that names a realm of experience within which multiple forms of *feeling the other* are given: friendship, love, compassion, attention, care, respect, regard."[3] Empathy, therefore, is an emotive participation in the experience and feelings of the other, despite being a "vicarious" emotion, that is to say, an emotion that is equal or similar to that of the other and nevertheless requires the clear perception of the distinction between self and other. In short, empathy presupposes the recognition of the other as being distinct from us, although gifted like us with feelings, thoughts, and volitions in which we are able to participate.

We agree, therefore, with Michael Slote when, positioning care ethics within the tradition of moral sentimentalism, he argues that the "caring motivation is based in and sustained by our human capacity for empathy with others."[4] He proposes here the concept of "empathic care."[5] We have also seen, however, that empathy does not automatically translate into an ethical response, as it does not imply a value judgment on the other's emotion and experience. In other words, empathy, understood as a fundamentally social capacity, allows one to understand, to "participate in the affective situation of the other and to adopt their perspective."[6] As Hoffman notes, it is "the spark of human concern for others"[7] and, therefore, represents the condition for the emergence of emotions that inspire moral action. Yet, empathy alone is not sufficient for moral action, since it is not itself a moral sentiment.[8] As confirmed by many authors, we must not confuse, for example, empathy with sympathy, which, as already mentioned, in its current usage refers to "the mode of being *for* the other, in favor of the other"; or with compassion, which means feeling sorry for the suffering of the other; or with *love*, which aims to promote the well-being of the loved one.[9]

Furthermore, it is equally legitimate to say that, as we have seen, empathy presides over the demand for justice whenever we witness situations of injustice and we put ourselves in the shoes of those who suffer them. Empathy is, undoubtedly, the necessary condition for thinking of a subject that recognizes itself as constitutively in relation with others. Yet empathy is not sufficient to explain the different emotive configurations that govern the relationship with the other.[10] In other words, very different emotions can arise from empathy.

In sum, empathy is a morally neutral affective state that can give birth to a variety of emotions (even negative ones), and this variety depends, now and again, on who the other is and on the kind of relationship one has with such other. Consequently, it is not enough to argue that care presupposes the capacity for empathy. We must also ask ourselves what emotions are activated in care relationships in their various forms, and which ones are desirable insofar as they are ethically oriented. The quality of these emotions will inform the relationship of care and one's ability to practice good care. On this last point, it becomes therefore necessary to integrate the reflections of care theorists.

We have seen that what brings together, even though in their differences, various forms of care theories is the recovery and elaboration of the affective dimension as the foundation of ethics. Gilligan values the role of compassion and attachment in moral choice. Kittay brings care work back to love, as the title of her book suggests (*Love's Labor*). Held points out that individuals are motivated not only by self-interest and selfish passions but also by moral emotions (from empathy to sensitivity/receptivity/responsiveness) that can play a positive and essential role for the care of the other.[11]

The reference to the dimension of emotions nevertheless remains, for the most part, generic. One can also see the tendency, on the part of some care theorists (for example, Joan Tronto, Patricia Paperman, Sandra Laugier), to hold a kind of prudent skepticism toward feelings. This certainly does not deny their importance, though it prevents the danger that they become the only and most important foundation of care.[12] Tronto argues that the devaluation of care coincided, in modern thought, with the devaluation of emotions[13] understood as negative poles within dichotomies specific to Western thought (masculine/feminine, public/private, reason/passion, mind/body). Consequently, to base care (only) on feelings entails the risks of reaffirming the traditional reductive image of care as a private and feminine dimension and precluding its necessary extension to the public and social spheres (as well as to the opposite sex), ultimately preventing its desirable universalization. Therefore, as Paperman remarks, we can recognize the importance of feelings for the care perspective only insofar as they are "put back in their place" (*remis à leur place*), that is, reconnected to the fabric of practices and relationships that form the context of care, because it is only inside this context that they take on meaning and value.

I fully share the foregoing perspective, but I think it could be further supported through a more accurate and detailed investigation of the sentiments that motivate care. In other words, I think that we need to overcome what, I believe, is still an overly generic understanding of the category of "feelings" (or emotions or passions) and draw deeper distinctions, as is the case for the ethics of justice. This task is necessary to bring to light their risks and potentialities, their negative and positive aspects, while understanding more fully the role emotions can play in an ethics of care.

Recognizing and distinguishing the different emotions that moti-vate people to care can be enlightening for at least three fundamental reasons. First, it can help distinguish various forms of care and propose a broader and more complex concept of it. Second, it will help differenti-ate between emancipatory aspects and negative aspects of care. Third, it will allow us to identify the strictly ethical dimension of care. In other words, addressing the issue of care from the point of view of emotions enables us to focus better on the image of *good* care. We can do so by exploring, as we are about to do, three variations of the relationship of care that I consider exemplary, namely, *private*, *social*, and *global*.

These three typologies of care certainly do not exhaust the vast multiplicity of possible forms of care,[14] but, through specific variations, they allow us to focus on the role of the emotions and the diversity of motivations. Let us consider, then, the first two typologies, which mirror each other as they represent, the first, a form of care that presupposes a preexisting affect and, the second, a form of care in which affection arises later, within the relationship itself.

The first type, which concerns the private sphere, is the *care out of love*, that is, the care for someone to whom we are linked by a personal relationship (husband/wife, son/daughter, friend, brother/sister). This case consists of a relationship in which the affective bond precedes care, regardless of whether care is occasional, transient, or constant.

The second type, which concerns the social sphere, is what we can define as assisted care, that is, the care of the disabled, the sick, and the elderly. It is that form of care that we properly call "work" and that also implies some form of remuneration. Here, feelings can only follow the relationship, possibly arising within the relationship itself.

Which emotions preside over each of these relationships? Love or compassion, generosity or gratitude? And what bestows an ethical value on these emotions? I think that a first response can be found, albeit indirectly, in Simone Weil's reflection on *attention*. Weil defines attention as the "rarest and purest form of generosity"[15] in that it implies not only the capacity to understand and emotionally participate in the experience of the other (as is the case with empathy) but also the ability to welcome the other, the willingness to make space for the other, in their naked truth, in the void left open by the ego.[16] In other words, attention reveals the first, fundamental sign of morality;[17] attention testifies, and more intensely so than the neutral attitude of empathy, to the possibility of really accessing ethics and moral sentiments. In fact, it is the confirmation and unequivocal testimony of "decreation,"[18] that is, of the capacity of self-suspending the self, which is a radical act of generosity and which, in care relationships, finds its utmost place of both concrete and symbolic representation.

Caring Out of Love

Let us begin our analysis with the exemplary case of a care relationship grounded on the existence of a feeling that precedes it, of a relationship in which we take care of someone because we love the person, whatever the archetypal form of love that binds us—*eros* for a partner, *philia* for a friend, or *agape* for a child.

Undoubtedly, the latter, that is, agapic love, is the most traditional image of love that cares, that is, an agapic love that is purely altruistic and devoted, ready for sacrifice and self-denial. Women are well-aware of this form, and it is women whom I would now like to take as an exemplary case of care out of love, as they have always been identified with it in the name of an alleged natural destiny of the female species. Women have had to renounce the excesses of eros, seeking refuge in the consolation, not without traces of rhetoric, of philia and sisterhood. One could just think of the modern conception of conjugal and maternal love, which is viewed as feminine; in this framework, for the first time, women are seen as subjects but they are simultaneously confined to a self-sacrificing image. I refer here to the Rousseauian vision of the woman as wife and mother, which has deeply influenced the trajectory of modern thought: the idea that women are naturally disposed to love and take care of the other as a way to realize women's own authentic nature, identity, and destiny. Love, understood in the altruistic and self-giving sense, has ended up becoming a vehicle for inequality between the sexes, for sacrifice, and for patriarchal domination. In the name of love, women have not only been relegated to the marginal function of care subjects, confined to the private sphere and forced into a position of subalternity, but have also been deprived of the passionate dimension of eros and desire, thereby seriously mutilating a fundamental aspect of their identity.

Drawing from insights of feminist thought, it can certainly be argued that the first answer to the problem of averting the sacrificial risk of the traditional idea of care consists of reappropriating rights and justice, as care theorists suggest when they distinguish between a feminine and a feminist ethics. Women's struggle for equal opportunities, for access to the professional sphere, and for the recognition of their role within the public sphere has been, for long, the legitimate response to the condition of subordination and exclusion.

In my opinion, though, this is not enough and it is necessary to rethink the very nature of love. The conquest of dignity and rights in the public sphere does not automatically amount to a transformation of the imaginary and of the emotive sphere. One cannot deny that there exist contradictory realities that clearly reveal the discrepancy between the public and the private. A woman may have obtained prestigious positions in the professional sphere and even leadership roles in the public sphere, but she may continue to suffer forms of oppression in the private sphere, where she is not able to affirm a woman's rights as she undergoes, in the name of love and relationship, the emotional blackmail of a partner. This discrepancy is attested by extreme forms of oppression such as the recent radicalization of male violence against women and the worrisome spread of a phenomenon that, deploying a neologism, has been called femicide and that can be retraced, at least partly, to a distorted and possessive idea of love. A further attestation comes also from more invisible and daily forms such as the refusal on the part of men to accept a just division of labor within the domestic sphere due to the persistence of an image of women as self-giving and caring.

As Anthony Giddens argued already a few decades ago,[19] it is true that we have been witnessing for some time a profound transformation of the nature of intimacy, which women have helped significantly alter with their unprecedented achievements, thereby resulting in a crisis of the traditional model of romantic love, which is founded on a strong asymmetry within the couple and on the subjection of women. It is evident, that is, that currently there increasingly exists the possibility of a "pure relationship" between the sexes that is free from the chains of reproduction and gender stereotypes. But it is also true that, in the name of love, despite the acquisition of previously nonexisting rights, women risk remaining imprisoned in forms of emotional subjugation that are the more powerful the more they are disguised under the veil of legal and social equality.

It becomes important, then, to draw upon the concept of capability proposed by Martha Nussbaum.[20] Despite the legal and social recognition of certain rights, it may happen that a woman does not have the "capability" to exercise them in the sphere of intimacy, precisely because of a distorted vision of love of which she is unable to break free. The difficulty of exercising one's autonomy in the private sphere, therefore, risks returning women to the traditional and Rousseauian image of care, understood as that purely altruistic and sacrificial dimension that finds further support in the rhetoric of maternal love, and that today paradoxically ends up coexisting with the achievement of rights.

Together with the sacrosanct defense of rights, it becomes necessary, therefore, to retrieve the complexity of love, which, as Georg Simmel reminds us, remains love only if, in its historical manifestations and concrete epiphanies, it effectively safeguards the wealth of its archetypal forms (agape, eros, philia) and combines them in infinite forms.[21] This becomes possible only by taking up, once again, the importance of that often-neglected dimension, if not the object of blame and guilt, of self-love, as some philosophers suggest, from Spinoza to Rousseau himself to, more recently, Harry Frankfurt. Against a Kantian ethics founded on the opposition of egoism and altruism, it is indeed possible to affirm, as Frankfurt suggests, that self-love does not contradict love;[22] rather, it is the elementary form of love, for self-love is the first manifestation of taking to heart, of taking care of any thing or person we love. Self-love is nothing else than the desire to love.

However, even if this definition seems a bit paradoxical, we can at least affirm that self-love is what allows us to free care from the aspects of sacrifice and domination. One could simply recall here the words of Amy, the little girl and protagonist of the moral dilemma presented by Gilligan. Her words are very effective, in their spontaneity, in affirming the necessary connection between caring for others and caring for oneself: "If you have a responsibility with somebody else, then you should keep it to a certain extent, but to the extent that it is really going to hurt you or stop you from doing something that you really, really want, then I think maybe you should put yourself first."[23] If, on the contrary, this right to self-love is sacrificed or underestimated, there emerges the risk of the flourishing of negative emotions (such as resentment, anger, disgust), which pollute or radically compromise the care relationship.

In other words, if it is to be good care, caring for the beloved (a partner, one's children) cannot be founded on a purely altruistic and agapic idea of love, understood as a natural dedication and forgetting of oneself. In this case, good care requires adopting a critical-reflective attitude with respect to one's emotions in order to overcome the obstacle of a sacrificial idea of love and, ultimately, make love the object, in Simmel's sense, of a conscious choice. In this choice, attention to the other does not exclude self-respect and self-awareness, and love for the other does not mean renouncing self-love. This also allows one to recover the right to passion and to eros, with all its excesses, ambivalences, and transgressions—a right that was stolen from women in the name of an alleged natural disposition to self-dedication and self-forgetfulness, to a wholly and only positive feeling.

Attendant Care

In its various dimensions, attendant care expresses what is, properly, care work. This is the form of care on which contemporary reflection—both theoretical and empirical—has mainly focused; it includes, in addition to multiple remunerated service activities (education, childcare, health, care for the elderly), the work of the unpaid attendant.[24] To distinguish it from love care, I will focus here on salaried care work, with particular reference to the work that is carried out in the presence of the contingent, and sometimes extreme, need of the other, be it the disabled, the elderly, and/or the sick.

Here, the first problem comes to the fore through the presence of a paid salary. Various authors ask whether it is possible to reconcile care and money. On the one hand, as some argue, this implies the risk of commodifying affective work, as a material and utilitarian aspect inserts itself in the care relationship, thereby corrupting, as it were, the affective bond between the caregiver and those who receive care. Contemporary capitalism, Michael Hardt and Antonio Negri argue,[25] possesses the particular feature of putting affections, bodies, and emotions to work, thus exploiting for its own purposes (of acquisition and profit) the emotional component and people's abilities to create relationships. Hence, it is legitimate to speak of a biopolitics of work. Pay for affective work, or for the work of care, does entail exposing it to commodification[26] and to the risk of alienation for those who perform it.[27]

On the other hand, according to the "love and money frame"[28] perspective, some thinkers contest the dualistic vision of love versus market. They argue that money and care are not necessarily antithetical and that the presence of remuneration does not corrupt the affective ties.[29] They even suggest that fair compensation, as a sign of respect and appreciation for the work of the caregiver, can foster the emotional bond with the care receiver and save that "invisible heart" that feeds the relationship of care.[30] In support of this position, let us recall that, traditionally, the absence of remuneration has been precisely what, in some cases, has penalized the caregiver in this kind of work, which was largely reduced to nonwork. One could think, for example, of the free assistance provided by women to elderly and disabled family members or sick people. Fair remuneration can counteract the traditional devaluation of care work mostly associated with women,[31] as it implies that state and institutions recognize the dignity of the caregiver, their time and competences, thereby ensuring adequate remuneration and protection of rights. Here, not only does cash payment not contradict the emotional relationship but also "the more that pay is combined with trust and appreciation, the less it drives out genuine intrinsic motivation—especially important in care work."[32]

Without neglecting the risk of commodifying emotions, I think that one can support this position, which defends the possible coexistence of a double motivation, both extrinsic and intrinsic, of care work. However, the initial question remains: What is this intrinsic motivation? In other words, what emotions inspire care work? If we consider many of the empirical works examining the link between compassion and care,[33] we can legitimately affirm that the emotion that guides attendant care, or, rather, the type of care work on which I am focusing, is compassion. As I mentioned earlier when I distinguished it from empathy, compassion means that one feels sorrow for the suffering of the other.

Following Nussbaum's definition, compassion is a painful emotion provoked by the awareness of the undeserved suffering of another person, which arises when one stands as an impartial observer but is also induced by the awareness of one's own vulnerability. Compassion testifies to the ability to get out of one's selfishness/narcissism, to renounce one's omnipotence, to recognize oneself as vulnerable. In short, it is one of those passions that "expand the boundaries of the self." A moral sentiment par excellence, compassion presupposes the ability to identify with the discomfort and suffering of the other, placing oneself in their place, while remaining aware of the distinction between self and other.[34] And it simultaneously testifies to both the expansion of the self and the attention to the other as an important part of one's range of interests and purposes, or as part of one's own "circle of concern." This means that compassion is not to be understood in terms of the charity and altruism of pity, but rather like a *cum-patire*, a co-feeling or feeling together that derives from the judgment of the other's undeserved suffering. It is a feeling-together that implies the recognition of a common humanity.

Therefore, it is legitimate to expect that those who offer care, especially in the face of another's serious suffering and extreme fragility, are motivated by compassion for the care receiver. In other words, this is what we could judge to be the "just emotion" fit for attendant care.[35] It is undeniable, however, that multiple obstacles to compassion can arise—obstacles visibly due to the asymmetry of the care relationship.

A first obstacle is essentially psychological and is produced by what I would like to define as the rejection or fear of vulnerability. At best, this may generate an absence of empathy that translates into the habituation to suffering that is typical in some health-care professionals, or into the selfish drift due to emotional overinvolvement. At worst, as Kittay observes,[36] the caregiver or, better, the dependency worker, as she calls them, abuses their own power, thereby establishing a relationship of domination with the other, perhaps even of violence. It can be assumed that this is due to the disgust for the other's dependence and to the desire to exorcise it through an emotional detachment that converts empathy into negative empathy. But the opposite may also occur: the care receiver, especially when they perceive the hostility of the other, may exert power over the caregiver in tyrannical ways and through emotional blackmail that tend to humiliate the giver. In this case, we can assume that the care receiver is motivated by feelings of anger and resentment toward the person they perceive as the one who decides on their well-being and controls their life.[37] In both situations, what emerges, ultimately revealing the dark aspects of the care relationship, is the rejection of vulnerability, which is exorcized or exploited by exercising power over the other.[38]

A second obstacle to compassion can be essentially material and social in form, as it originates in the differences of class, status, or race. Sensitivity to the suffering of the other can be compromised by social inequality and the highly disadvantaged status of the caregiver. To take a contemporary example, one can think of migrant women who come from poorer countries to assist the sick and disabled in wealthy families residing in rich countries. An unprecedented phenomenon produced by globalization, the case of migrant women evidently constitutes a challenge to the care relationship.[39] These are often underpaid women, who fill the gaps of a social state unable to provide adequate support for the problem of dependence. These women leave their families for long periods to live with other families (live-in workers) and, in turn, entrust their children to other women. Eva Kittay describes the situation as a "global heart transplant"[40] within what Arlie Hochschild calls "global care chains,"[41] of which these women represent the weak link, as they are forced to sacrifice their own ties with their family of origin. It is easy to imagine how the emotional bond with the care receiver, the compassion for their suffering, may be hindered by this sacrifice as well as by the fact that their sacrifice is not compensated by adequate financial support and legitimate public recognition of their work.[42]

It is therefore necessary to restore dignity to care work. This requires, first, that we address a problem of justice, namely, the enactment of policies that guarantee the caregiver material and legal justice (defense of fundamental rights, fair remuneration)—underestimating this aspect would be serious. A profound cultural and symbolic change is also required, though: what is needed, as many care theorists (from Eva Kittay to Marian Barnes) argue,[43] is a recognition of the dignity of dependence and vulnerability. The myth of autonomy and independence, on which the figure of the modern subject was built,[44] has produced the removal of the reality of reciprocal dependence and our constitutive "neediness"; it has overshadowed the fact that we depend on each other, and not only when we are in conditions of extreme need (such as disability). Due to this suppression, we see the emergence, in care relationships, of negative drives and feelings of disgust and fear that—though they may not degenerate into forms of violence such as physical and, more strikingly, emotional abuse (on children, the elderly, the handicapped) repeatedly reported by the media or the various websites of medical and psychological associations—compromise the very possibility of an emotional bond supported by "right emotions" such as compassion and sympathetic participation.

These risks are intrinsic in that constitutive aspect of care that is the unbearable burden of its everydayness. The daily aspect causes care work to be experienced as a duty and a routine, thus exposing it to the emergence of forms of domination and negative feelings, such as disgust or resentment toward what is perceived as the blackmail that comes from the vulnerable other (one could just think of the disconcerting case of so-called "bad mothers").[45] This possible drift is further aggravated by the overlapping of multiple "circles of concern," of potential circles of care (domestic, professional, public, and environmental) in which we are involved and that are very difficult, if not impossible, to reconcile (like being, at the same time, a good mother, a good teacher, and a responsible citizen).

In this second paradigmatic case, that is, in the case of attendant care, good care requires therefore that we overcome the obstacles to compassion and put ourselves in the condition of cultivating this intrinsic motivation, ultimately counteracting the reciprocal reactions of disgust and resentment. Consequently, good care can avoid a double and opposite risk: domination (on the part of the caregiver) and humiliation (on the part of the care receiver); and it can promote a spirit of cooperation on the part of both parties of the relationship.

In conclusion, these two typologies certainly do not exhaust the multiplicity of care relationships that shape our private, professional, and social lives. Yet, as I mentioned earlier, they are typologically exemplary, due to their specular structure: in the first, affectivity precedes and, in fact, favors the relationship of care; in the second, the affective bond can possibly arise only later, within the relationship. Both typologies may bring forward a fundamental aspect that characterizes the ethical relationship—a relationship that is anything but easy, peaceful, and definitive, for it always contains a potential challenge that derives from negative and even unspeakable impulses and that, therefore, demands that we resist our negative emotions by cultivating our positive ones, such as compassion, and orienting them consciously and reflectively toward good care.

Five

Global Perspectives

Care and Justice Confronting the Challenge of the Spatially *Distant Other*

Do I exhort you to love of your neighbour? I exhort you rather
to flight from your neighbour and to love of the most distant!

—Friedrich Nietzsche, *Thus Spoke Zarathustra*[1]

New Figures of the Other

At this point, I would like to call attention to what I have introduced
as the third exemplary typology of the relationship of care, that is,
the *global* relationship. The challenge it faces becomes decisively more
difficult due to the peculiar character of the figure of the other that
emerges from, and is structured by, the unprecedented social transformations of our contemporary age. I am alluding here to the one whom
we can call the *unknown and distant other*.[2] This is definitely a current
figure, which emerges in correspondence with the development of our
globalized society and the radical changes that it introduces in the very
concept of distance. In the present and next chapters, I will investigate
two fundamental variations of this figure.

The global epoch is characterized by the interdependency of events
and lives due to some kind of paradoxical coexistence between erosion
of borders and contraction of a world that we perceive as increasingly
smaller and narrower.[3] Due to "space-time compression,"[4] globalization

compresses and reduces distance, thereby producing an unprecedented condition of interdependency that makes relevant for us events and subjects that, up to this point in time, had been perceived as distant and uninfluential. In terms of events, we can think of some macroscopic phenomena such as an economic-financial crisis (in 2008), a nuclear accident (Fukushima in 2011), or an ecological catastrophe (the fires in the Amazon in 2019). Originating within spatially circumscribed situations, these events are destined to trigger uncontrollable chain reactions that affect our entire planetary space, breaking boundaries and trespassing territorial borders.[5] In terms of subjects, we currently witness a multiplication of the figures of the other due to the fact that we live in an interconnected global space. Within it, not only familiar, close individuals or people we somehow know become relevant for us but also people who are distant and whom, up to a few decades ago, we could easily ignore or target as essentially dismissible, as they were confined, for us, in a nebulous elsewhere. I am referring here to two increasingly ineludible and structural variations of the distant other, which we can synthetize in the two figures of the other distant *in space* and the other distant *in time*. In the first case, which I will address in this chapter, we find the poor and disadvantaged populations of the planet, which are affected by wars, hunger, and famines, as well as those individuals who have been struck by catastrophes or traumatic collective events (such as earthquakes, tsunamis, and environmental disasters). In the second case, which I will address more in-depth in the following chapter, we find future generations, that is, those who, given the disquieting expansion and violence of the environmental crisis, will inevitably suffer the negative effects of our current actions and will inherit the world as we will have handed it down to them.

All this implies not only an indisputable widening of the figure of the other but also an extension of the other who is potentially significant to us.[6] Briefly, globalization, on the one hand, breaks the spatial boundary between outside and inside through which the context of state and territorial modernity had been configured; on the other, it shortens the temporal gap between current and future humanity because of the acceleration of time and the processes of speed.[7] Due to globalization, for the first time the distant other objectively becomes part of our increasingly wider "circle of concern." This means that, currently, the other is not only the one for whom we take charge in a face-to-face relationship and in a context of proximity. The other is also, indeed, the unknown and distant other who, in some way, irrupts into our life and calls us to a concern and an answer that become unavoidable.

The problem that immediately arises, however, relates precisely to the cogency of the response to it, that is, to the degree of ineluctability of the problem. The emergence of the distant other very much complicates the question of moral obligation. It seems reasonable, then, to deduce that globalization posits the objective conditions necessary to ground the justification of an obligation toward the distant other. Yet, it is also true, as we shall see shortly, that this does not automatically translate into a response by the subject. The issue of the motivations that move us to the demand for justice or to practices of care toward those who live in remote places or are not yet born is, theoretically as well as politically, one of the most arduous challenges of our age.

Why should human beings mobilize for individuals to whom they are not tied by an affective connection, a professional relation, or a direct generational bond? Why should they be concerned with their needs, take to heart their suffering and their destinies? What motivations and emotions are enacted in relation to the unknown and distant other? Can we rely here on the same passions of justice and care we have described thus far?

Trying to confront this issue requires, to my mind, two preliminary clarifications. First, we must take a step back, return to the function of empathy, and ask whether it can generally function in a relation of nonproximity. Second, we must keep the two figures accurately distinct, namely, the other distant in space and the other distant in time, in order to highlight the peculiar difficulties that each figure implies at the motivational and moral levels.

The theme of the expansive potentiality of empathy was already present in Hume, Smith, and moral sentimentalism, as we have seen.[8] Hume claims that we tend to feel sympathy more for those to whom we are close and with whom we are familiar than for strangers, more for our fellow citizens than for foreigners; in short, for those who are part of our closer circles of mutual recognition. The circles can be expanded, however, as Peter Singer recently suggests: "The circle of altruism has broadened from the family and tribe to the nation and race, and we are beginning to recognize that our obligations extend to all human beings. The process should not stop there."[9] That is, we can always progressively widen the range of those toward whom we acknowledge a moral obligation:[10] from our family members to our fellow citizens to humankind; from animals to the environment, all the way to future generations.

This widening of obligation is far from spontaneous, though, as we can gather from our contemporary context, where what often prevails is a sentiment of indifference and extraneousness (for example, toward the environment and future generations) or fear of the other, especially when the other (for example, the migrant who crosses our borders) becomes dangerously close, thereby abolishing distance and challenging our immunitarian defenses. We can think, here, of ethnocentric out-bursts, discrimination against what is different, racist regressions, or the increasingly extreme forms of ethno-religious intolerance—phenomena that lead us to have legitimate doubts about the empathic capabilities of humankind.[11]

We certainly take comfort, therefore, in recent analyses such as those by the anthropologist Frans de Waal, who tries to show the natural and universal character of sympathy through his investigations of the animal world.[12] Yet this character does not amount tout court to moral agency, as some critics of de Waal have promptly noticed while invok-ing Hume's reflective faculty.[13] Moreover, it does not tell us how and why empathy should extend to the distant other. On this topic, Jeremy Rifkin's diagnosis, which is attentive to our historical-social context and its epochal changes, seems more convincing to us.[14] Rifkin explicitly links the universal potentialities of empathy to humankind's entry into the global age and its possible positive aspects. He seems in fact to suggest that the global age makes possible the resurfacing of motives that have always been constitutive of human beings but have long been obscured and sacrificed to the acquisitive yearnings of homo oeconomicus and to the predatory hubris of homo faber. Paradoxically, thanks to the very same challenges that jeopardize its survival, for the first time in history, humankind has the opportunity of rediscovering the empathic capability that the sciences themselves currently acknowledge as constitutive of human nature. As Rifkin claims in his formidable epochal diagnosis of the history of humankind, we are about to enter "an empathic civiliza-tion" grounded on the awakening of the sense of sharing, that is, on the emergence of an empathic awareness that predisposes us to sociality and solidarity. Paradoxically, he adds, this possibility opens up at the very moment when we witness (and pay for) the very high cost humanity had to pay to be able to access such an empathic civilization, such as the pillage of resources and the insane consumption of energy—what has been called "the tragedy of the commons."[15] Empathic consciousness, which the progressive development of complex and technologically advanced societies has made possible, must reckon with the negative and catastrophic effects of such development. That is, it must confront the parallel and specular tendency toward "entropy" that currently yields to the extreme danger of the self-destruction of humankind and the planet. Briefly, empathy, which implies the development of a self that is open and sensitive to the destiny of the other, has grown in direct proportion with the entropic damage produced to the environment, the biosphere, and living beings: "We are at a decisive moment in the human journey where the race to global empathic consciousness is running up against global entropic collapse. While our empathic gains are impressive, our entropic losses are equally foreboding."[16] We face an opportunity that is up to us to seize. The gamble here lies with the possibility of breaking the binary empathy-entropy relation, thereby initiating the new age of *homo empathicus*—the human being who, on the ground of the awareness of one's constitutive connection with the other and the mutual interconnectedness, is capable of avoiding the catastrophe facing living beings.

In other words, it is legitimate to hope that the very fact of living in an interdependent world may open us up to the possibility of a greater awareness of our relational condition and participation in one single humanity[17]—a humanity that is exposed to the same challenges and the same destiny and shares the same condition of vulnerability, beyond all differences and even prior to inequalities. This amounts to claiming that the global age produces favorable conditions for the reflective sympathy Hume considered capable of expanding our empathic capability and generating an impartial viewpoint. The global age thus creates the presuppositions for the inclusion of the distant other into our empathic circles.

An additional proposal that aims at valorizing the aforementioned diagnosis comes from an interesting context of postmodern sociological reflection, in which some thinkers representative of so-called "aesthetic cosmopolitanism,"[18] including Scott Lash, John Urry, and John Tomlison, have emphasized the positive potentialities of the global society. Thanks to the erosion of spatial and cultural boundaries, the global society enables the diffusion of a multiplicity of symbols, cultures, and lifestyles that end up generating a new and widespread sensitivity, open to the encounter with diversity. Whether it is direct and concrete, as experienced in our everyday reality, or virtual and media channeled,[19] the contact with the different other creates the exposure to diversity that ends up stimulating, according to these authors, an *emotive curiosity* for alterity. I would like to emphasize that perhaps such a curiosity does not necessarily translate into empathy toward the new figures of the other; yet, it can nonetheless favor a deeper interest and even moral attention toward those *others* who become, now and again, significant for us.

The Other Distant in Space

Let us consider how the possibility of expanding the circles of empathy may function in the case of the other distant in space. Once again, it is Peter Singer who leads us in this direction when, in his book *The Life You Can Save*, he proposes a very elegant and clarifying mental experiment.[20] Let us imagine, he tells us, that we pass in front of a pond where a child is drowning. It is more than likely that we would not hesitate to jump into the water and save the child, even though this ended up ruining the expensive shoes we wear. Seeing the child and the child's fear and hearing the child's screams generate in us an instinctual and immediate response that, at that very moment, puts on the backburner our other needs or preferences (especially when futile). Singer wonders, though, whether we would do the same for African children who suffer and die because of poverty. Would we feel equally involved and ready to intervene here in some way? Evidently not, as attested by the fact that poverty is increasing exponentially, producing more victims on a planetary scale. We know that, in remote parts of the world, there are suffering and death; we even see media images of them on a daily basis; yet, we are not moved in the same way, because distance enables us to activate defense mechanisms, such as denial, aimed at nullifying the reality, thereby allowing us to return to our reassuring routines.[21]

This is partly understandable, if not legitimate, as claimed by some of Singer's critics. Among them, we are not surprised to find Michael Slote, who is convinced that a moral obligation exists only for "the near and dear": "We (normal humans) generally feel more empathy, and more empathic concern (or caring), for those whose plight we witness than for those whose plight we merely know *about*, and for those who are related to (or intimately involved with) us than for strangers and people we know only by description."[22] Furthermore, as Singer himself does not fail to remark, even in the most well-intentioned people there arise doubts and perplexities that are not entirely specious, for example, the fact that saving one child is easier than saving thousands, that we do not know strategies to save thousands, and that often we do not even trust humanitarian associations. Yet, Singer concludes, in order to eliminate the problem of poverty, it would be sufficient that citizens of wealthy countries made a small donation that would not even require a sacrifice of our own interests or lifestyle.

In sum, on the ground of de Waal's and Rifkin's overall considerations as well as Singer's more targeted diagnosis, it seems legitimate to suppose that the circles of empathy can be expanded to the other distant in space, especially in a world like the global one that compresses distance and creates unprecedented planetary connections. We have seen, however, that even where it is the outcome of a reflective path and an impartial gaze, empathy is not sufficient to ground moral obligation.[23] Empathy is, in fact, a neutral mechanism that in itself has no motivational force unless it is translated into a specific emotion or moral sentiment.

Indignation and Compassion

We inevitably come to ask the same question we posed at the beginning, this time taking into account the global context: Is it possible to pre-suppose the self-activation of emotions or, better, of empathic emotions, when confronted with the need and suffering of others that are distant in space? If so, which emotions? Can we still count on the insurgence of those emotions that earlier we connected to the demand for justice, namely, indignation and compassion?

I think there are no apparent doubts with respect to indignation. Contemporary reality attests to the global diffusion of this passion as one of the growing phenomena of our times. This diffusion imposes on us the need for a more accurate diagnosis than what transpires from its various media-based expressions. Indignation is undoubtedly the passion that inspires the multiple protests against the various forms of injustice present on the planet and that acts, to use Manuel Castells's words, as the emotional "spark" from which contemporary social movements arise.[24] From the 1999 Seattle protesters to the various incarnations of Occupy that have truly proliferated in recent years,[25] these movements are characterized from their outset by an evident heterogeneity while at the same time always sharing an emotive origin. As Castells remarks with reference to the theory of emotive intelligence, it is for the most part a matter of episodes in which the reaction against an unjust event yields to an explosion of rage that at first enables a collective overcoming of fear and then coagulates in forms of mobilization inspired by enthusiasm and sustained by a rebirth of hope.[26]

This second effect seems to have weakened, at least in part, during the revolts and protests of the last decade. Due to the global financial crisis—which started in 2008 and is heavily responsible for new forms of poverties and inequalities—and following the often intolerable conditions generated by the crisis, "the cauldron of social and political indignation reached a boiling point." It is also true, however, that it seems to settle for claims that are more selfish and circumscribed in comparison with Seattle's initial ideal inspirations. Castells argues that, in actuality, things are not this way insofar as contemporary social movements share a set of positive characteristics due to the fact that they are networked movements [in rete]. This implies a set of particular features. They can afford not having an identifiable center while ensuring, at the same time, functions of coordination and deliberative process thanks to the interaction of a multiplicity of nodes. Their decentered structure "maximizes chances of participation in the movement, given that these are open-ended networks without defined boundaries." Their horizontal and multimodal networks create "togetherness. This is a key issue for the movement, because it is through togetherness that people overcome fear and discover hope." "The horizontality of networks supports cooperation and solidarity while undermining the need for formal leadership." Finally, which is what interests me the most here, they can count on the viral impact of their message on their multiple recipients, "whose emotions connect with the content and form of the message."

Indignation can coalesce in structured global associations such as OXFAM or Global Justice Now, or it can give rise to more informal demonstrations and ensue in legitimate and contingent explosive reactions such as in the case of the already mentioned gilets jaune in France. It is certain, however, that its spark seems to spread, through networks, into the global space, giving voice now and again to protests against various forms of injustice—whether this is suffered personally or is witnessed more or less directly by us. In short, the just anger animating contemporary movements originates not only from the (by all means legitimate) protest against the end of welfare, from the fear of poverty, or from the loss of that minimum level of well-being we thought was a given; it also originates from more exquisitely ideal perspectives and the desire for a better world. These are goals that require a fight against "the new spirit of capitalism" and its lethal consequences, trust in global solidarity, the awakening of forms of cooperation, and the sharing of a different image of the world. We can recognize these goals in the very recent Fridays for Future and Extinction Rebellion or, in agreement with Alain Touraine, in the different expressions of women's movements (from Se non ora quando [If Not Now When] to MeToo).[27]

Whereas the current reality attests to the widespread and active presence of indignation, the role of compassion in the face of the distant other seems to be more problematic. There is no doubt that compassion does not entail the risk of a unilateral folding onto one's own interests, as compassion is a more "altruistic" passion than indignation. Compassion arises only in the presence of the other's suffering and thus, using Nussbaum's words on this topic, it is one of those passions that expand the boundaries of the self. Compassion is particularly representative of such passions. Nevertheless, Nussbaum herself does not fail to remark on the limits of compassion, quoting Adam Smith.[28] The limit of this passion that we want to highlight here is precisely its presupposing the proximity of the other, the face-to-face relationship, and the view of the pain and discomfort in the other's material and bodily marks.

How can we think, then, that compassion may be activated toward a remote and anonymous other, whose suffering we cannot perceive except in the abstract? Actually, we do indeed have powerful media instruments that daily present us with images of amassed, humiliated, wounded bodies (from migrants to victims of wars, tsunamis, poverty): through internet and the social networks, which certainly encourage forms of active participation, as well as through TV images, which abruptly break into our lives and, despite us, perturb our passivity.

Interesting and convincing is the proposal that sociologist Luc Boltanski advanced already a few years ago, in which he revaluated what he called a "politics of pity,"[29] calling for its decisive and urgent retrieval in face of the pressing needs for humanitarian protection. Boltanski challenges, first and foremost, the increasingly widespread conviction that we are victims of an addiction to media images, so much so that we are impermeable to their crudity and violence. As already mentioned, this conviction inspires, for example, Susan Sontag's harsh criticism on the limits of compassion,[30] and finds confirmation in the psychological theory of "compassion fatigue" (or compassion stress disorder), which alludes to the anesthetization and decline of empathic emotions when they become the object of repeated and excessive stimuli.[31] According to Boltanski, if, on the contrary, we posit ourselves as critical spectators, we become capable of letting ourselves become emotionally involved by "spectacles of suffering." We can respond to these spectacles with a "politics of pity" that does not aspire to impartiality and equality, like the politics of justice, but rather implies a sort of mobilizing asymmetry that joins with the spectator's emotive involvement. In short, Boltanski points to the need to rethink the politics of pity in new terms on the ground of the paradoxical reality that it is called to resolve.

The paradox lies precisely in "distant suffering," that is, in the fact that the global age introduces distance between spectator and sufferer. On the one hand, distance makes possible a political use of pity (there is no politics without distance, Boltanski reiterates in evident agreement with Hannah Arendt); but, on the other hand, distance renders the spectator's moral commitment evidently problematic. Consequently, Boltanski asks: What form can commitment take up when the one who should act is distant from the one who suffers? When we come to know someone else's suffering only as it is channeled to us through mass media information and images? According to Boltanski, a politics of pity must satisfy a double need. On the one hand, to activate pity, it cannot leave aside individual, specific cases that have the power of affecting the sensitivity of the observer (no one is moved by cold statistics about poverty!). On the other hand, however, as politics, it must be able to generalize and treat individual cases as exemplary instances. Here, in the "paradoxical treatment of distance," the role of emotions becomes fundamental— emotions that are filtered through Adam Smith's requisites of reflection and moral consciousness that Boltanski does not fail to invoke, thereby grounding moral obligation and the birth of a community of observers. The sharing of information created when one is faced with the media transmission of the spectacle of suffering translates into collective respon- sibility on the part of informed and conscious spectators. It is therefore possible to conceive of a coordination of spectators through speech, through communication with others, within the public space, of what has been observed (for example, through television images). It is indeed the case of "effective" speech, which implies the affective involvement of the spectator faced with the spectacle of suffering, favoring the move from individual speech to collective commitment.[32]

I argue that Boltanski's proposal can find an additional reason for its effectiveness if we situate it explicitly within the context of the global age. The hypothesis that the expansion of pity to the distant other and the break of the wall of indifference originate in the possibility of self-recognition as members of a single humanity gains substance within such a context. In this case, pity would shed all traces of hierarchical difference (between those who feel pity and those who are subjected to it) that makes it suspect to its critics and take up the broader sense of compassion, *cum-patire*, suffering-with.[33] This sense is implicit in its very etymology and implies sharing suffering with the other (even the remote and unknown other) by virtue of a shared belonging in humankind (and the living world).[34] It would be the expression par excellence of what Etti Hillesum referred to as a basic love for humanity.[35] Currently, this love is no longer simply the wish and gift-giving act of sublime individuals; rather, it is a sentiment that has the chance to unite individuals into a mutual bond insofar as they objectively are, and self-recognize as, members of a single humanity and inhabitants of a single planet.

Fear and Resentment

The issue gets to be more complicated and the chances of compassion drastically diminish when the distant other becomes, as it were, proximate and approaches us by crossing our borders and penetrating our territories in search of refuge, work, and hopes for survival. That is, when the other becomes the person whom we can define as "the internal stranger," the person "who comes today and stays tomorrow," to use Georg Simmel's expression.[36] The problem becomes more complicated when the distance that is abolished at the spatial level is reproduced in more radical forms at the symbolic and cultural levels. Thus, indifference to the person who is distant in space—that is, the person who does not involve but also does not threaten us insofar as we are protected by territorial borders—is replaced with fear of the proximity of the different [*il diverso*]. Or, better, a diffused feeling of anxiety spreads in front of an object that appears the more threatening the more it is indeterminate:[37] fear of siege, of the loss of borders, fear, as I have suggested elsewhere, of contamination by someone who embodies an ineludible difference and challenges our immunitarian certainties.[38] The border that, when associated with state and territorial modernity, evokes the idea of a fixed and reassuring demarcation has been replaced with a *limes*, a line that is undefinable and unrecognizable, that excludes but does not separate and no longer ensures immunity.[39] The internal stranger (the immigrant, the refugee, the clandestine) is the one who can be neither assimilated—as the person resists with his, her, or their identity, tradition, and culture—nor expelled as, within the global society, there is no longer a sharp border between inside and outside. Paradoxically, the case is that of a presence that is simultaneously internal and distant, close and foreign; or, better, it is the more foreign and threatening the more it becomes internal and proximate. Due to massive forced migrations investing our territories, thereby challenging any immunitarian delusion, (European, Western) individuals feel besieged by the stranger, threatened in their own safety and privileges. The other, the different, is perceived as the one who invades our borders, takes work and resources away from us, and, above all, with his, her, or their diversity produces effects of contamination threatening our own identity. Briefly, we could say, with Émile Benveniste, that from *hospes*, guest, the other becomes *hostis*, enemy.[40] The outcome is a defensive response that consists in the radicalization of the immunitarian mechanism in an aggressive direction; that is, it consists in constructing scapegoats supported by "attacks on minorities"[41] or inventing enemies and forming "communities of fear"[42] based on the contraposition us versus them[43]—in other words, converting fear into hatred, spite, and misrecognition.

This is not all, though. Mirroring the destructive dynamics of fear is the reply by the other, the stranger, who reacts to humiliation and exclusion by harboring sentiments of rancor and hostility; that is, resentful passions, ready to explode sooner or later into violent and conflictual forms.[44] We have examined how resentment is a reactive passion that responds to an insufferable sense of powerlessness and inferiority through, at times, even extreme forms of retaliation and vengeance. Whether, with Sloterdijk, we conceive of it as a deformed and involved variation of rage—insofar as, unlike rage, it is void of any ability to innovate and change—or we regard it as an enduring and rancorous filiation of envy, resentment seems currently to produce a "metaphysical revenge bank."[45] That is, it produces an ideology that has lost all ability to make legitimate claims—such as those arising from "just anger"[46] and righteous claims to recognition—and instead is only capable of nourishing spirals of violence, as seemingly evident in the terroristic drifts of Islamic fundamentalism and the cyclical revival of atrocities as well as in the outbursts of racism and xenophobia.

Confronted with this bleak alternative of fear and resentment, which is produced by the proximity of the different and in which the space for empathic passions seems irremediably eroded, the question of whether an appeal to compassion is still possible becomes inevitable. An initial answer could be to adopt a *homeopathic* strategy; that is, to interrupt the *allopathic* dynamics of immunization and oppose it precisely with openness to contamination and availability to a contagion with alterity, thereby accepting the challenge that comes from difference. To use Judith Butler's words,[47] the matter would be that of an exposure to the transformation coming from contact with the other, letting the other act as factor of permanent contestation. In short, it would be a matter of risking oneself in front of the other's difference and of recognizing such difference also as a potential resource in order to avert the absolutization of identity that constitutes the very source of conflict and violence.[48]

Such is also the sense of Jean-Luc Nancy's paradoxical invitation to let the stranger preserve his, her, or their strangeness, to let him, her, or them be "an intruder."[49] It is, paradoxically, from the strangeness of the other or, better, from the irreducible truth of the other's strangeness that an awareness may emerge regarding the contingent and relative aspect of our own identity. This concept finds confirmation in sociological and anthropological reflections such as, for example, in James Clifford's claim that we must preserve the concept of alterity understood as difference and "radical irreconcilability" because these are the only ways to "make any assimilative synthesis impossible" and keep open "a space that makes the other's positioning possible,"[50] that is, the other's ability to assume an active role within the power dynamics that rule the struggle for recognition.

The other resists us, compels us to take stock of his, her, or their ineludible presence and accept the contamination that comes from difference. I want to stress that this does not mean giving up aspects of one's own identity that are rightly dear to us (such as rights and freedom); rather, it means rejecting their self-referential logic and immunitarian closure and opening oneself up to the confrontation with the different. The confrontation is evidently not void of anxiety [*inquietudine*], as suggested again by Nancy when he claims that the advent of the other will not "cease being in some respect an intrusion."[51] Nevertheless, or perhaps precisely because of this, it is a confrontation open to alteration. Anxiety, as the *perturbing* Freudian effect produced by the challenge of the different, is what compels us to keep identity open, to measure up with its frail, provisional, and contingent character, thereby preventing its immunitarian closure and preserving it from absolutistic temptations and desires for domination.

To expose oneself to the contamination of one's identity is the precondition for overcoming fear, interrupting negative projections onto the different, and reconverting the *hostis* into a *hospes*, the enemy into a guest. It is, in other words, the presupposition for hospitality.

Hospitality and Recognition

What does hospitality mean? Currently being a crucial notion to understand the status of the other distant in space and the relationship that we can establish with this figure, hospitality has more ancient origins. Ever since ancient Rome, it included recognizing the rights of the foreigner, which were equal to those of the Roman citizens. These rights are sanctioned normatively and are circumscribed by a pact of reciprocity (of rights and duties) with any foreigner who possesses identification documents.

Yet, as Jacques Derrida claims, to be truly the case, hospitality can neither be limited by rights nor be conditioned by a pact-based and symmetrical logic.[52] It rather presupposes a break with such logic in order to become absolute, unconditioned, and indiscriminately welcome "the new arrival."[53] The law of hospitality

> seems to dictate that absolute hospitality should break with the law of hospitality as right or duty, with the "pact" of hospitality. To put it in different terms, absolute hospitality requires that I open up my home and that I give not only to the foreigner (provided with a family name, with the social status of being a foreigner, etc.), but to the absolute, unknown, anonymous other, and that I *give place* to them, that I let them come, that I let them arrive, and take place in the place I offer them, without asking of them either reciprocity (entering into a pact) or even their names.[54]

Hospitality can only adopt the asymmetrical logic of the gift and move beyond justice;[55] or, at least, beyond justice that is limited by bonds, calculations, and duties of right.[56] It can only start earlier than any identification, before the symmetrical and equivalent criterion of justice is instituted. As Derrida asks, "Is hospitality *rendered*, is it *given* to the other before they are identified, even before they are (posited as or supposed to be) a subject, legal subject and subject nameable by their family name, etc.?"[57] In its paradoxical emphases, among other things, Derrida's invitation has the merit of reconfirming, even in the case of the other distant in space, the limitations of the symmetrical logic that subtends the paradigm of justice (understood in its abstractedly normative variation) and the need for an openness to the gratuitousness of hospitality. These limitations appear again in the case of the other distant in time (and of future generations), for whom, as we shall see, a more adequate response can be found in the ethics of care and responsibility.

Nevertheless, I argue that Derrida's proposal with regard to the other distant in space necessitates two substantial integrations that return us to the passions. First, we could reiterate that *this* (gift-giving and unconditioned) hospitality that Derrida advances cannot do without the empathic disposition of putting oneself in the place of the other and without a motivational drive that originates in the emotive spark of compassion. The hospitality without conditions or reciprocity of which Derrida speaks can only arise from the activation of empathic passions, capable of contrasting indifference, diffidence, and fear when faced with the suffering of those who cross our borders and appeal to us with the extreme eloquence of their wounded, tortured, abandoned bodies.

Second, if the unconditioned character of hospitality implies rejecting the symmetrical logic of reciprocity that compels the other to a pact-like bond, this nevertheless does not entail denying the importance of recognition by the other—that is, by the guest, the one who is hosted—toward the host.[58] In other words, we should not underestimate the importance of the other's response, its role that is not only passive and receptive but also active and defining of relations. This is especially the case when the other, whom Derrida basically considers as "the new arrival," becomes also "the one who stays," to use Simmel's expression—that is, the one who as a temporary guest asks to become a permanent citizen, to enter permanently a new homeland, a new culture, and a new lifestyle. This is the decisive point at which the host's overcoming of fear and welcoming can be met with the guest's overcoming of resentment and negative projections. As we have seen, resentment is a regressive passion that arises from a deep sense of powerlessness and congeals the interlocutor in the static and definitive image of an enemy to dare and strike, in a vengeful spiral. We witness this spiral, in its extreme forms, in the demonization of the Western world and the terroristic drift that is becoming increasingly endemic and unpredictable. So that a sustainable coexistence may be possible, there is at least one ground of reciprocity that the guest is called to practice when faced with the host: turning the host into the object of a form of recognition that liberates the host from the deleterious image of being the incarnation of evil and a pure instrument of oppression.

This means, however, that the one who receives the gift accepts the gift of hospitality and is willing to return it through the recognition of the donor. I call this situation *asymmetrical reciprocity* insofar as it demands unconditioned welcoming on the part of the host and, on the part of the guest, acceptance of the gift on the ground of a position of social and identitarian disadvantage. The risk is that the gift may be perceived as a heavy burden, thereby assuming the aspect of a perverted gift[59] and generating, in the case that it hides traces of pity, negative passions such as humiliation, resentment, and hatred, which are always potentially liable to light the fuse of violence.

To avert such a risk, the recipient of the gift must feel that justice has been ensured, because only in this case will they be able to afford feeling gratitude and recognizing their debt, as suggested by Simone Weil in *Gravity and Grace*: "In order to feel true gratitude . . . , I have to think that it is not out of pity, sympathy or caprice that I am being treated well, it is not as a favour or privilege, nor as a natural result of temperament, but from a desire to do what justice demands."[60] In other words, the gift cannot be perceived as charity, as a unilateral act that, as Marcel Mauss argues, ends up humiliating and wounding the receiver. Receiving the gift—and returning it without the fear of feeling and acknowledging even gratitude toward the one who welcomes us—allows us to complete the cycle of the gift understood in Mauss's sense of a structure of reciprocity.[61] By averting interruption in the cycle of the gift, it is possible to prevent the potential explosion of negative passions and violence, ultimately laying the foundations for dialogue and negotiation.[62]

I will return to the paradigm of the gift in relation to the other distant in time. What I want to underline here is that the matter is not that of hypothesizing some kind of peaceful acquiescence and passive habituation. This is especially the case when, toward the different that has become an internal stranger, the host enforces dynamics of power and misrecognition by denying rights and justice. Here, it would become legitimate for the guest to react with those "tymothic" passions (such as anger and indignation) that, without giving up conflict, nevertheless do not yield to resentment and violence. It would thus be possible to move from irreducible antagonism to constructive agonism.[63] In this case, the guest could rediscover the constructive energy of just anger, shifting the gaze from the other to the self, in order to become again protagonist in legitimate struggles for recognition—being animated not by a will to annihilate the other, but rather by the legitimate desire to assert one's own dignity and difference.

One could object by claiming that this conversion of the other's passions (from resentment to indignation) can only be hoped for and that, given the global context—certainly not encouraging, as it is made of retaliations and violence—there is not much hope with respect to this point. Our alleged powerlessness can, however, be overcome if we start acknowledging our own responsibilities, and even our guilt, in provoking the other's aggressive response and if we are willing to put ourselves personally at stake. We must be the first to try and change our negative emotions and convert indifference and fear into compassion[64] and, even earlier, into shame [vergogna], because shame is, in this instance, the passion that can arise from the awareness of creating intolerable inequalities and from the fear of incurring on the other's judgment.[65]

The fact remains, however, that even when this conversion is successful, thereby favoring the awakening of positive motivational forces, this does not automatically translate into a move to action. The ability to feel and participate empathically in suffering, overcoming the obstacle of compassion fatigue even with respect to the distant other, does not necessarily imply mobilization and engagement. On the contrary, as Susan Sontag remarks with heartfelt disenchantment, it can turn into some form of self-exemption from all responsibilities or authentic involvement: "But if we consider what emotions would be desirable, it seems too simple to elect sympathy. . . . So far as we feel sympathy, we feel we are not accomplices to what caused the suffering. Our sympathy proclaims our innocence as well as our impotence. To that extent, it can be (for all our good intentions) an impertinent—if not an inappropriate—response."[66] This holds true both for the distant other at the territorial level, that is, the one who lives beyond our national borders and moves us through media images, and for the refugee or the migrant who lands on our territories and to whom we offer emergency responses and survival kits.[67]

It becomes imperative, therefore, that we ask ourselves which possible strategies can be deployed to shift to engagement, understood as a continuous and incisive practice that certainly is nourished with the initial spark of passion but is also capable of moving beyond pure feeling. As far as the other distant in space is concerned, I would like to suggest two strategies; they would require the involvement of political subjects as well as institutions, of individuals as well as citizens, thereby reconfirming the necessary alliance between justice and care.

Frequently, we hear heartfelt and emotional announcements by various European politicians confronted with the proliferation of extreme images of suffering: the Syrian young boy who was found lifeless on a Bodrum beach in Turkey in 2015, which became the symbol of the humanitarian tragedy of migrants; the young girl who died in a fire in the hell of the Lesbos refugee camp in Greece in March 2020; or the images, which rarely filter through, of the torture of migrants in Libya's detention camps. Compassion does not seem to be followed by coherent and effective action, though. On the contrary, the measures taken mainly by the European countries are fueled by the radicalization of the immunitarian logic that, paradoxically, intensifies the more illusory and ineffective it proves to be, ending up shattering the very same structures of justice it seeks to preserve and create. As I have already suggested earlier with respect to gratitude, it becomes pressing to reinstitute justice as a right and as guarantee of rights. Out of love for paradoxes, Derrida proposes to overcome it,[68] but without it there can be neither common rules to appeal to nor cooperation and, therefore, there can be no real hospitality.[69]

At the same time, hospitality cannot be limited to emergency and provisional welcome—which, by the way, often justifies inhuman conditions and harms the dignity of the individuals who are the recipient thereof. Hospitality must instead transform itself into attention to the others' needs while respecting their dignity on the base of the awareness that one is often dealing with someone who "comes to stay." And one must be aware that our role is not exhausted by our coming to the rescue and providing means to satisfy some primary needs; rather, we must take responsible charge of the other, and envision daily practices, adequate structures, and abilities to plan future developments. In other words, hospitality must become care.

I will return later to the theme of care as a dimension of action and commitment toward the distant other when I address the other distant in time. It is appropriate to clarify immediately, however, that despite the prevailing skepticism about theories of care, which seem to bind it to face-to-face relationships,[70] care is not limited to the "near and dear" and to relations of proximity. In other words, care is not "parochial," as Fiona Robinson correctly claims when insisting on the need to expand the ethics of care to the global level insofar as it is capable of responding effectively also to distant relationships.[71] One can therefore suppose, and wish, that care may work not only toward those who are close and familiar to us, or toward the internal stranger with whom we create, albeit with difficulty, relations of proximity,[72] but also toward the distant other in geophysical and territorial senses, of whom we only see images from afar, mainly blurred and short-lived, channeled through the media.[73]

Undoubtedly, the forms of care and the practices that ensue from it change for each of these figures. As we shall see shortly with respect to the other distant in time, what joins all of them, though, is the idea that, within the global society, not only *feeling* but also *acting* and the commitment toward the other can be constantly expanded as long as they are nourished by some form of feeling. Thus, they become increasingly more inclusive of those who are not known, proximate, or familiar to us.

Six

Global Perspectives

Care and Justice Confronting the Challenge of the Temporally *Distant Other*

Intergenerational Justice

As we have seen, it is not easy to identify the motivations and passions that are the foundation of moral action directed toward the other distant in space. This is even less the case for the other distant in time, who can be legitimately recognized as the radical challenge of our time. What can push us to worry about future generations, that is, for the unborn, who have neither face nor name and whom we can easily confine to a nebulous and remote future that, to deploy Jacques Derrida's provocative expression, does not regard us?[1] In short, is there an obligation of responsibility toward future generations?[2] What might be its motivations? We can indeed develop a deep sense of empathy and community for the spatially distant other, that is, for the poor of the world, refugees, and migrants; we can mobilize up to risking our own life to create networks of solidarity with those affected by war, exile, hunger, and humiliation. And, nevertheless, we can simultaneously remain indifferent to the fate of those who will live after us in a remote future. It is no coincidence that the so-called "motivation problem,"[3] which underscores the weakness (if not the absence) of reasons to justify the responsibility for future generations, precisely concerns the other distant in time. We must therefore identify the factors that can motivate individuals not only to accept responsibility for the future in the abstract but also to adopt responsibility as part of their moral identity and, consequently, take appropriate action.

The question about motivations had already emerged, starting from the second half of the twentieth century, in the philosophical reflections of Günther Anders and Hans Jonas when facing the emergence of two unprecedented planetary environmental challenges: the threat of nuclear power and the ecological crisis. The question was evidently implicit in the Stockholm Declaration of the first environmental summit of 1972, in which the responsibility for future generations is recognized as an inescapable imperative, given the enormous impact that, for the first time in history, the action of present generations may have over those of a distant future.[4] Currently, this imperative assumes further cogency due to the multiplication and radicalization of threats and risks stemming from the dizzying speed of the processes of globalization. Climate warming and resource erosion, ozone holes and soil depletion, waste and slag disposal, nuclear power and the threat of global nuclear conflict, and climate migration of biblical scope, these are the increasingly evident manifestations of the growing pervasiveness of global environmental risks,[5] which endanger, if not the life of future generations, at least their right to a life worth living. The need for intergenerational responsibility is, therefore, now the object of widespread attention, even when not of broad consensus.

Increasingly in the minority[6] seem, in turn, to be some positions that can be brought back, despite their differences, to what a couple of decades ago Giuliano Pontara defined as "the thesis of nonresponsibility."[7] This thesis may be grounded on a trust in divine providence capable of guaranteeing progress to a better state no matter what; or it may claim the impossibility of knowing today what the preferences of future generations will be; or it may rest on the absence of motivations for caring for individuals who do not yet exist; or it may deny the relevance of an ethics of the future compared to that of the present. But this is not all. Insufficient are also the theories that propose forms of partial or reduced responsibility. Exemplary in this regard is the theory of John Passmore, who, however, deserves credit for paying early attention to this topic.[8] Even though he recognizes the obligation not to harm posterity, Passmore argues that we can never foresee whether our actions will have a positive or negative impact on it; we can, however, be pretty sure about the fact that we ourselves would be harmed now by certain choices made for the sake of future generations. Consequently, the one responsibility that is reasonable to assume is toward immediate posterity: if every generation cares about those immediately following it, as is likely to be the case by virtue of an affective bond, a chain of love may be created that will reach generations furthest away in time.[9]

Reservations and cautions seem in turn to fall away, parallel to the progressive maturing of an ecological conscience, in the face of the increasingly visible signs of the damages to the planet caused by our actions. The belief is growing that an ethics capable of living up to the global challenges must now include future generations. In other terms, the concept of the future, as Hans Jonas had already proposed in the last century, must fully enter the horizon of our moral obligations.

Unsurprisingly, scholarly contributions confirming the spreading of the aforementioned position have multiplied in recent decades, so much so that it would be impossible to give an account, even partially, of the debate on this issue. From the now classic 1978 text of R. I. Sikora and Brian Barry, *Obligations to Future Generations*, to the *Handbook of Intergenerational Justice*, edited by Jörg Tremmel and published in 2006, from Avner de-Shalit to Dale Jamieson and the now multiple analyses of climate change,[10] the attention to these issues seems to have grown exponentially,[11] so much so that it has also given a new twist to theological-religious reflection. Such a reflection has moved away from referring to the action of the divine providence and has become aware, as evidenced by the important encyclical of Pope Francis, of the urgency of the environmental problem and even of its dignity as the moral problem par excellence for our times.[12]

The diagnostic awareness of the problem carried out by theoretical reflection currently leads to a regulatory concern about the strategies to be adopted, which start with some more or less shared slogans such as the need for sustainable development and the recognition of the rights of future generations, the reduction of emissions responsible for global warming and the fair distribution of burdens, an awareness of the limits of natural resources and the guarantee of equal access to resources for all. Together, these strategies form what we can call, drawing on Giuliano Pontara's lexicon, the "thesis of (full) responsibility."[13]

Yet, I would like to point out here that the scenario is more complex and impervious than what it seems: not only for the variety and multiplicity of answers offered, often in conflict with one another, but also for the difficulty that each regulatory approach visibly faces when dealing with this problem, along with the radicality of the challenge that it poses to traditional paradigms,[14] especially that of justice. It is sufficient here to recall some of the most frequent objections advanced even by those who nevertheless appear determined to find some answer: first, the possible conflict between the interests of future individuals and the interests of those living in the present, as both are legitimate recipients of moral obligation; second, the impossibility of knowing what the effects of our actions will actually be, given the speed of technological development and its ability to keep up to date with respect to the emergence of new obstacles; and, last but not least, the speciousness of currently favoring a certain choice A (for example, a choice to save) over another possible choice B (for example, a choice to waste), as if only the former were capable of protecting future individuals and, therefore, of being morally acceptable. Here, we confront what Derek Parfit has called the "non-identity problem," that is, the fact that, if one makes choice A, the individuals who will exist in the future will anyway be different from what they would be if choice B were made[15]—a fact that would end up exempting the present generation from responsibility for future generations.

Mainstream normative theories, which for some time have treated systematically the problem of intergenerational justice—whether they are deontological theories such as contractualism or consequentialist theories such as utilitarianism—try to respond to these objections. In both cases, the difficulty arises when an attempt is made to reconcile the presuppositions constitutive of each paradigm—an action is right if it respects certain moral principles, in the case of deontological theories; if it produces beneficial consequences, that is, the maximum well-being for the greatest number of people, in the case of utilitarianism—with the specific needs and objectives of the intergenerational perspective.

Let us try, without any pretense to present a complete picture, to reflect on these two proposals, starting, first, with Rawls's neocontractualist view developed in his *Theory of Justice*.[16] As we know, Rawls develops the model of a just society by assuming an agreement on the principles of justice on the ground of two fundamental premises: first, subjects are conceived of as existing within the context of an originary position in which they will have to make decisions starting from a "veil of ignorance" (about what their status, values, and talents are and the generation to which they belong), which guarantees the impartiality of the agreement; second, the subjects of the pact are perfectly rational, that is, they are motivated not by the passions (such as envy) but essentially by the pursuit of their interests (primary goods, rights, opportunities). These assumptions can only lead to a universal consensus on the decision for an equitable distribution of resources that is mutually beneficial, in which the only legitimate inequality would be, according to the "principle of difference," the inequality that would reward the most disadvantaged.

This scenario, however, does not seem to include intergenerational justice,[17] since it runs into the difficulty of considering as parties in the pact generations that are not coeval as well as of conferring the status of contracting party to not-yet-existent generations. Although Rawls clearly poses, out of respect for the principle of fairness, the problem of the extension of principles of justice to future generations, invoking the principle of just savings in their favor, he also is aware of its inapplicability, as this would be contrary to what is assumed as the dominant tendency of the parties, namely, the tendency to maximize their own present interests with total indifference toward those who will come after them.[18] Rawls, therefore, is, so to speak, forced to modify some assumptions of his theory regarding the motivations of the parties in the initial position. He hypothesizes, then,[19] that the subjects of the agreement are no longer single individuals that only seek to satisfy their own self-interests; rather, they are the heads of families motivated by a "natural enough" concern for the well-being of their children and grandchildren.[20] This solution is simultaneously incongruous and ineffective:[21] it is incongruous because it presupposes a sort of loophole, an ad hoc response, as noted by Brian Barry among others,[22] that cannot be inferred from the presuppositions of his theory (that is, contemporaneity of the parties and symmetry); and it is ineffective because Rawls seems able to solve the problem of moral obligation to future generations even less than Passmore, with whom he actually shares the idea of the chain of generational proximity; in comparison with more proximate descendants, future generations could in fact suffer different effects that may be even more devastating than certain choices of the current generations.

The utilitarian paradigm of justice seems to cohere better with the adoption of a theory of intergenerational justice, since, unlike contractualism, it includes the foregoing element in its own premises on the ground of Jeremy Bentham's well known "hedonistic calculus."[23] As already mentioned, for utilitarianism, a society is just if and when it promotes the maximum happiness for the greatest number of people. Henry Sidgwick argues that the achievement of happiness is a universal value; hence, it follows that the factor of time becomes completely irrelevant in this regard, since the well-being of future individuals legitimately matters as much as that of present individuals.[24]

Despite the greater compatibility with the intergenerational perspective, utilitarianism too runs into a series of problems that compromise its normative effectiveness. The first problem concerns the very notion of happiness or well-being, that is, the difficulty of defining what constitutes the well-being of future generations, given that we do not yet know their tastes, needs, and preferences. A second problem, repeatedly emphasized by scholars, stems from the absence, in the utilitarian approach, of distribution criteria. Axel Gosseries notes: "Yet, it is entirely true that this theory of justice is not primarily concerned with the *distribution* of welfare among the members of society. What matters is the size of the welfare pie from which society as a whole will benefit, not the relative size of the pieces of that pie each member will be receiving."[25] The impact on the level of intergenerational justice consists in the fact that the criteria used to evaluate the fair distribution of costs and benefits between generations are lacking. This means that the present generation is required to adopt savings policies necessary for the maximization of intergenerational well-being,[26] with very costly if not outright sacrificial outcomes. Rawls himself notices this when he remarks that utilitarianism is a theory that is excessively demanding to present generations.[27]

Finally, utilitarianism incurs on what (again) Parfit defined as a "repugnant conclusion,"[28] namely, the completely unacceptable outcome that stems from the absence of any concern for distributive justice. In other words, since, according to utilitarianism, the well-being of the world can grow without the growth of the well-being of each individual, it follows that the choice to increase the quality of life thanks to a simple quantitative increase in individuals would be preferable over a choice that lowers the total level of the quality, but increases the average one.[29] We would be faced with the paradox according to which, as Parfit writes, "[f]or any possible population of at least ten billion people, all with a very high quality of life, there must be some much larger imaginable population whose existence, if other things are equal, would be better even though its members have lives that are barely worth living."[30] Neither contractualism, even in its most sophisticated Rawlsian version, nor utilitarianism, despite its interest in the happiness of humankind, succeed in providing a valid justification for our moral obligation to future generations. Furthermore, neither the partial "correction" of the rationalistic assumption of symmetrical reciprocity nor the naturalistic premise of an automatic inclusion of future generations in maximizing well-being are convincing.

More effective is, in my opinion, the communitarian approach, in particular, that proposed by Avner de-Shalit a couple of decades ago in his widely discussed *Why Posterity Matters*.[31] In showing the inadequacy of conventional theories of justice, de-Shalit reiterates that the obligation to future generations remains a matter of distributive justice (understood primarily as equitable access to natural resources) and not of *caritas* or supererogation. He proposes to retrace the moral foundations for it in the idea of a "transgenerational community," which also includes generations temporally more remote while justifying the choice of certain environmental policies. De-Shalit certainly does not deny the difficulties inherent in this special case of justice, and he takes care to premise that, where needs and interests of the current individuals conflict with those of future generations, it is necessary to give reasonable priority to the first ones.[32] However, probably aware of the possible objections to this premise—given that, as we have seen, the conflict between generations is precisely one of the significant challenges that intergenerational justice must face a priori—de-Shalit corrects the apparent naivety of his arguments through two fundamental additions.

The first consists in affirming that we have always and in all cases strong "negative" obligations to future generations, which essentially consist in avoiding harming them.[33] The second tends to emphasize that, where there is no conflict, we have no excuse for not fulfilling our obligations,[34] which arise precisely from the common belonging to a transgenerational community. This is an interesting concept—first, because it restores an (albeit indirect)[35] motivation for the obligation to future generations; second, because of the particular version of it that de-Shalit proposes. The normative prerequisite is that, if we recognize the community as the foundation of our identity, it would be absurd to deny an obligation to it.[36] But, which community is this? Definitely opting for Michael Sandel's vision of a *constitutive* community that seeks to avoid any deterministic connotation,[37] de-Shalit emphasizes its rational and reflective character that arises from the critical capacity of its members as well as from the constant willingness to review the ideas and values that ground it. Though it assumes a "moral similarity," that is, the sharing of principles and values, the community must be the outcome of a choice:

of a rational choice that arises from free critical examination, through various cultural interactions, of its founding elements and principles, be they traditions, feelings, and/or customs.

On these same grounds it is possible to found the concept of a transgenerational community that extends into the future, albeit in the absence of the daily interactions that characterize the very idea of community. Already a few decades ago, Ulrich Beck spoke of a "community of destiny."[38] We can bring this idea of community back to an anthropological, and even ontological, foundation. As human beings, we tend to project ourselves (into) and worry about the future, considering it as constitutive for our identity, especially because presupposing the unity of the self over time allows for the mitigation of the fear of death, but also because we are pushed to a sort of "self-transcendence" that allows us to move outside ourselves and think of a broader image of the self.[39] In short, we are creatures psychologically capable of concerning ourselves with, and taking care of, the future: "We are creatures who are capable of caring about and feeling concern for the future; this is one of our basic characteristics as human beings, and this is part of what defines our personal identities. By this we can enlarge our conception of our 'self,' our identities: we include in it the future of objects—human and non-human—that are part of us. And by this we mitigate—at least to some extent—our fear of mortality, of death."[40] This is not enough, however, to justify the obligation to future generations. Nor can we appeal to sentiments, de-Shalit adds, referring to what he calls the "fraternity model."[41] He gives two reasons for this: first, it is not possible to experience love and empathy for persons not yet born and whom we will never know; second, sentiments in and of themselves neither mobilize nor motivate action. I shall return later to this crucial point, which I do not wholly share. Here, it is important to underscore what de-Shalit claims in order to ground his normative perspective, namely, that obligation can stem only from the recognition that we are members of a transgenerational community that we understand as constitutive of our identity by grounding it on cultural exchanges and moral resemblances.[42] Concerning the latter, far from identifying with static homogeneity, resemblance must continuously be kept open and reflectively challenged in light of the changes in history and identity. Regarding the former, cultural interaction must be conceived as a logical implication of the interaction we have with the past through an unending debate that runs, precisely, across generations.

These are generally convincing arguments that could, in my opinion, be reinforced by the fact that globalization, which here is understood as the emergence of a global ecological crisis, creates the emergence of a new subject, namely, the human kind, which is joined beyond all differences by the same challenges and destiny, and which is called to respond to the very same moral imperatives. This point was perfectly grasped both by Hans Jonas, when he underlined the ethical potentialities of the environmental planetary challenge, and by Günther Anders, when he maintained that the nuclear bomb and threat have rendered us, for the first time, one single humanity.[43] The communal exposure to what, following Ulrich Beck, we call "global risks,"[44] *objectively* creates, given their radicality and pervasiveness, an intrinsic communal bond that could and should become stronger than differences. This would be the case—we must reiterate this—provided that some macroscopic and unacceptable inequalities are remedied at the same time; for instance, and referring to a topic of great importance, starting with the recognition on the part of the rich countries of the Global North of an "ecological debt" toward the poorer countries of the Global South, which not only have been exploited and robbed of their resources but whose populations also constitute the majority of those currently affected by the effects of the ecological crisis produced mainly by the aforementioned rich countries.[45]

The Responsible Subject and Indirect Reciprocity

The question, however, is whether this objectivity can translate into subjective awareness, and whether we now have available a subjectivity capable of grasping the opportunity of recognizing itself as a member of a transgenerational community that also includes future generations. De-Shalit himself explicitly discusses the problem when he argues that his communitarian theory of intergenerational justice presupposes a conception of the human being that is capable of going beyond its own selfish interest: "Hence, I shall begin by putting forward a "communitarian" theory of intergenerational justice, which is based on a conception of human beings seeking a moral environment transcending self-interest. Analyzing the concept of a "transgenerational community"—one that extends into the future—I argue that it reflects this conception of the person, that it is morally desirable, and that it justifies a belief in obligations to future generations."[46] Here, however, de-Shalit's argument stops, effectively leaving open the reflection on the question of the subject: What form of subjectivity do we need for individuals in the globalized world to be able to think about themselves and act as a single humanity?

This is a topic that is still entirely to be tackled. Nevertheless, we do have some answers that, albeit from very different perspectives and languages, converge on the need to rethink the subject departing from the inadequacy of the mainstream paradigm formalized during the unfolding of modernity. This is the paradigm of homo oeconomicus and the rational choice of a sovereign, self-referential subject that is concerned only with pursuing its own interest and that, paradoxically, if we investigate the pathological drifts that affect it from the second half of the twentieth century on, ends up becoming obtusely short-sighted, especially with respect to the future.

An essential answer is the one that comes from the philosophies of alterity influenced by phenomenology, from Levinas to Ricoeur to Jonas,[47] all centered on the relevance, if not on the primacy, of the figure of the "other" in the very constitution of the subject: be it the affirmation of the precedence of the other and the ethical power of the other's call (Levinas), be it the emphasis on human frailty and the condition of mutual dependence (Ricoeur).[48] But it is Jonas, in particular, who, with his pioneering insight into the new risks and challenges that loom over humanity and the living world, extends this ethical perspective into the future by proposing the idea of a subject that responds to the call of an other distant in time, to the silent but unavoidable appeal of future generations. Not only does Jonas catch the explosion of the contemporary ecological crisis at its birth—a crisis that now becomes more and more visible through the multiplication of extreme events—but he also presents the reasons for it, which are attributable to the pathologies of homo faber, to its Promethean omnipotence fueled by technology, and to the disconnect between one's actions and the consequences of such actions.

This theme unites Jonas's thought with Günther Anders's insight about the splitting, the "Promethean difference," between doing and foreseeing, which permeates the subject from the moment it has lost touch with the purpose and sense of its own acting, perverting itself from homo faber into *homo creator*.[49] The radicality and destructiveness of these challenges can only be countered by answering the call of the other distant in time, which works as a provocation, an injunction that forces us to responsibility.[50] This call cannot be escaped, says Jonas, as it comes from a vulnerable other, from a fragile, imperfect, and transient object,[51] which, precisely by virtue of its fragility and imperfection, has the power to bind us and demand our attention: "Yet just this far from 'perfect' object, entirely contingent in its facticity, perceived precisely in its perishability, indigence, and insecurity, must have the power to move me through its sheer existence (not through special qualities) to place my person at its service, free of all appetite for appropriation."[52] The force of the vulnerability of the other, Jonas claims with an eloquent oxymoron, is equal to the force that leads parents to take care of a newborn who, by simply "breathing," imposes on them the charge to take care of its life, thereby establishing itself as the "timeless archetype" of responsibility and care.[53]

This is a powerful proposal. We can find some echoes of it in contemporary reflections,[54] and, moreover, it does not fail to summon the emotive dimension, as it identifies fear for the other (which I will address later) as the motivation impulse to responsibility for future generations. The limit of Jonas's argument consists in the presupposition of a purely altruistic subject capable of welcoming the appeal of the other while not being fully capable of accounting for it, oscillating, in fact, between affective reasons that require an intellectual operation (the heuristics of fear) and metaphysical-deontological ones (we have the duty to be responsible toward future life, as the value of being is superior to nothingness).[55]

Jonas presupposes the existence of an altruistic, duty-bound subject whose motivations remain partly opaque. We can nevertheless integrate his position with others, even within various philosophies of alterity that, though they do not treat the problem of the future, still enable us to uncover the sources of the responsible subject that lie neither in an abstract ethical imperative nor in an altruistic sentiment, but in the subject's very own perception of its own vulnerability and recognition of its own dependence (and interdependence).[56]

From the point of view of Emmanuel Levinas, the extremely radical affirmation of the primacy of the other amounts to presupposing a subject stripped of its pretensions of sovereignty and expropriated of its foundations—a subject that is constituted by the ethical break of the absoluteness of identity and its hybris.[57] This is what, in her intense discussion of Levinas, Judith Butler calls the "necessary grief" for the death of the subject—not of the subject tout court, but of the sovereign subject.[58] This mourning foreshadows the possibility of thinking a different structure of the self, that is, a self that is aware of its constitutive dependence, of its unbreakable link with the other in a relation of reciprocal interdependence. The self, in other words, is constituted by an originary "impingement" of the other—an intrusion that gives rise to the subject at the very same moment that it expropriates the subject of its identity, that it violates it, thereby causing a decentering, a wounding of the subject itself.[59] Here, the subject is consigned to a state of vulnerability.

Butler often returns to this concept that, as we have seen, brings together most feminist thought, and she investigates its various versions (ontological, ethical, and social). Vulnerability is a primary, originary situation; so much so that we can recognize in it the very mark of the human, of the constitutive, inescapable fragility of the human condition. It is something we can never escape, as, "when the human . . . refuses the way it is impinged upon by the world, it ceases to be human."[60] We cannot even trace its origins, as it is coeval with the origins of life itself and precedes the very formation of the subject. "That we are impinged upon primarily and against our will is the sign of a vulnerability and a beholdenness that we cannot will away."[61]

To recognize one's own vulnerability means recovering the truth of the inherent sociality of the human condition that shows us to be truly dependent on one another, exposed to the risk of relations, tied by a bond that connects our lives in an unbreakable and reciprocal link. This "does not dispute the fact of my autonomy, but it does qualify that claim through recourse to the fundamental sociality of embodied life, the ways in which we are, from the start and by virtue of being a bodily being, already given over, beyond ourselves, implicated in lives that are not our own."[62] Vulnerability is, therefore, a resource, "one of the most important resources" that the self must seize and value in order to recover its relational nature and its sense of being in the world.[63] It is, in sum, an ethical resource in which resides the source of responsibility. It is in the very being exposed to the other and in "the failure" of its sovereign position that the subject finds the sources for its responsible acting.

The connection between vulnerability of the other and vulnerability of the subject lies also at the center of Paul Ricoeur's thought. In a perspective similar to that of Jonas, Ricoeur affirms that the "fragile," that is, "what is perishable by natural weakness and threatened by the blows of historical violence," has the power to reawaken our feeling, provoke our pain and indignation, our concern in the face of something that we "experience as deplorable, unbearable, inadmissible, and unjustifiable,"[64] and that, consequently, demands our care. There is no responsibility except where "we feel" that we are made responsible by someone who, on account of their fragility, trusts in our help while asking us to take charge of their destiny.[65] At the very moment it accepts responsibility, the subject constitutes itself as such, not as a sovereign and autonomous Cartesian subject, but as a *relational subject*, which is aware of the condition of reciprocal dependence characterizing the human. Different than Jonas and similar to Levinas, Ricoeur dwells on the subject and on its ability to respond to the call of the other insofar as the subject recognizes itself as constitutively *indebted* to the other.[66] The particular relevance of the notion of "debt" is confirmed by the fact that, in "Love and Justice," Ricoeur builds on it his criticism of the idea of justice. Rawls's model of distributive justice creates, in the best-case scenario, a society in which "the feeling of mutual dependence . . . remains subordinate to the idea of mutual disinterest." It is not that the idea of reciprocity is absent from this model, Ricouer claims; but "the juxtaposition of interests prevents the idea of justice from attaining the level of a true recognition and a solidarity such that each person feels indebted to every other person."[67]

A fecund concept, debt is deployed to reconstruct the very idea of a social bond and solidarity, as long as it is purified of the negative connotations of burden and guilt—along with the specter of its infinite insolubility—hanging over a single subject isolated from the community; and as long as it is reimagined from the point of view of its communitarian root. This is what has been recently proposed by David Graeber, who sees in debt a condition that, now more than ever, unites us and can therefore be understood and experienced no longer as a burden that weighs on the individual and for which one must answer individually, but as the shared basis on which to re-found the cohesion of the community and the value of solidarity.[68] Albeit in a different context, this theme returns in Roberto Esposito who, explicitly referring to Graeber, proposes to transform debt into an instrument of sharing by recovering its original meaning as *munus*: that which is a debt but also a gift.[69] This gift is to be understood in its negative meaning, always favored by Esposito, as what unites us all through the sharing of a lack, a void, a duty by subjects dispossessed of their sovereignty, of "*not*-subjects" subjects, connected by a reciprocal commitment that unites them precisely insofar as they are "missing from themselves" and that shatters the illusion of all individual absoluteness.[70] The gift as a debt, as that which "one *cannot not* give,"[71] emerges, in other words, as what interrupts the "immunitary project" of modernity and of modern individualism, returning human beings to the duty that binds them to one another, emptying them of their objective presumption of sovereignty, and exposing them to the "contagion of the relation with others."[72]

The notion of debt is also at the center of many reflections on the gift aimed at enhancing the ontological status of dependence and bond that connect individuals in a network of reciprocity in which everyone is always, simultaneously, donor and donee.[73] In fact, as Jean-Luc Marion would say, the one who gives has been in turn donated (*adonné*),[74] if only because they received the gift par excellence, which is the gift of birth and life. This is the great Debt, as Jacques Lacan calls it,[75] which binds us all to an inescapable origin, a creaturely origin that we cannot disown.[76]

For Paul Ricoeur, it is the awareness of our ontological condition of debt that allows us to move not only beyond the hegemonic paradigm of individualism, inspired by a purely utilitarian vision, but also beyond the paradigm of justice, which is always inscribed, Ricoeur emphasizes, in the "logic of equivalence" and anchored to an idea of symmetrical reciprocity. The recognition of the mutual debt allows us to enter the "logic of overabundance," which is asymmetrical and not bound to the response of the other,[77] inaugurating what Ricoeur calls "a gift economy." Here the gift should not be understood as a gesture of pure altruism but, more precisely, as a structure of reciprocity; or, better, of that peculiar form of reciprocity that Mauss-inspired gift theorists define as "enlarged reciprocity," in which what matters is not "mutual advantage," but the creation of a bond and the reaffirmation of the intrinsic value of the social bond.[78] Ricoeur uses an intense and eloquent expression in this regard when he speaks, in another text, of the "more or less umbilical relation of beings to each other."[79]

Enlarged and generalized[80] or unconditional[81] reciprocity—in which the very essence of the gift is expressed, so to speak—implies not only deferment over time but also the possibility of giving back not to the one from whom one received the gift, but to someone else. And this evidently suggests that the impulse to give does not come, in this case, from a direct motivation toward its recipient, but from the subject's awareness of its own vulnerability and indebtedness. However, being in debt loses all traditionally negative connotations in order to assume, on the contrary, the positive connotation of the logic of the gift, as Mauss first recognizes: "In the distinctive sphere of our social life we can never remain at rest. We must always return more than we receive."[82]

In this regard, Godbout speaks of "the tension of the reciprocal debt," and writes that "the true obligation is not just to give back but to give back even more. . . . [T]he obligation to give back more amounts to our becoming donors in our turn, not in order to do away with the debt but to permanently (re)fuel it."[83] It is, therefore, a debt that one does not feel the need to discharge; on the contrary, one wishes to prolong it, as it attests the valorization of one's own constitutive dependence and establishes a circuit of reciprocity based on that essential component of the social bond that is *trust*.[84] As Godbout remarks, "At a general level, this is the way in which we can make sense of the actors' discourse when they express their trust in a network in which things circulate and, somehow, work out—some kind of a general law of the universe or society that makes it so that one gives because one wishes to be part of such a system, because one feels that this is part of the conditions of being part of society."[85] Giving within a circuit of extended reciprocity therefore means thinking of oneself within networks of interdependence, exposing oneself to the risk of the other's response, and betting on the social bond.

Now, it is interesting to note that Mauss had insightfully thought of this form of reciprocity as the one that presides over the relationship and the gift between generations. In a text following the essay *The Gift* and recently brought back to attention by Marcel Hénaff,[86] Mauss distinguishes two forms of reciprocity: the first is direct, symmetrical, and dual; the second is instead temporally deferred and indirect, as it implies the presence of a third party in the dynamics of the gift. It is what Mauss calls precisely "indirect alternative reciprocity,"[87] according to which B returns to C what it received from A, and C in turn will return to D what it received from B, thus inaugurating a chain that extends infinitely in time. This chain therefore seems to be perfectly adequate to describe intergenerational responsibility, as it pushes the link between generations well beyond direct parental or family proximity. It is a "paradoxical reciprocity," which Hénaff calls *mutualité*, mutuality, and which facilitates the transition from a "logic of replication" to "an ethics of sharing," since "we do not give back to those from whom we have received, but to those who have not yet given."[88]

In truth, as Mauss reminds us, this usually happens when we transmit, mostly involuntarily, knowledge and beliefs, customs and values to those who will come after us, even in the distant future. But the gift of the future, I would like to add, the one that saves the future of humanity, requires an awareness that goes beyond any automatism. It requires trust in the social bond and a sort of morality of respect for things not yet born.[89] This awareness—it is legitimate to hope—could be currently favored by the globalization process and the unprecedented transformations that follow from it. This is primarily the case because, given the ontological condition of reciprocal debt, globalization also confers an anthropological and social status by virtue of the condition of interdependence and concrete vulnerability that it produces.

Mauss's intuition and the gift paradigm, if founded on the idea of vulnerability and debt, can provide a motivational context and a plausible justification for some theories of intergenerational justice that, albeit from different perspectives and without any reference to Mauss, in fact, currently repropose the idea of *indirect reciprocity*. It is a nonsystematic and nonuniform set of proposals united by the idea that each generation feels, now and again, the obligation to pass on to future generations what it has received from previous generations, according to a descending chain of obligations fueled precisely by the indirect character of reciprocity, not surprisingly called "descending reciprocity."[90] The most interesting aspect perhaps lies in the phrases of some authors whose thought in no way aligns with the paradigm of the gift. In them, we find the contestation of proprietary individualism and the invitation to think of ourselves not as owners but as guardians of what we have received. Annette Baier maintains:

> We all inherit a social order, a cultural tradition, air and water, not as private heirs of private will-makers but as members of a continuous community. . . . In so far as such inherited public goods as constitutions, civil liberties, universities, parks, and uncontaminated water come to us by the deliberate intention of past generations, we inherit them not as sole beneficiaries but as persons able to share and pass on such goods to an indefinite run of future generations.[91]

This is an explanation that even an author like Brian Barry, one of the most renowned supporters of social choice theory, is forced to admit, moving away, albeit reluctantly, from its rigorously rationalistic assumptions. He writes, "I must confess to feeling great intellectual discomfort in moving outside a framework in which ethical principles are related to human interests, but if I am right then these are the terms in which we have to start thinking. . . . [T]hose alive at any time are custodians rather than owners of the planet, and ought to pass it on in at least no worse shape than they found it in."[92] Incidentally, it is worth noting here the close similarity, also in the lexicon, with the vision of an integral ecology proposed by Pope Francis in his encyclical *Laudato si'*: "The world we have received also belongs to those who will follow us."[93]

However, all these proposals still do not sufficiently account for the motivational foundations. Further integration and taking another step are necessary. We saw that the first step implies an awareness of our reciprocal debt. As an integration to the paradigm of the gift, I want to reiterate that this awareness is nourished by the unprecedented conditions produced by the global age,[94] that is, by the urgency of the challenges and the interdependence of events and lives that transform the vulnerability of individuals into a condition that is not only onto-logical-symbolic, but concrete and real, and unite humanity in what Ulrich Beck called a "community of risk" or a "community of destiny."

There is a second and decisive step, though, which requires awareness of the fact that we ourselves are responsible for the risks to which the life of future humanity is exposed. In fact, it is because of our unlimited power that, for the first time in history, the risk of humanity's self-destruction is no longer just an apocalyptic fantasy, but a real danger. This is undoubtedly one of the most effective intuitions of Hans Jonas, who identifies the fundamental novelty of the global age in the nexus between power and responsibility: "The altered nature of human action, with the magnitude and novelty of its works and their impact on man's global future, raises moral issues for which past ethics, geared to the direct dealings of man with his fellowmen within narrow horizons of space and time, has left us unprepared."[95] Because of homo faber, who perverts himself into an "unbound Prometheus," we now have the power to jeopardize the very possibility of the survival of humanity and the living world, since we have lost, together with the meaning and purpose of our actions, the ability to imagine their consequences. The obligation to take charge of the destiny of the world and of the future of humanity derives from the fact that "modern technology . . . has enhanced human power beyond anything known or even dreamed of before."[96] It is a power without limits that produces "unintended and unwanted" effects,[97] all the more dangerous, the more they are precisely unintentional, that is, neither voluntarily nor consciously produced. In other words, the fate of future generations concerns us[98]—Günther Anders states, unhesitatingly tracing an unprecedented connection between the present and the future—as it depends on our actions and our present choices: "In fact, they occur now because they depend on the present moment; and as they happen now, they concern us because we initiate them already now through what we are presently doing."[99]

It is therefore our current power to decide on their lives that also makes us indebted to future generations. It is this power that ensures that, unlike our position with respect to past generations, future generations have rights and can legitimately claim them "against us," according to Annette Baier's eloquent expression: "It is possible that we stand to future generations in a relation in which no previous generation has stood to us; so that although we have no rights against past generations, future generations do have rights against us. . . . Our knowledge and our power are significantly different even from that of our grandparents' generation, and might be thought to give rise to new moral relationships and new obligations."[100] In sum, what drives us to assume responsibility toward future generations is not a direct motivation—whether it be the pursuit of one's interest, a personal and emotive bond, or the emotional reaction to the experience of suffering—but one or, rather, many "indirect motivations," as Dieter Birnbacher defines them, that is, motivations that produce a certain good or value as a side effect.[101] As I have tried to argue, some of them are, in my opinion, more convincing than others, for example, the awareness of sharing a condition of mutual debt fueled by feeling oneself a member of a community of global destiny, or the acknowledgment of the potentially irreversible risks and damages produced by our power.

If it is therefore true that what drives us to act responsibly toward the other who is distant in time is, unlike the case of the other distant in space, an indirect motivation, it cannot be ruled out that emotions may be activated also in this case. Without emotions—it is perhaps superfluous to repeat it here—the main motivational resource would be lost. Birnbacher himself does not fail to specify that indirect motivations are supported by a wide range of emotive factors, which end up constituting those motives that he defines as "quasi-moral," and in which he recognizes, within moral action, an importance equal to other types of motives.[102] This diagnosis, in my opinion, is largely acceptable, even though, once again, it stops at a generic reference to "altruistic" emotions (love, compassion, solidarity)[103] without introducing the necessary distinctions among the emotions themselves. The question we need to address here is: What emotions are we dealing with?

Global Passions: Fear for the World, Love of the World

It is perhaps not superfluous to reiterate that asking this question means implicitly presupposing the possibility of feeling empathy as the essential core of emotions, even toward the other who is temporally distant. It is not superfluous to repeat this, because, on this point, even those reflections that are most sensitive to the problem of intergenerational justice—and that are convinced of the potential constitution of a "transgenerational community," including, as we have seen, de-Shalit—seem to hesitate and be rather inclined to skepticism. The important concept of an "extension of the circles of empathy" proposed by Peter Singer, even though it does not exclude future generations from this process, explicitly refers to the spatially distant other.

However, we have available a decidedly more favorable approach to the possibility of extending the capacity for empathy to include the temporally distant other. In this approach, the tradition of moral sentimentalism and the ethics of virtue that I have mentioned previously converge, thereby confirming their mutual affinities also on this theme. Adopting Shaun Nichols's reflection on the development of morality,[104] Eugenio Lecaldano argues that it is precisely thanks to empathy that moral history undergoes continuous evolution, producing values and norms that tend to gradually eliminate everything that causes harm and suffering to living beings (from slavery to torture, to cruelty toward animals).[105] This does not mean, in my opinion, that this process always results in a linear and purely evolutionary history. In fact, we observe, clearly and in every age, cyclical and unexpected regressions that are difficult to reconcile with any form of Enlightenment optimism. It is true, though, as we have seen, that the process of empathic inclusion tends to involve ever new figures of otherness and that these figures become, now and again, "significant" for us. In other words, these figures and experiences are capable of mobilizing a reflective and extended empathy/sympathy—that is, that peculiar form of empathy that Hume saw as "the chief source of moral distinctions,"[106] as it is capable, through the imagination, of overcoming one's limits and correcting one's biases to access the impartial dimension of morality. It is no coincidence that precisely the lack of this reflective vision in the conception of empathy pushes, for example, an author like Michael Slote—even though he is a strong advocate of moral sentimentalism as a normative theory—to have evident hesitations and ambiguities regarding the potential usefulness of the notion of empathy as foundation of care for the other distant in time.[107]

A potentially open and impartial empathy is one that can intercept social turning points and changes and that, adopting the point of view of Smith's "impartial spectator," can respond emotively to unprecedented events, thereby broadening the range of those who are destined to become the object of attention and responsibility. It is the empathy that gets currently activated not only toward the stranger and the other distant in space, overcoming discrimination and borders, but also toward the potential future victims of the ever accelerating and disturbing ecological crisis. Phenomena such as climate change, to cite the most macroscopic effect of environmental challenges, inaugurate a new era by now commonly called Anthropocene.[108] This is the era in which human action has such a radical effect on the climate and on the ecological balance of the planet that it makes possible the very self-destruction of humanity and the entire living world. This translates, following Jonas's diagnosis, into the need for a further expansion of our responsibility toward future generations, which becomes more and more urgent. For this reason, as the proponents of virtue ethics propose when contesting the singularly selfish vision of the rational choice paradigm, we need a virtuous character capable of responding adequately to the transformations taking place.[109] That is to say, we need a type of character that can live up to the globalized and interconnected world. We need, as Dale Jamieson points out, a character endowed with those "green virtues" (such as humility, temperance, thoughtfulness) that confirm our willingness to commit ourselves to defending the planet and concretely transforming our ways of life for a sustainable future. In short, we must change ourselves in order to change the institutions, which in turn must be able to promote virtuous characters, in order to nurture that mutual cooperation between the individual and the community that alone can foreshadow a responsibility for the world.

The foregoing proposal may be read as an "ideal vision," as Jamieson calls it, which, on the one hand, is undoubtedly acceptable, both because it restores trust and value to the subject's empathic capacities against the reductively selfish vision of homo oeconomicus and because it underscores the very current potential of these capacities in facing what is the most difficult challenge of our time. On the other hand, however, in my opinion, this vision brings forward two problematic aspects. The first concerns a metaethical problem that I limit myself to mentioning here, namely, the perhaps too-demanding nature of the very concept of "virtuous character." To give an example, one could just think of the fact that a person who is very attentive and sensitive to the sufferings of others distant in space can remain indifferent to the fate of future generations, given the effect, even more powerful in this case, of defense mechanisms such as denial and self-deception, which I mentioned above. The second problematic aspect concerns the limits of empathy as a source of motivation. Indeed, we have seen that empathy is a neutral state that acquires motivating force where and when it gives rise to ethically oriented emotions, that is, where and when it translates into real moral feelings. It is therefore necessary to renew here, contextually speaking, the question we have already formulated several times: What emotions motivate us to be concerned with the other distant in time and to take charge of future generations?

We cannot propose here the same passions that we have seen functioning both in the demand for justice and in certain forms of care, such as compassion and indignation, because they presuppose, if not the presence and proximity, at least the existence of the "other," as in the case of the other distant in space. In other words, one cannot count on the emergence of compassion toward the unborn, since compassion always springs from witnessing, albeit from a distance, the suffering of another in flesh and blood, a victim of concrete and localizable events, for which it is possible to verify and measure the extent, time, and place (How many victims of wars or humanitarian catastrophes? Where? When?). In other words, compassion is what we could define as a passion of the present, always and in all cases aroused by being spectators of a current situation of suffering. This also applies to indignation, an eminently reactive passion that responds and rebels against a current and clearly identifiable situation of injustice, which can affect a people, a social category, or an ethnic group—in all instances, someone to whom we can attribute a name, a face, and a body. Neither compassion nor indignation can therefore be inspired by a future evil, nor can they be mobilized toward someone who has no name or face, as this person is still enveloped in the indeterminacy and abstractness of the not-yet.

If we return instead to the two main characteristics of the global age, namely, our unlimited power and our condition of mutual indebtedness, we can presume that the awareness of both these aspects may lead to the activation of those passions endowed with what we could define a self-critical reflectivity: for example, the feelings of guilt and shame, which, not by chance, have been defined as "self-conscious emotions," since they make us reflect, in the specific case, on the damages that our hubris and power have inflicted on the entire living world. These are two representative cases of those "negative" passions—also evoked, albeit fleetingly, by some scholars of intergenerational responsibility[110]—of which we can make "good use" by enhancing their positive qualities and directing them toward morally appreciable results.[111]

Yet, the most exemplary case of the ethical function of a negative passion is, perhaps, that of fear. It is worth dwelling on this passion both because it has been consecrated as a social and political passion from Thomas Hobbes to Hans Jonas[112] and because it is perhaps the most eloquent example of a *paideia of the passions*, an education of the passion or, rather, of the need to take care of the passions, to which I will return later.[113]

It is good here to immediately highlight a difference. The fear to which Jonas entrusts a fundamental role in his foundation of an ethics for the future is a very different passion from the classic Hobbesian fear in that it is not fear for oneself and one's own death, but fear *for the other*. In short, unlike Hobbes's selfish fear, it is an altruistic fear that arises in the face of the ecological crisis and the completely unprecedented danger of humanity's self-destruction and "loss of the world." It is a fear *for* the world and *for* those to come, which arises from the awareness of our power and of the negative effects our actions and choices may have on future generations.

This particular twist on fear, which turns it into a passion that I would not hesitate to describe as empathic, is anything but active and immediately available, though. Jonas is perfectly aware of this limit and sees its cause lying in the temporal distance of the evil, in its belonging to a remote future, which decisively reduces its impact and intensity. This is a fundamental aspect of the psychology of fear, which is fully intuited by Hobbes when he discloses to us that the fear of a future evil is weak and ineffective with respect to the passions and interests of the present. In other words, when it comes to choosing between a present passion and pleasure and a possible future good, human beings tend without hesitation to choose the first option, even if this means exposing themselves to inevitably negative consequences: "[M]en cannot put off this same irrational appetite, whereby they greedily prefer the present good (to which, by strict consequence, many unforeseen evils do adhere) before the future."[114] But that is not all. The desire for an immediate good is so powerful and blinding that it pushes people to deceive themselves about the negative effects that the attainment of that good could cause in the future, or, at most, to believe that it will in any case be possible to find strategies to avoid them, so as to weaken and render fear ineffective.

Now, if this irrational mechanism of self-deception and neutralization of fear holds true for choices concerning one's individual life, as happens in the Hobbesian scenario, it is legitimate to suppose that it works even more, as Jonas intuits, when our choices concern, first and foremost, the life of others, and of future others, with respect to whom we can invoke our objective impotence with impunity, or laugh it off as some form of catastrophism. In short, fear does not arise when danger affects the fate of future generations and of the planet more than our own lives; that is, when it affects a fate that "affects neither me nor anyone else still connected with me by the bonds of love or just of coexistence" and, consequently, "does not in itself have this influence upon our feelings."[115]

Günther Anders too insists on the unavailability of fear for the world and future generations when, as we have seen, he reflects on the risks of the atomic age,[116] identifying their roots in that split between doing and foreseeing, between knowing and feeling, which he calls the "Promethean gap"—a pathology of the global age that inhibits the emergence of fear despite the fact that the hubris of homo faber has ended up exposing humanity to the risk of self-destruction.[117] Anders intuits, in other words, the psychic roots of that powerful defense mechanism that Freud called denial of reality (of which self-deception is, so to speak, the most active manifestation). A different and more complex mechanism than repression, which in fact implies the oblivion and confinement of an uncomfortable or painful content in the unconscious, denial presupposes a split between the cognitive sphere and the emotive sphere. This means that we know what is happening, we know reality as we continuously receive flows of information that we cannot escape, attached as we are to increasingly pervasive computer prostheses. And yet, we deny reality, we prevent this knowing, this knowledge, from reaching our feelings, our emotive sphere. This may also be the case because our psyche is incapable of conceiving such a huge and definitive event as the destruction of humanity and the planet. We "react as we do not know what we know," states Stanley Cohen, who, starting afresh from Freud, has intuited the subtle ambivalence of denial and has grasped the pathological drift of this defense mechanism, especially when it becomes collective.[118] It is because of this split that we are unable to recognize and admit the dangers that threaten us.[119]

Consequently, we do not experience that mobilizing fear that would allow us to reappropriate the future: "At the idea of the Apocalypse, the soul remains inert."[120] In the case of the other distant in time, in fact, denial allows us to enact an anesthesia of fear. Even though the end of humanity and of the living world has now entered the realm of the possible, and even though human beings themselves are responsible for it, their psyche escapes the very idea of this possibility, inhibiting the onset of fear upstream. It is the beginning of that "great derangement," as Amitav Gosh recently defined it, that currently prevents us, as stubborn defenders of unsustainable lifestyles, from recognizing the ecological challenge and the devastating effects of climate change, thereby dragging us inexorably toward self-destruction and depriving humanity of its future.[121]

The future, as Anders had already warned us, "no longer 'comes'; we no longer consider it as something 'that comes': we make it. And we do it in such a way that it contains within itself its own alternative: the possibility of its cessation, the possible absence of a future."[122] Regaining the future, therefore, means recomposing the Promethean gap, putting our faculties back in touch, recovering the ability to imagine the possible consequences of our actions. Imagination—understood here, in a more daring and radical sense than the Humean one, as an *anticipatory faculty*—is the faculty that we can and must reactivate in order to relearn to be afraid,[123] even though it is a different fear from the Hobbesian one, that is, a fear "of a very special kind. . . . A life-giving anguish, since instead of locking us up in our rooms it makes us go out into the squares; a loving anguish, which fears for the world, and not only for what might happen to us."[124]

It is again to the imagination that Jonas himself entrusts the possibility of feeling fear for future humanity: an absolutely vulnerable humanity threatened in its very survival. In other words, there is a need for a "heuristic of fear," which makes use of the imagination as a faculty capable of reactivating fear in its appropriate forms, and of finding a powerful stimulus in the vulnerability of the other, in the silent but inescapable appeal that comes from future generations. Jonas affirms, normatively sanctioning fear as a necessary prerequisite for the ethics of the future and of responsibility, that "bringing ourselves to this emotional readiness, developing an attitude open to the stirrings of fear in the face of merely conjectural and distant forecast concerning man's destiny—a new kind of *éducation sentimentale*—is the second, preliminary duty of the ethic we are seeking."[125]

Jonas's proposal is undoubtedly interesting. Yet it rings, as we have already mentioned, of excessive altruism, for which he is unable to fully establish motivations. If it is true that the prefiguration of the vulnerability of the other is what can interrupt the destructive spiral triggered by homo faber, it is also true that this can only happen if the subject gives up the hubris of limitlessness to recover the sense of limit and vulnerability of the human condition.[126] In short, it is the awakening of the awareness of one's own fragility and limitation that makes the subject sensitive to the fate of the other and capable of responding to the other's appeal.

This perspective finds resonance in the reflection of Anders, who goes further, to the point of assuming what we could define as a nostalgia for vulnerability, which draws its legitimacy not (only) from a generic human condition, but from the assumptions of a particular historical era: ours. Faced with the destructive effects of our limitlessness, he affirms, faced with the excess of our titanic omnipotence that threatens to reduce us to helpless "pygmies," a new yearning seems to emerge that opens up an enormous distance between us and the generations that preceded us. While the latter, in fact, were driven by a Faustian aspiration to infinity and ultimacy, we, the first Titans, are driven on the contrary by the "desperate desire" to recover the limit that restores us to our human condition. Although they are scarcely aware of the direct connection between their "omnipotence" and the specter of the Apocalypse, human beings currently live in the paradoxical situation of a "Titan who desperately desires to return to being a human being,"[127] motivated by the "boundless nostalgia" for human limitation, fragility, and vulnerability. We can therefore assume that, in this desire to eradicate titanism in order to recover one's human limitations, lies the source of that awakening of fear that allows human beings to heal the Promethean split and worry about the fate of the world.

Perhaps, especially with the hindsight of the present, when human hubris does not seem at all to have completed its insane parabolic rise, it seems too optimistic to assume a desire for vulnerability. Yet the mere perception of one's vulnerability would be enough, in a world crossed by unprecedented global risks, to produce the awakening of fear: of a fear adequate to the challenges of the present; a fear that, acting as a *passion for limits*, can counteract the Promethean subject's vocation to limitlessness while functioning effectively as emotive source of an ethics of responsibility.

Does all of this mean that responsibility toward the other distant in time can only rely on "negative" passions, assuming that we know how to make good use of them?

A first answer, which leads us once again to the more sophisticated aspects of moral psychology, is already partially implicit in Jonas's arguments, in which he actually claims that a fundamental impulse toward responsibility for the world comes from the desire to preserve what is worthwhile for us. In other words, the fear that arises in the face of the specter of the "loss of the world" is inspired by the fact that we confer a value on the world (understood as nature, life, humanity) and that, by virtue of a basic psychological mechanism, the more we risk losing it, the more we appreciate it: "This (evil) is perceived first and teaches us, by the revulsion of feeling which acts ahead of knowledge, to apprehend the value whose antithesis so affects us. *We know the thing at stake only when we know that it is at stake*."[128] The prefiguration of evil makes us recognize and appreciate the good. This means that the fear of the "loss of the world" is transformed into the desire to preserve it thanks to the intrinsic value we attribute to it. It would be the case of one of those indirect motivations, inspired in this case not by people but by the good things that we value, here and now, and that we want to preserve, as we consider them essential also for future generations.[129]

This means, as has recently been suggested,[130] that the question that we must and can ask ourselves is not how to calculate, through the imagination, what might be in the interest of future generations, because we will never be able to answer this issue. The question, which we can reasonably answer, is rather the following: In what kind of world would we like our posterity to be able to live? And this implies at least two presuppositions from which it is possible to start, while also rejecting the specious objection of the "ignorance excuse."[131] The first, which brings us back to Jonas's imperative, concerns not acting in a way that harms posterity. The second concerns not depriving posterity of basic opportunities (such as the right to a functioning ecosystem or access to vital resources). But perhaps, faced with the specter of the loss of the world, we could abandon useless hesitations and ask ourselves a more risky question, without letting ourselves be stopped by that fear of deciding for future humanity that so worries some sophisticated champions of theories of justice: What aspects of the human, which ideals, practices, and resources, are worth saving in order to prefigure what, from our point of view, is a life worth living? Responsibility toward the future in fact also means assuming the courage of one's beliefs, opinions, convictions, even if we know that future generations may judge them insufficient or even wrong—this is the only criterion we have to try to avert the destruction of the living world.

The question posed above is, in other words, unavoidable in the epoch of the Anthropocene. In it, to quote the words of Serge Latouche, the human being "has become a telluric power capable of interfering with the great planetary cycles"[132] and an increasingly probable destruction and artificialization of the natural environment threaten to deprive future humanity of everything that forms the very matter of the world we love, of that irreplaceable set of flavors, smells, and sounds that mark our lives from the moment of birth. In the Anthropocene, the wager concerns—as the recent "visionary" reflections of Dale Jamieson and Bonnie Nadzam suggest[133]—our own ability to feel and love, the modalities of loving and being in a relationship within a totally denaturalized world. The reduction of nature to a pure "extension of ourselves"[134] and our desires deprives us of a vital and independent interlocutor, thereby enclosing us more and more in the sterile cage of narcissism: "In losing nature as a fully independent partner, we will have lost our best teacher for learning that something other than ourselves is real and thus a profound opportunity for learning how to love."[135]

It becomes therefore impossible to predict whether love will save the world. If that were the case, it should certainly be the kind of love that can only interrupt the self-referentiality of our self and act as that Platonic cohesive force that places us in an intimate and profound relationship with the living world and all that constitutes our dwelling.[136] It should be a love that, first of all, is connoted as love of beauty,[137] which arises from the contemplation of the beauty of the loved object, and which finds its energetic impulse in such an object. Like beauty, this love seems to have left the world; therefore, recovering the former means reaccessing the latter. We love the world, James Hillman reminds us in his heartfelt appeal for the return of beauty, "because it is beautiful, its sounds and smells and textures, the sensate presence of the world as a body."[138] One could certainly object that the appeal to beauty appears weak and purely tangential in the face of the radical nature of contemporary challenges. Yet, it is our sensitivity to beauty, our need for beauty that makes us love what surrounds us.[139] Consequently, the more the world becomes, as it is currently, an orphan of beauty—through the violation of the landscape, polluted waters, poisoned air, impoverishment of resources, disruption of seasonal cycles, and the degradation of cities—the more it becomes an orphan of love. In short, as Hillman writes in a passage that is only apparently daring, "Below the ecological crisis lies the deeper crisis of love, that our love has left the world. That the world is loveless results directly from the repression of beauty, its beauty and our sensitivity to beauty."[140]

We live today in a condition of anesthesia, of profound ignorance of aesthetic sensibility.[141] Therefore, caring for the world cannot be just a moral imperative, but requires recovering this sensibility, being able to rediscover the path indicated by the love of beauty, an indispensable presupposition of participation and commitment.[142] In short, the invitation is to believe, still now, that "beauty will save the world," as the Dostoevskyan title of a recent work by Tzvetan Todorov allusively states.[143] Referring to Iris Murdoch (whose entire work is pervaded by the theme of beauty), in a few essential words, Todorov indicates that, in the discharging of oneself from selfishness and in the attention to the world, the fulfillment of the relationship between aesthetics and ethics, between the beautiful and the good occurs: "The writer Iris Murdoch reflected on it, coming to the conclusion that the beautiful and the good go hand in hand precisely because they indicate an escape from an egocentric cocoon, as they accord priority to the world. Only in this way can true beauty be produced."[144] Perhaps Hannah Arendt herself, in her invitation to act "for the love of the world," would have welcomed the idea of summoning beauty, if it is true, as Hillman says, that for love to return to the world, beauty must return first.

It is therefore evident that, compared to the figure of the other distant in space, the other distant in time presents us with a much more difficult challenge. In fact, it is not enough to extend to the distant other feelings that are active and available anyway, such as compassion and indignation; rather, it is necessary to awaken passions that have been repressed, if not even extinguished, such as the love of beauty, or to activate new ones, such as the empathic fear for another without name or face.[145] In both cases, we must presuppose the subject's ability to transcend itself, to break through the narrow confines of the ego in order to respond to the call that comes from otherness. But in the case of the distant other in time, we cannot count on the immediately mobilizing impulse that springs from the vision of suffering and injustice. Even the acknowledgment of one's condition of debt, if this is understood only in a negative sense, would not have the strength to rekindle dead passions or to germinate new passions.

It is therefore necessary—and the concern for future generations proves this more than anything else—that, in going out of itself, the subject find its own gratification. This truth, on which, as we have seen, the gift paradigm itself is based, was already implicit in that ancient moral paradox according to which the most satisfying life is achieved when we are capable of self-transcendence. As Ernest Partridge says, a self-transcending concern toward future generations is not only possible, but healthy for the very realization of the self.[146] Certainly, to believe that this capacity for self-transcendence could be the result of the "normal process of maturation and socialization" would be too optimistic, in my opinion, unless this implies, as Partridge himself suggests, the commitment to adopt educational measures or institutional reforms capable of fostering this ability.[147]

The theme of the importance of a paideia of the passions therefore emerges again; I will return to it shortly. First, however, I would like to underline a further step, which I believe is necessary to complete the path toward an ethics of responsibility. I would like to define it as the passage from emotion to commitment and action.

Promise and Care

As we have already seen with regard to the other distant in space, the risk lies in stopping our argument at the pure dimension of feeling. This risk is even greater in the case of the other distant in time, where the object of the emotion itself does not have the disruptive force of concretely witnessing (even if from a distance) situations of suffering and injustice. In short, if this risk holds true for compassion in the face of the experience of suffering, it will be even more valid in the case of empathic fear for others who will live in the distant future, or in the case of shame for the harms that our actions will potentially cause to humanity and to the planet. Where everything (the object, the goal) is more indirect, it appears more difficult, assuming one manages to access the emotion, to translate it into mobilization, commitment, and action, given the uncertainty and distrust in the future and the difficulty in identifying the right strategies.

This difficulty, which, however, does not authorize us, as many authors rather hastily do, to liquidate the ethical function of the emotions with the accusation of weakness and ineffectiveness, can be addressed by activating some strategies that strengthen the capacity for commitment, since (1) they bind us to our own emotions and (2) they push us to take charge of the problem individually without delegating to others or waiting for institutional responses, be they local or global.

I especially think of promise and care. From Nietzsche to Derrida, from Arendt to Ricoeur, promising or, rather, the ability to promise, emerges as the faculty par excellence that allows us to face the uncertainty of the future. Making promises and keeping one's word means committing oneself, assuming responsibility for the future, "set[ing] up islands of security," says Arendt, in that unpredictable dimension par excellence that is the time to come. But it also means committing oneself to someone, binding oneself to someone, since no one would feel responsible for a promise made only to oneself.[148] Compared to Nietzsche's emphasis on the promise as the endowment of the autonomous and sovereign individual who, in respect of one's word, finds first and foremost the confirmation and growth of one's own power,[149] Arendt underlines the necessarily relational structure of the promise: "Binding oneself through promises serves to set up in the ocean of uncertainty, which the future is by definition, islands of security without which not even continuity, let alone durability of any kind, would be possible in the relationship between men."[150] Promising therefore means, first and foremost, recognizing the other and feeling bound to them by a commitment that extends to the future.[151] It is no coincidence that Paul Ricoeur makes it the foundation of that identity (*ipseity*) which is capable, precisely, of persisting in its own identity and being faithful to its word.[152] The promise is one of the powers of the "capable" individual: capable of speaking, acting, narrating, as well as being accountable for one's actions and being responsible for oneself.[153] But this individual is also capable, within the dynamics of recognition, of committing to someone and being faithful to that "promise that precedes any promise making," which consists in keeping one's word over time.[154] However, Ricoeur points out, partly inspired by Nietzsche, the promise is *fragile*, it can be broken by the betrayal of one's word.[155] Jacques Derrida also warns us about this danger when he states that a promise is "[a]n impossible act, therefore the only one worthy of its name."[156] As it is exposed to unpredictability and uncertainty, the word that promises may become corrupted and, consequently, it may interrupt that openness toward the other in which lies the fruitful potential of its giving quality.[157]

Arendt, perhaps too confident in the ability of the promise to "master this . . . darkness of human affairs,"[158] could not foresee this possible corruption. I would like to add, here, that this corruption becomes not only possible, but highly probable in the case of the promise to future generations, where there is no concrete subject that can call us back to our commitments and duties, nor can it threaten sanctions. In this case, therefore, the promise runs the risk of being broken in that phenomenon of weakness of the will, which has its ancient roots in the Greeks' *akrasia*. Consequently, the promise needs support, that is, it needs tools and devices that guarantee its fulfilment and protection.

Exemplary in this sense is self-binding, that psychological mechanism thanks to which we bind ourselves to protect ourselves from our own inability to keep the promise, whether this inability is due to trivial opportunism or to deceptive blindness toward the future. Evoking it precisely with regard to intergenerational responsibility, Dieter Birnbacher reminds us of its multiple and complex nuances.[159] Self-binding can be internal, when individuals rely on their own conscience to be protected from themselves and from possible deviations from their own principles and goals through the activation of emotive sanctions, such as guilt and shame, which I have already mentioned. Or it can be external, when we delegate to (legal, constitutional, educational) institutions the necessary sanctions for our short-sighted behavior toward the future. This is the model of Ulysses-and-the-sirens, certainly more effective and constricting than the imponderable punishments of conscience. Moreover, we already have some operational examples of this model (from the constitutional courts to the Kyoto Protocol and the subsequent summits on climate, from transnational organizations to the many research institutions and think tanks).[160]

Yet, in my opinion, we must recognize that, at least so far, the power of these institutions appears too weak to entrust them with the protection of the future and the ability to enforce our commitments toward the next generations, unless we are simultaneously able to develop, starting at the subjective level, *a culture of care*, which fills the void between the purely inner dimension of conscience and the external dimension of institutions, to become confirmation and testimony, in the present, of a determination to keep one's word through concrete and even daily acts.

In other words, the promise becomes reliable and effective if it can be translated, here and now, into care practices, into an active and concrete commitment aimed at preserving the world as a planet, as a home that hosts life, thereby guaranteeing future generations not only survival but also the possibility of a life worth living.

Care, Form of Life

We have already seen, with regard to the other distant in space, that care is not "parochial," that is, it is not limited to the "near and dear." On the contrary, it can always potentially extend beyond the narrow confines of proximity, provided that the other becomes significant to us. There are also those who argue, like Maurice Hamington, perhaps with an excess of optimism, that the ethics of care, unlike traditional (Kantian, utilitarian) ethics, contains, in its very ontology, concern for future generations and attention to sustainability regarding the environment: "An ethic of care is also much less likely to struggle conceptually with the problem of having moral obligations to future people and beings. . . . The practice of caring involves caring for future generations, some already existing and others that have projected existence. In maintaining relations, care ethics promotes practices that are more likely to project the existence of future generations, and in so doing, dependency relations are established that bring with them normative obligations."[161] However, what forms can the care of the distant other take over time? It is undeniable that, whereas it is easy to imagine forms of care that we can activate with respect to the spatially distant other—such as, for example, saving them from suffering or even from death due to wars, poverty, or ecological disasters, or providing them with help to soothe the wounds of the body or granting them a dignified welcome—it is more difficult to imagine to which practices we can actually commit ourselves in relation to an incorporeal other, who lives in the dimension of the not-yet. Yet, it is precisely here that care can show, in my view, its genuinely moral quality.

In fact, caring for the other distant in time clearly differs from the two forms of caring analyzed above, in that this kind of care is not preceded, like caring out of love, by a personal feeling toward the other, nor is it "contaminated," like attendant care, by a remunerative aspect. But it also differs from caring for the other distant in space since, in order to be activated, it cannot count either on the vision of the other's discomfort or suffering or on the mobilizing power of urgency and contingency. Together with the imaginative effort that activates the empathic passions, it therefore implies and demands the determination to commit oneself as a permanent quality of a relational subject, as a virtuous endowment capable of conferring attention to the other (in Weil's sense) a constant and widespread statute; capable of being activated, paradoxically, even in the absence of the other.

Unlike caring for the spatially distant other, which tends to be activated in a more episodic and fluctuating way, after the occurrence of specific events and on the wave of an appeal that arrives, now and again, from the emergence of suffering, deprived, tortured bodies (as in the case of the cyclical mobilization toward migrants), care for the temporally distant other can only be preventive. In other words, it can only mobilize, in order to be effective, before the events occur,[162] since these are potentially irreversible and irreparable events that can compromise the very future of humanity and of the living world—events that arise, as we have seen, from the pathological twists of modernity and the dominant model of homo oeconomicus. In other words, care can provide a decisive critical point of view on what has been configured since modernity as a real *form of life*—based on the hegemony of the economic and on the pervasiveness, at an individual and social level, of capitalist logic—potentially responsible for the loss of the world.

It is impossible to account here for the complexity of the concept "form of life," which has garnered renewed and widespread attention. We can only recall the element common to the various lines of interpretation, namely, that in all of them there "emerge the relationship between the level of social ties and the natural and biological dimension."[163] It is undoubtedly the particular approach of the critical theory tradition that poses the problem, to which I would like to draw attention here, of the legitimacy of the *critique* of the forms of life.[164] Let us simply evoke the main theses of Rahel Jaeggi's recent work.[165] The first is that a form of life presupposes not only certain values and beliefs, but also their deposit in institutional structures, as well as their materialization in practices, actions, and attitudes that concern the cultural and social reproduction of human life.[166] The second is that there is a multiplicity of forms of life that, now and again, have the task of facing and solving the problems connected with the maintenance of a given historical-social context.[167] The third is that it seems legitimate to subject any form of life to criticism when its inadequacy emerges or, rather, its failure to carry out the task for which it was intended, thereby proposing an immanent critique.[168]

Based on these premises, care can be taken as the ethical perspective that is capable of denouncing the pathologies of the modern and capitalist form of life, revealing its aporias and contradictions, and showing its inadequacy, even before subjecting it to a value judgment, in the face of the new challenges of the contemporary age.[169] By placing the accent on vulnerability and interdependence, on attention to the other and the conservation of the world, the ethics of care seems to be evidently not the only but a privileged point of view on which to base the critique of a form of life that is no longer able to give effective responses to the problems that emerge from the sociocultural context that hosts and mirrors it. This inadequacy is all the more paradoxical, I would like to add, in that these are problems that it itself has generated. In other words, the ethics of care can be the foundation for the legitimate critique of a form of life, which, to return to Arendt's metaphor, is no longer able to keep its promises, namely, the progress and well-being of humanity. It therefore requires, together with a change of perspective and paradigm, the activation of practices, attitudes, and purposes that are alternatives to those already in force, thereby contrasting the hubris of homo oeconomicus with the dependence and fragility of the human condition,[170] the blindness of technical action with the awareness of limits, indifference with concern and attention toward the fate of the other and of the world.

In other words, care appears particularly effective in countering the pathologies of the global age, as it is itself a form of life. The strength of the ethics of care lies in sinking its roots not in normative precepts or in deontological imperatives, but in material and symbolic forms of organization of one's life and one's world. As Sandra Laugier has rightly emphasized in the context of Wittgenstein's philosophy of life forms,[171] the particularity of the ethics of care is its pursuit not so much of what is right as of what is important.[172] It allows us to recognize what appears far from evident to the average consciousness, in that it has the power to direct "our attention towards the ordinary, towards what we are not able to see but which is before our eyes."[173] The ethics of care is the concrete manifestation of a sensitivity and an attention, as Iris Murdoch would say,[174] to detail, to the particular, which makes it possible to reveal and give importance to what is generally overlooked, that is, that microcosm of needs, expectations, and bonds that we tend to forget and devalue, to relegate to an area of opacity and invisibility, despite the fact that they form the daily fabric of everyone's life, the living matter of our existence. Care is everywhere, says Laugier, effectively recognizing the consistency and universality of a form of life.[175] "[Care] is present so pervasively in human life that it is difficult to see it for what it really is: a variety of activities with which we try to organize our world to be able to live in it at best."[176] Care can therefore counteract the growing diffusion of contemporary neglect, first and foremost, because it translates into a daily commitment,[177] into practices characterized by continuity, constancy, and an ontological statute, as it were, of permanence.

If, in a sense, these qualities belong to all dimensions of care, they appear even more constitutive and indispensable for the care of the temporally distant other. In fact, this kind of care loses all features of contingency and episodic character, which, despite everything, can characterize other forms of care,[178] to become a permanent attitude based on a vision of the world and on the will to commit oneself, even in the absence of the other, to daily practices capable of "promising" the survival of the other and of the world and a successful life. The daily commitment that we are currently able to offer is, in other words, the only proof of our determination to take care of the world and of future generations, the only confirmation of our will to keep a promise. This becomes all the more appreciable when we know that, in this case, we will not be exposed to any sanction and any reproach that can directly affect us.

Care for future generations is, in short, particularly exemplary of care as a form of life, since it requires an immanent critique of the dominant forms of life, a radical change of mentality, and the adoption of alternative practices and behaviors starting from daily commitment. In short, it requires a different way of thinking about the world and of being in the world that inspires our actions and transforms their deep roots.

There is perhaps no more effective example, in this regard, than the evocative images of two recent films, from which emerge that unique and extraordinary synthesis that care always promises to actualize between the concrete and capillary dimension and a strongly symbolic and transformative impact. The first film is Wim Wenders's *The Salt of the Earth* (2014), inspired by the photography of Sebastião Salgado, which through the latter's monumental work tells the beauty of the world in all its forms, natural and human, and its devastation and destruction at the hands of humans (an example is the photo of the half-naked child who, with his dog, observes the land parched by drought). This film opens onto hope, in that it ends with a narration about the project for the reforestation of the Atlantic forest in Brazil (*Recreate the Earth*), carried out by Salgado together with his wife. The second film is *Tomorrow*, a 2015 French documentary, whose directors travel halfway around the world in search of constructive examples against the destruction of the planet, focusing on five sectors: agriculture, energy, economy, democracy, and education. Among the exemplary experiences presented, particularly striking is the one that shows the possibility of achieving nothing less than the audacious goal of solving the problem of world hunger by carpeting our cities and metropolises with small green and cultivable spaces. This image can undoubtedly appear utopian, if it were not for the fact that it communicates the power of a real and concrete initiative. All of this evidently requires making a "bet," to use a metaphor dear to gift theorists,[179] on the effective possibility of translating into effective action and commitment what risks stopping at a virtuous potential.

It is therefore important to reiterate not so much that care goes "beyond justice,"[180] but rather that care is just as necessary as justice. This is the case not because care has the exclusivity of affections and emotions, but because it is based on emotions and feelings—such as love, gratuitousness, attention—which allow us to set different, yet equally precious, objectives from those that occupy justice. Among such objectives are not only the recognition of the debt to nature and the living world, based on the awareness of the ontological condition of interdependence and vulnerability, but also attention to everydayness and permanent commitment, the ability to create, in ordinary situations of life, that capillary fabric of mutual belonging that arises from valuing relationships.

Having entered into the merits of the passions and feelings that underlie the two different ethical perspectives allows us, in sum, to confirm the initial premise relating to the need for their mutual integration: justice and care operate in different fields, have different motivations, and set different objectives. It makes no sense to oppose them or to consider one more effective or adequate than the other nor, even less, to assume, in Aristotelian terms, that one can be self-sufficient and do without the other. In fact, we always need both. We need the impartiality and aspiration to fairness that are expressed in the passions of justice, as well as the capillary solicitude and excessive affectivity that manifest themselves in care. Our task is to try to identify, now and again, the strategies that make the two ethical paradigms more effective, and to understand which passions we can mobilize to make them operational.

Seven

For an Emotive Subject

Taking Care of the Passions

A *Paideia* of the Passions

Adopting a moral psychology perspective allows us, as we have seen, to let emerge the affective motives and motivations that inspire our moral actions, thereby recognizing the ethical role of the emotions. We have also seen, however, that this role does not reside tout court in the automatic moral relevance of natural sentiments; rather, it rests on our ability to orient ourselves consciously on the slippery terrain of emotive life in view of a reflective adhesion to what we call "moral sentiments." In other words, we cannot rely on a conciliatory naturalism but, rather, on the possibility of *cultivating* (to use the term introduced by Martha Nussbaum) the ethical quality of our emotions.[1] As Nussbaum claims, we learn from Aristotle, in contrast with Kantian rigorism, that we can cultivate emotions so that we can turn them into an essential component of the moral sphere, which is otherwise incomplete.[2] This is indeed a thought-provoking proposal, which, however, requires that we answer a series of necessarily ensuing questions. What does cultivating emotions properly mean? What faculties and strategies are at play? What subjects are called to take charge of them? What are the normative presuppositions?

Following a hypothetical, inevitably informal map, I would argue that the first presupposition is a dynamic and contextual view of the emotions that enables us to intervene in, and educate, orient, and transform, them. This requires, first and foremost, that we eliminate the prejudice concerning the unmodifiable character of the emotional sphere. Such a prejudice has forever been implicit in the dualism between reason and the passions and in the devaluation of the latter component, frozen under the rubric of irrationality and lack of temporality.[3] In short, we must do away with the idea of the ahistoricity and static nature of the emotions and regain trust, in Edgar Morin's words, in the possibility of "progresses of the human spirit" and transformations of "its psychic interiority."[4] Emotions can be assimilated neither to the rigid inexorability of instincts nor to the blind force of irrational drives. They are historical-social constructs, affective manifestations of an open and malleable nature such as human nature, always exposed to change and becoming. This diagnosis finds its most complete expression in some important twentieth-century theoretical perspectives: from German philosophical anthropology[5] to Freud and psychoanalysis, from phenomenology to María Zambrano, from Deleuze to the theory of the posthuman. As attested by Freud's very concept of the "drive" (*Trieb*), understood as a synthesis of the somatic and psychic, its plasticity and malleability find their origin first and foremost, or better, at first, in the fact that emotions depend, now and again, on our beliefs, convictions, and world images. And, with them, emotions share their historical and contextual character, as reiterated by Anders: "Feelings are not less historical, less modifiable, less ephemeral than ideas whose transformation is described by the history of philosophy and religion. . . . From a historical-philosophical viewpoint, it would be naive to believe that human beings remain emotionally constant. It is out of the question. Emotions depend rather on the existing historical situations, above all on technical tools."[6] Thus, we can act on emotions, thereby escaping the idea of the inexorable passivity of a subject that is enslaved to blind and incontrollable forces. This does not mean that we can control the passions, in the reductively rationalistic sense of the term; rather, we can take care of them. This expression is not simply another way of formulating the invitation to cultivate positive sentiments;[7] simultaneously, it also hints at something more. If we return to the double etymological meaning of the term "*care*" as concern [*preoccupazione*] and attention [*sollecitudine*], taking care emphasizes more carefully the complex and chiaroscuro character of this operation, the need better to understand how one should position oneself as a subject in order to identify the necessary strategies and steps for a path that is not void of obstacles, risks, and opaque zones.

The second step can be generally synthesized in the formula of *mindfulness*, that is, the strategy of self-awareness and attention to the self that currently sees a multiplicity of theories and practices—from the classic psychoanalytic exploration of the self to new forms of self-discovery within the varied archipelago of contemporary techniques of self-understanding.[8] I want to stress that awareness appears as absolutely necessary in a world like ours, where emotions are subjected to all forms of manipulation: instrumentalized by politicians, subtly imposed and even created by mass-media, or simply frozen in the inertia of stereotyped images. Awareness means, first and foremost, acceptance, the nonjudgmental openness toward one's own experience and one's own emotional lived world; yet, at the same time, it aims at an authentic transformation of the self.

We must, of course, find our way within a galaxy of thoughts and practices that, contaminated by fashion, often run the risk of simplifications when they do not become outright quick instant-guides with attached instructions for the attainment of well-being. To immunize ourselves against this risk and save, at the same time, the goal of self-understanding, we can evoke, albeit briefly, a seminal and quite distinguished source, namely, Spinoza's philosophy and the path he proposes in order to "understand" the passions.[9] Legitimated as expressions of the *conatus* to persevere in one's being, the passions become destructive only when they are blind, unaware of themselves, sources of the opacity of the I that leaves us prey to obscure and chaotic forces. To understand passions amounts to liberating them from such opacity, as psychoanalysis will claim centuries later. It amounts to emending them of their negative aspects in view of increasing one's own *vis existendi*, one's own power to exist, without giving them up or, even less, repressing them.[10] As Antonio Damasio suggests in his anti-Cartesian valorization of Spinoza's vision,[11] this means trusting the power of the mind not as separate from but, rather, as rooted in the body,[12] with the goal of fighting negative passions with positive passions.[13] Or, in more exquisitely Spinozian terminology, with the goal of combating "sad" passions, a source of the self's disempowerment, with "joyful" passions, which, on the contrary, increase the power of existing as they are enlightened by reason.

Beyond all dualisms, Spinoza teaches us that the understanding-knowledge of the passions yields to the subject's ability to distil their positive aspects not through opposition but through a mutual alliance of passions and reason that can valorize the function of each within the context of a necessary complementarity. We know that Spinoza's lesson has not enjoyed much popularity in the subsequent reflection on the passions, where what has prevailed has been a split between a rationalistic approach, more classically modern, and an expressionist approach, more particular to the postmodern perspective. The matter is that of overcoming this dualism that opposes, on the one hand, (illusory) trust in the control of the passions and in self-mastery, grounded on the primacy of reason, and, on the other hand, the emotivistic exaltation of the irrational, which, in the best of cases, can attain the undifferentiated justification of the effects of any emotion as long as the specific emotion reasserts the basic primacy of allegedly authentic and emancipatory forces.[14]

Understanding the passions also means recognizing that they are not immune to our ability of enacting a critical gaze that can also valorize their ethical potentialities, as Hume and Smith had already intuited. This argument has been recently reproposed, as we have seen, by Amartya Sen and Peter Singer, who claims that "we can't take our feelings as moral data, immune from rational criticism." In fact, as Singer says, alluding to a famous work by Thomas Nagel,[15] "I feel, but I also think what I feel" and it is precisely this fact that distinguishes me from a bat.[16]

Our passions are the emotive expression of what we think and believe. In other words, we feel on the basis of what we think as well as on the ground of the legacy of traditions and archetypal images we have inherited, which are destined to an ongoing and, mainly, unconscious labor of reenactment. Using Max Weber's terminology, we could also say that emotions and feelings depend on the historically variable images of the world that constellate our lives and the epoch in which we live.[17] And we could also add that, as Singer reiterates, any ethical perspective can only be the outcome of the reciprocal cooperation of reason and compassion. "Were we incapable of empathy—of putting ourselves in the position of others and seeing that their suffering is like our own—then ethical reasoning would lead nowhere. If emotion without reason is blind, then reason without emotion is impotent."[18] Once we recognize that the complex set of beliefs, convictions, and world images are, within any social-historical context, at the root of our emotive life, we can then subject it to a critical-reflective gaze. This way, we can determine and actually select the objects of our fears, the targets of our anger, or the recipients of our compassion (just to name a few exemplary references). We should not forget, of course, that the passions exert a decisive impact on reality, orienting and modifying it in a mutually dynamic action that is constantly renewed.

Based on this critical awareness, we can also learn to differentiate among the passions so that we can contrast those that are selfish and destructive with those that are "reasonable" or empathic, as Spinoza teaches us.[19] This way, we can enact that dynamics of counterbalancing, which we evoked earlier, that we find at the very origin of modernity (from Hobbes to Freud) and that consists in fighting the passions with the passions (the desire for power with fear, self-love with love of the self, sad passions with joyful passions, thanatos with eros).[20]

All this is not enough, though, to ground a moral perspective that, in order to arrive at the most authentic meaning of the term *paideia*, requires at least one last step, namely, the ability to translate understanding and critique into the ability to learn to act according to ethical parameters. In other terms, it is the ability to adopt practices that, when the subject recognizes such a need, enable us to initiate an active process of education-transformation of the passions.

Exemplary, in this sense, is Günther Anders's invitation to enact a practice of self-expansion that enables individuals to live up to the tasks of their times[21]—as long as we, evidently, free ourselves of the prejudice that the realm of sentiments constitutes "the *non-historical* element in the history of humankind."[22] According to Anders, if there is a moral task for the individuals, it consists in some kind of emotive learning that leads them to "widen the extension of the common performances of their imagination and feelings"; that is, that leads them to "engage in exercises in order to transcend the apparently fixed human *proportion* of their imagination and feelings."[23]

Even though it has never been consecrated as such, I would not hesitate to define such a practice as "ascetic." It clearly presupposes Arnold Gehlen's image of the human being as deficient and world-open, as the one who "does not *live* but *leads* a life" and whose task is "twofold: precisely because he is 'world-open,' he must discover, appropriate, and work through the uncommon fullness of the world with no help from instincts. And in this task, he meets another: to make himself ready, since he is unready, to gain control of himself and develop a whole range of controlled abilities."[24]

The very same presupposition grounds, more or less explicitly, the philosophical proposal of two contemporary authors, namely, Michel Foucault and Peter Sloterdijk, whom I would like briefly to consider at this point. Starting from the critique of the present, they both return, somewhat unexpectedly, given their overall philosophical proposals, to emphasize the subject while simultaneously deconstructing the hegemonic and sovereign image of modernity and finding precisely in asceticism the power of a radical discipline aimed at a self-completion that is also a self-transformation.

Intrinsic in the critical perspective of an "ontology of actuality,"[25] the possibility of thinking and building "new forms of subjectivity"[26] appears in Foucault as the indistinguishable corollary of the ascetic practice that requires that the subject be preliminarily capable of self-distancing (*se déprendre de soi-même*), thereby breaking with normative prescriptions and dispositifs of power. Foucault applies his genealogical gaze to this practice, full of Nietzschean and Bataillean echoes; he shows its origin starting with Greek and Roman antiquity, and he unfolds the "hermeneutics of the technologies of the self"[27] on which a subjectivity autonomous from the power of discourses has been built. Against power, which imposes a single regime of truth, the Western subject arrives, through the ethical injunction to "know thyself," at a different order of truth on which to build different and "more just" forms of governance of the self and others.[28] Yet, this "Cartesian moment"[29] that modern thought has definitely privileged must be situated again within a context that is properly ethical insofar as it implies the subject's ascetic exercise in view of its own self-transformation.[30] The self is not a substance, an originary entity or a self-enclosed identity; rather, it is a work-in-progress, the result of the subject's incessant work on itself—"it is a process of becoming more subjective."[31] As tools of such a process of self-constitution and transformation, the technologies of the self "permit individuals to effect by their own means or with the help of others a certain number of operations on their own bodies and souls, thoughts, conduct, and way of being, so as to transform themselves in order to attain a certain state of happiness, purity, wisdom, perfection, or immortality."[32] This explains why Foucault especially valorizes the Hellenistic model of the care of the self. It is the exemplary model of an ascetic ethics that finds its inspirational core not in abstract precepts but, rather, in the capillary work of the subject upon itself through "a historical-practical test of the limits that we may go beyond, and thus as work carried out by ourselves upon ourselves as free beings"—that is, through criticism of what one is and creation of what one wants to and can be.[33] The care of the self amounts to the construction of an active subject, capable of enacting a return to itself, a "conversion" (*epistrophé*) that allows it to escape the dispositifs of power and give itself its own rules.[34] This is so that it can attain "the full enjoyment of oneself, or the perfect supremacy of oneself over oneself."[35] Being the protagonist of an "aesthetics of existence"[36] that is nourished with a daily and incessant practice, the subject that is *"maître de soi,"* master of itself, becomes its own work, shaping itself in order to learn the art of self-governance and invent its own lifestyle. It is not only a "resistance" to the domination of ruling canons; rather, it is also a self-constitution that is simultaneously a self-transformation. Briefly, a patient and continuous work upon itself allows the subject "to subtract itself to itself" through a process of desubjectivation that breaks open the essentialist limit of the identitarian subject and unlocks the freedom of creation and transformation, enabling the irruption of what is other than oneself.[37]

The care of the self inaugurates a form of ethical self-subjectivation that foreshadows the critique of power. It delineates itself as a particularly necessary task starting with modernity, as modernity is characterized by the pervasiveness of sophisticated and devious biopolitical forms of control and normalization of subjects and the entire living world.[38] This task belongs first of all to philosophy when philosophy presents itself as ontology of actuality and critical theory. Yet, Foucault clarifies that it will have to be a different kind of philosophy and of critical theory. In other words, unlike mainstream thinking, it will have to be willing to be concerned with "what we are willing to accept in our world, to accept, to refuse, to change, both in ourselves and in our circumstances. . . . Not a critical philosophy that seeks to determine the conditions and the limits of our possible knowledge of the objects, but a critical philosophy that seeks the conditions and the indefinite possibilities of transforming the subject."[39] The emphasis on the subject and on the ascetic techniques of subjectivation is precisely what brings Foucault's diagnosis into proximity with Peter Sloterdijk's proposal of an acrobatic asceticism—an explosive proposal both for the radicalness of the critique and for the originality of the solution.[40]

The deafening and false asceticism of our contemporary times—of this last "sphere"[41] that has reduced all spiritual need of verticality to performance and all aspiration toward what is better to caricature drifts of fitness—can no longer be opposed with traditional proposals of evading the world, escaping the passions, and finding refuge in atemporal spiritual spaces, which, on the contrary, seem doomed to lethal evanescence. As Sloterdijk writes, "[T]he meditative enclaves gradually become invisible, and the residential communities of unworldliness disband. The beneficial deserts are abandoned, the monasteries empty out, holidaymakers replace monks and holidays replace escapism. The demi-mondes of relaxation give both heaven and Nirvana an empirical meaning."[42] We must answer, then, by inaugurating new practices or, better, new "anthropotechnics" that lead us toward a radical process of transformation.[43] First, we must reaffirm human beings' constitutive dimension, namely, their "acrobatic" tendency to elevation and their aspiration to improvement.[44] Second, through repetitive and progressive exercises, we must enable the subject to attain, now and again, a superior level, thereby retrieving the pathos of distance and dissociating itself from a world that exalts obtuse and narcotizing keywords such as efficiency, wealth, and consumerism.[45]

It is necessary to operate a "secession" from the imperatives imposed by that new authority that is the global crisis or, better, catastrophe, which is given an aura of unthinkability until now reserved only to transcendent powers.[46] We could add that this authority is the more domineering the more it is, to deploy Foucaultian terms, not coercive but, rather, persuasive, anonymous, and only with difficulty an object of imputability. As Sloterdijk claims, "The concern of the most resolute secessionaries is not simply a fascinated retreat from a reality that no longer invites participation, but rather a complete reversal—a turn away from the superficially manifest, which means a turn towards something that is better, true and real on a higher level."[47] Evident here is the emphasis on the Platonic movement of a "turn," a "conversion" (to which I will return later) that gives back to the subject's autonomy the imperative "You must change your life." Like Rilke, who could not subtract himself from the voice that appealed to him at the Louvre Museum, we cannot escape such an imperative. It requires that the subject, if it wishes to be such, distance itself from the various external "trainers" and immunize itself against the authorities and government issues to which we are all, more or less, currently subjugated.

The subject constitutes itself, self-produces itself, precisely as Foucault claims, through *askesis*, understood properly as exercise, as repetition of practices and rituals aimed at reactivating and promoting the tendency toward verticality, toward ameliorative self-transformation. "Practice is defined here as any operation that provides or improves the actor's qualification for the next performance of the same operation, whether it is declared as practice or not."[48] It is not the case of a neutral practice. The practice that grounds acrobatic ascesis is, evidently, a *good* practice. As elevation technics, it amounts to a *good* anthropotechnics, endowed with an unequivocally ethical value. It is a secessionist ethics that, as we have seen, is capable of reactivating old lifestyles in order to create new ones and enable human beings to exit no longer from the world but from "dullness, dejection and obsession."[49] That is, from that layer of skepticism, apathetic addiction, and unavowed impotence that prevents them from taking seriously the signs of the catastrophe—signs that are, at most, absent-mindedly perceived as "a form of horror-genre documentary."[50]

What is required, therefore, are more audacious answers that, as Hans Jonas had already intuited, are not content with traditional virtue ethics[51] but, rather, ask us to enact the conversion—understood here as move from passivity to activity, as double movement of exiting the passive modality of existence and entering the active mode—through which one properly becomes a subject. In one of the most explicit definitions of the concept, Sloterdijk clarifies that subject becomes "anyone who takes part in a program for de-passivizing themselves, and crosses from the side of the merely formed to that of the forming."[52] Subject is the one who, centering its life on exercise, is capable of enacting a set of practices of self-formation and self-transformation that enable it to "eventually be superior to its life of passions, habitus and notions."[53] Thanks to the overcoming of all oppositions between internal and external, personal and global spheres, *this* subject becomes the pivot of the creation of a co-immunitarian global macrostructure. Reiterating the urgency of conversion in light of global challenges and the specter of the catastrophe, Sloterdijk asserts that this subject's "monastic rules must be drawn up now or never"[54] so that they allow us to "take on good habits of *shared survival* in *daily* exercises."[55]

It is obviously impossible, within the current context, to tackle proposals that are so thick and totalizing. And it is even more impossible to show their critical points except for one aspect, which is the one I am interested in underlining here by returning to Anders's reflections. This aspect is crucial and concerns the very structure of the ascetic subject. We can immediately summarize it in a synthetic formula: whereas, for Foucault and Sloterdijk, self-transformation requires, among other technics, the control and mastery of the emotive sphere, for Anders there exists the possibility of transforming the emotive sphere itself and inaugurating new forms of feeling.

As we have seen, Foucault's subject is the one who tends to self-mastery (*enkrateia*). As in the Greek-Roman period, this translates, among other things, into practicing one's ability to free oneself from enslavement to the passions. The care of the self is that set of practices through which the subject becomes master of one's own self, by governing one's own passions, learning to make good use of one's pleasures and desires (as in the case of governing sexual pleasures). This does not mean that the transformation of the self occurs through repressive technics; nor that it takes place within the enclosed space of a substance-subject, solipsistic and, in a Cartesian mode, alien to all relations or dependency. One could just think of the importance of the role of the teacher (understood as spiritual teacher and conscience director) or, even, of a simple friend in the process through which the self acquires the ability and the courage to tell the truth (*parrhesia*) as a royal way on the path of subjectivation.[56] It is in *parrhesia*, in fact, that the self exercises its freedom through the critique of itself and others. It is undeniable, however, that one of the presuppositions—and of the technics—to access the truth and acquire the awareness needed to realize a good life remains the domination of the passions, according to a classic Stoic postulate.

This last *topos* is shared also by Sloterdijk, who seems to reassert its centrality in the constitution of the acrobatic subject. This subject is master of itself, capable of breaking open passivity and inertia in order to exit the current life and "cross to the other side" with respect to what it finds within itself.[57] It is a secessionist self, which elevates itself, thereby freeing itself, over the communitarian habit that has sedimented within its interiority. To change one's life, means, first of all, to fight against "the two-headed *daimon*" that holds us in its domain, whether it is the power of the passions that seethe within us or the routine force of inertia to which we are pushed by habit.[58] To change one's life means to enact the conversion that enables us to become masters of what controls and subjugates us, namely, one's habits and ideas as well as, precisely, one's passions, which, not by chance, are referred to as the first "side" over which we must elevate ourselves. "By noting how passions are working within them, they understand that they must reach the other side of passion so that they do not simply suffer from the passions, but rather become skilled at suffering."[59] The need for this conversion holds also for the only passions Sloterdijk is willing to consider and valorize, namely, the thymotic passions (from Plato's *thymos*: rage, courage, and pride), which he proposes in *Rage and Time*[60] and which, if controlled and oriented in a proper way, can constitute a relevant energetic resource in the process of self-transformation. Critiquing the hegemony of "erotic" passions that have been the main focus of Western thought up to Freud and psychoanalysis, Sloterdijk decisively brings back to the fore the role of *thymos* as a possible foundation of the desired conversion. "Thymotics discloses ways for human beings to redeem what they possess, to learn what they are able to do, and to see what they want."[61] Even though thymotic passions are currently subjected to a process of dispersion and regressive involution that prevents them from coagulating into "rage banks" producing emancipatory movements—as was the case, on the contrary, in the twentieth century—it is always possible to regain control of them and convert them into tools for secession from what exists, into emotive sources of ascetic elevation. Briefly, rage "belongs to the renewable energies."[62]

All this means not only reasserting the need of verticality even at the emotive level, but also confirming the image of a strong and volitional subject that abandons the muddy and passivizing regions of eros in order to assert itself proudly by resuming control of the thymotic passions. It is a sovereign subject, which builds itself in the solitary space of its own interior acropolis dissociating itself from sedimented habits and ideas and governing its own emotive life from on high.

One could immediately object that, as we have seen for Foucault, this does not amount to reproposing either the substance-subject or the atomistic and solipsistic individual of modernity. The presence of an opening of the subject to alterity is, in fact, undeniable in Sloterdijk, and this manifests itself explicitly in two fundamental places. First, in an anthropological perspective according to which alterity appears as constitutive of the subject ever since its origins and biological dimension; that is, ever since that prenatal condition in which the placental bond with the mother structures the subject as double (or, better, as a "nobject").[63] This bond will then be lacerated by the trauma of birth, thereby inaugurating the succession of "spheres" as answers to the loss of the originary microsphere. What follows is that the quest for the other, which the subject will pursue through the construction of various cultural systems (from religion to art), will essentially be a process of replacement of the other—a process nourished more by a physiological need of self-completion than by a really relational, reciprocal, and interactive dynamics.[64]

Second, the opening to alterity is present in Sloterdijk, as well as also in Foucault, in the importance given to the figure of the teacher: the "trainer" who guides the subject engaged in the care of the self toward an ascension and who guards such a subject by offering it a mirror image to imitate. Whether the matter is that of spiritual trainers (from gurus to sophists) or pragmatic trainers (from sport coaches to professors),[65] their role is that of the *other*, understood as an exemplary figure "whom one supposes already to have achieved ethical reform"[66] and who can consequently enable the subject, through an "ascetic pact," to complete its own self-poietic journey.

As has been correctly noted, though,[67] this means that the other plays a fundamentally instrumental role. It is the exemplary model that, as a mirror image, has the task of supporting, orienting, and confirming the I in its process of self-transformative performance. Clearly, this instrumentality is quite different from that belonging to possessive individualism or to the sovereign subject of modernity; in fact, it does not aim at utilitarian goals or the conquest of power but, rather, the improvement of the self (and the world). There is no alteration, however, in terms of the image of a self-centered subject;[68] it remains a subject that, with the other, does not establish any truly dynamic and horizontal relationship—a relationship exposed to the unpredictability of mutual transformation—and a subject that, in its verticality, preserves the need to dominate what lies Platonically (or Stoically) below, such as, precisely, the passions.

Different is, on the contrary, Günther Anders's perspective, as I have anticipated. In it, the subject is configured as capable of interacting dynamically with its own emotional life, thereby transforming it.

Anders clarifies that this operation is not easy for at least two fundamental reasons. The first, to which I have already hinted, consists in the difficulty of dismantling the consolidated prejudice regarding the alleged naturalness and ahistoricity of the passions, from which derive their resistance to all attempts at modification.[69] The second reason, more directly linked to contemporaneity, consists in the fact that the vertiginous developments of technology have created a scission, a gap between, on the one hand, the unlimited expansion of making and producing and, on the other, the limited elasticity of feelings, which in themselves have difficulties adapting to social changes.

It is true, Anders notes, that we can actually observe some kind of inertial rhythm in the development of emotive life and in its possibility of keeping up with the rhythm of the world. Yet, it is also true that, even though slowly, sentiments have always had a history, have always undergone a historical process of evolution and change. This is due to the fact that, as nineteenth-century philosophical anthropology explains, since they are indeterminate and lacking beings, human beings have always had, and have always been able to build, a world and adapt to it their own emotive life in an almost automatic way. This happens because "the formation of human beings is complete only when their feelings too are given shape."[70]

Currently, though, this process can no longer be entrusted to an unconscious automatism and the demonstrated human ability for adaptation to world changes. The gap, the scission between the human being as producer and the human being as sentient requires that the subject mobilize, voluntarily and consciously, its engagement and responsibility.[71] What emerges is, in other words, the "need to help [people] feel or declaredly look for sentiments," especially when the gap becomes, as it were, a real social pathology generating a political danger and preventing world change.[72] As we have already seen, the macroscopic example on which Anders's entire diagnosis focuses is the absence or, better, the anesthesia of fear. Fear is a pervasive passion and, simultaneously, the object of collective denial and of defense mechanisms inhibiting its productive functions, thereby obstructing the possibility of recognizing the risks to which we expose the entire humanity at a global level, and therefore preventing mobilization to fight against them.[73]

In short, as Rilke claims, whom Anders also curiously evokes, we must retrieve the ability "to know how to feel."[74] We have a primary moral task consisting in recomposing the scission between faculties through the "development of moral imagination," that is, through the ability to "voluntarily dilate the volume of our imagination and of our feeling."[75] We cannot be certain that this is possible, but we can test it by carrying out experiments, practices of self-expansion of the self. We can "try practices of moral expansion in order to attain access, thanks to techniques of self-transformation, to situations, regions, or objects from which we would be otherwise excluded."[76] In this regard, we could provide a multiplicity of examples from religion, magic, and mysticism, Anders claims. In truth, though, we also have at our disposal customary practices that are immanent to our life context, technics of expansion of the self that actually constellate our daily life: for example, when our psyche tends to expand while listening to a symphony or while contemplating a work of art.[77] This expansion contains the self-transformative opportunity that also foreshadows the creation of new sentiments: "Human beings are not confined to being content with a set of feelings that are defined once and for all; on the contrary, they invent ever new sentiments, and even sentiments that exceed the average volume of their soul and that require, from their abilities to understand, efforts that can definitely be called 'exceeding.'"[78] In this perspective, to change life does not require that we dominate the passions but, rather, that we shape and transform them to the point of disclosing the possibility of the emergence of new emotive dimensions, suitable to the needs of the current time.

Generative Sentiments

The practices Anders wishes for in order to fulfil such a creative-transformative process find their propulsive engine in the faculty of imagination. Here, imagination does not only perform the representational role that enables individuals to distance and emancipate themselves from the present and prefigure the future. It also plays a transformative role, for which it becomes the instrument par excellence for a different configuration of the self. This self is no longer divided but is rather capable of recomposition and a simultaneous new creation. In other words, the imagination's adaptation to action gives birth to a creative process that is kindled by the reenactment of trust in the possibility of the new, of change, of the transformation of the present, even when it is a matter of the complex and more inertial sphere of feeling.

We can note at this point a convergence with Arendt's idea of "a new beginning."[79] It is true that Arendt's first understanding of "imagination" has to do with a faculty that enables representation of the possible. It is also true, however, that in her reflection a second form comes to be delineated—one that emphasizes the transformative and emancipatory aspect of this faculty.[80] It is imagination that, in fact, allows us not only, in a Kantian way, to emancipate ourselves from the givenness of the present, thereby expanding our mentality,[81] but also to give birth to a transformation of the existing conditions through the representation of what is possible. "A characteristic of human action is that it always begins something new. . . . In order to make room for one's own action, something that was there before must be removed or destroyed, and things as they were before are changed. Such change would be impossible if we could not mentally remove ourselves from where we physically are located and *imagine* that things might as well be different from what they actually are."[82] Mainly a devalued concept in modern thought, imagination enables us to distance ourselves from what is given and introduce something new into the world—giving birth, precisely, to a new beginning, which opens up again the possibility of changing (and for the better) the existing state of things.[83]

Returning to Anders, in whom we can find a vision close to Arendt's, we can say that it is from the broadening and dilation of our psyche through imagination that we can legitimately expect, together with the overcoming of the scission, "new creations of sentiments" or, better, the creation of "new sentiments, adequate to our contemporary world"—that is, sentiments that are up to the unprecedented transformations we have produced.[84]

The issue is that, despite his fecund intuition regarding the role of the emotive life, Anders too actually reproposes the image of an autonomous and self-centered subject, engaged in a dynamic that seems to unfold only within the autarchic space of the self's relation to itself. This is what emerges in the eloquent image of the self's appeal to itself: "The one who experiments gives oneself the task of suggesting to oneself that which has not yet been imagined and felt in order to bring to the open the 'rogue' that hides within one's intimacy—sluggish imagination, lazy feeling—and force them to come to terms with the assigned task."[85] Undoubtedly, Anders has the merit of grounding the technics of self-dilation of the self on a paideia of the passions. Nevertheless, he seems, as it were, not to have taken full advantage of his original intuition, thereby ending up presupposing, once again, the figure of a vertical and volitional subject capable of self-transcendence, of self-exercise within the solitary space of its ascetic vocation. The significant and certainly fascinating example of an intense experience of musical listening confirms it.[86]

Once again, conversion is entrusted to the self-determination of a subject capable of driving out and eliminating its own resistances and inertial opacities, thereby drawing it to the task that awaits it. This operation resembles more an energetic surgical intervention than a maieutic process and leaves partly unsolved the problem of the motivation for self-transformation. Yet, if pushed to its most "natural" consequences, the emphasis on the passions could potentially be the royal way to think of a nonautarchic or nonvoluntaristic subject, as such a subject would be always already inserted within relational dynamics—a subject engaged in an emotive connection with an other-than-itself that constitutes the subject, thereby exposing it to openness and change.

We must turn to images and perspectives, other than those proposed by Foucault, Sloterdijk, or Anders, who actually remain within the ascetic paradigm—a paradigm not sufficiently adequate to respond to the pathologies of the sovereign subject of modernity. We must thus converge toward the relational subject whose possible different nuances we have observed in phenomenology and feminist theories. And we must pay attention especially to two perspectives that we can consider exemplary in view of the criticism, and the overcoming, of the ascetic vertical subject.

The first perspective is the one proposed by Simone Weil through the notion of "decreation." This is the process of suspension of the I that, as we have already suggested, foreshadows attention toward the others, a generous receptivity that nevertheless contains nothing passive or fusional, as it rigorously preserves a sense of distance. Here, we find an asceticism that not only descends into the world but is also founded on the love for the neighbor, empathic participation, and sharing—even though this ought not to be understood in an emotionally and sentimentally charged sense. In Weil, this love actually has nothing to do either with charitable and pietistic feelings or with passionate or possessive excesses.[87] It rather assumes an emotionally sober tonality that perhaps brings it closer to *philia*.[88] In this manner, together with the need for distance, it also preserves the equal autonomy and equal dignity of both parties (the I and the other) in the relationship.

The second perspective is the "inclined" subject proposed recently by Adriana Cavarero.[89] Cavarero's perspective is undoubtedly very apt in this context, as we can oppose it directly to the image of the ascetic subject. In fact, it dwells particularly on the "posture" of the subject. To the absolute hegemony of the "upright" or vertical subject in the history of Western thought, Cavarero opposes the image of an inclined subject; that is, a subject that is bent over, stretched toward something that is outside itself. This subject is inclined toward the other, where the other is especially the harmless, the vulnerable, as in the archetypical image of the mother inclined over the child as portrayed in a famous painting by Leonardo.[90] Cavarero's concern with freeing this image from identification with a trivial and peaceful altruism and from the stereotype of the self-giving feminine is immediately evident. On the contrary, she accentuates the centrality of relationship, within which both subjects find, and potentially build, their form as it symbolically emerges in the reciprocity of the look and smile between mother and child.

I think, however, that this image could be projected also outside the maternal metaphor, as this metaphor risks freezing the relational parts in the fixed roles of (inclined) subject and (vulnerable) other. Here, we encounter a consolidation of the universal status of a subject that is alternative to the ascetic subject; that is, a relational subject that is inserted in dynamics of reciprocity, in which the two parties are involved in a constant and involuntary exchange of roles or inversion of positions, depending on context and circumstances.

This is precisely what happens in emotive dynamics, not only because emotions are the very source of our neediness and fragility[91] but also because the condition of vulnerability may shift from the one to the other (one could think, for example, of love relations), pushing the subjects now and again to lean out, to bend one toward the other. This way, they reciprocally expose one another to the flow of a continual becoming, which is nourished with the eccentric movement—in the etymological sense of *ex-centricus*, outside the center—of emotions.[92]

Valorizing the emotive dimension, whose fecund implications seem to be of no interest to either Weil or Cavarero, allows us to configure a subject that finds an impulse to self-transformation in the ever-renewed game of reciprocal provocations and solicitations that takes place in the relationship with the other. This is an *emotive subject*, as I term it, which lands on metamorphosis, as it lets itself be decentered by the relational dynamics of the passions.[93]

In this sense, the perspective that sees the subject as inclined toward self-decentering and self-transcendence seems quite significant, because the human is ontologically characterized by its openness to the other and the world. This perspective is not at all univocal, as it gathers different idioms, which we have already partly mentioned—from nineteenth-century German anthropology to the relational approach of feminist thinking, from Max Scheler and the ethics of sympathy to the philosophies of alterity (Levinas, Ricoeur). These idioms share the idea of the subject's constitutive relationality, regardless of whether such relationality is ascribed, now and again, to the subject's anthropological status of lack, to its ontological condition of vulnerability, or to its capability for empathy, which finds an additional confirmation in the neurosciences and in Michael Tomasello's discovery of the biological grounds of cooperation.[94] Additionally, within the contemporary scenario, particularly effective is the image of an incomplete subject—advanced by Edgar Morin[95] and recently revived within the psychosocial reflection[96]—that opens to an "ecological" relation, not only with the other but also with the entire living world.[97] In any event, the matter is that of a subject that, on the basis of its incompleteness, is inevitably destined, to use Gehlen's expression, to "complete itself" in a never ending or definitive process and that is nourished with what María Zambrano calls "hunger to be fully born."[98]

To my mind, the emotive approach adds an essential aspect to our argument insofar as it displays relationality in its own becoming, as it were. It is in the emotive relation with the other or, better, in emotive sharing, that the self forms and transforms itself through a Socratic "*epoche of the ego*," as Guido Cusinato so eloquently phrases it.[99] This allows the subject to acknowledge its vulnerability and let its singularity flourish at the very moment when it transcends itself and opens itself up to the world. If it is true that the ability for self-transcendence is part of the human thanks to the constitutive openness to the world characterizing it, it is also true that this essentially occurs through emotive dynamics. It is in "sharing emotions"[100] that a true *periagoge*, a true conversion of the subject takes places; the subject leaves behind the "erective" and self-referential posture and opens itself to the destabilizing *pathos* of amazement, of *wonder*—an originary and surging passion without which there can be no transformation.[101]

Or, perhaps, it would be better to say that, without wonder, there would be no metamorphosis. This term is complex, rich with mythical-symbolic resonances, and I propose it here in its most extensive sense: (a) as a radical change in the subject that, however, is not born out of nothing but rather lets embryonic potentialities germinate (as zoology teaches us);[102] (b) as a profound change that presupposes, to evoke Elias Canetti, the subject's willingness to break open the identitarian chrysalis and become other than itself in the name of welcoming multiplicity and a liberating relationship with living alterity;[103] and (c) as an active change that attests the subject's ability to accept the labor of generating itself anew, of letting itself be regenerated by the continual and endless putting itself at stake in the emotive relation.

This requires, however, that we presuppose a peculiar and nonconventional vision of the emotions that underscores, as I have suggested earlier, their constitutively relational character, disclosing the limits of the Cartesian interpretation and tradition. Some (few) authors have the merit of advancing a social theory of emotions, according to which they "are never first *in me* and only later *among us* but, rather, simultaneously *in me* and *among us*."[104] An emotion is not a substance, it is not something that resides purely within the interiority of the subject;

rather, it is a social structure, a relational plot. It is the crucial place of interaction with the other.[105] We therefore need a social theory of emotions that sets forth their open and unpredictable dynamics, as the opportunities of the subject's transformations rest precisely on the openness and unpredictability of emotive interactions. This is not all though; sharing emotions means exposing oneself to a confrontation with the other that is also generative of unconscious dynamics and involuntary outcomes; it means to let oneself be transformed by a relationship that, in its own unfolding, takes us out, mostly unconsciously, of the narrow and static boundaries of our own self.

This is what ultimately happens in the multiple experiences of "resonance," as Hartmut Rosa calls them,[106] which remind us that a different relation between subject and world is always possible. In resonance as primary relation with the world, we in fact experience a relationship that is neither instrumental nor alienated—like the one we inherit from the bulimic logic of acceleration characterizing our modernity—but is, rather, disinterested, selective, and welcoming. We resonate with the world when we enter a relationship with someone or something else (a person, a book, an idea, a landscape) that can shake us up deeply and transform us in an unexpected and unpredictable manner. In this way, we reestablish an accord, a "vibrating bond," with ourselves and the world that lets us see or, even better, perceive alternative scenarios and possible images of a good life. Rosa's proposal is suggestive, as it reminds us that the experiences we make within the "axes of resonance" (love and family, nature and religion, culture and friendship) function as a compass that points us in the right direction and, from there, we can move to change our life and access a successful life.

The fact nevertheless remains that it is up to us, endowed with the compass, to translate the involuntary experiences into active choices and conscious practices of life. The passage from the involuntary experience of resonance to the voluntary construction of resonating relationships and a good life requires, in other words, that we travel a path. This travel is impervious, and its outcomes are far from guaranteed, as the path is marked by confrontations with alterity and include dissonant and conflictual moments in which the very core of the chance of transformation is at stake. That is, it implies a close confrontation with the passions—our own and those of others—and the ability to stay in a relationship, to break its opacities open, to disclose its ambivalences, and to enhance its potentialities. It is a confrontation with the tricks and dangers of emotive relationships. An emotive relationship is, in fact, also the place of conflicts and of what is upsetting, of disorientation and regressive temptations. It is the place where we are vulnerable to the other, exposed exactly to a *vulnus*, to the wound that the other can inflict on us, to the other's provocation and resistance. It is, as it were, the dimension par excellence in which there occurs what Georges Bataille calls the the wound of the acephale subject that necessarily exposes it to alterity.[107] Or, in other words, it is the place of the *"déchirement du Même par l'Autre,"* the tearing apart and laceration of the same by the other that, according to Emmanuel Levinas, deposes the subject from its presumptuous sovereign position and consigns it to the ethical relation.[108] Independently, and mostly against our will, the other irrupts into the satisfied autonomy of the I through the displacing force of the passions, which compels us to self-transcendence and inaugurates a process of self-transformation—first despite us, and then through a self-reflective moment that transforms the experience into an autonomous and conscious choice.

The passions are therefore the dimension par excellence in which the metamorphosis of the subject can take place and the creation of the new can begin—that is, the generation of new feelings, thoughts, and life forms adequate to the metamorphosis of the world and the challenges of the present time, which is rightly wished for also in the ascetic proposals by Foucault, Sloterdijk, and Anders. The difference is that, in this case, change occurs no longer through a monological and voluntaristic ascesis but, rather, through the relationship and the unforeseeable emotive interaction with the other. It is only in the emotive relationship with the other, and not in the endogamous relationship with itself, that the self can achieve the learning process that foreshadows transformation as it learns to know and acknowledge its own limits and vulnerabilities, its mistakes and blindness, and also its own potentialities. It learns to correct negative feelings and cultivate the positive ones, which are the source of a possible emancipatory process.

The other is the one who obliges me, the more cogently, the more involuntarily, to cultivate my emotions or, better, to take care of them. This does not mean either to practice a dutiful moral instance or to count on an altruistic inclination. Rather, it means to let oneself be "contested,"[109] wounded by the other,[110] thereby creating an opening for the appeal coming from the other. It is a matter, as it were, of taking advantage of the infinite plasticity of emotive life in order to scratch all resilient obtuseness of the self and put oneself at stake through the fluid dynamics of the confrontation-conflict with the force of the other's desire. The relationship with the other becomes the place par excellence of the paideia of emotions. This paideia finds a culminating moment in the active and reflective process, which Hume and Smith initiated, that foreshadows the conscious metamorphosis of the self. This metamorphosis is fecund though never final or linear, and it proceeds through progressions and regressions, resistances and new acquisitions. It is an ethical metamorphosis, as we have seen, which is nevertheless characterized by a path that can never be deemed complete, as it is always exposed to the unknown of the relationship with the other.

I wish briefly to mention here that this foregoing aspect is absent not only from deontological ethics but also from virtue ethics, which nevertheless shares with the perspective I am advancing at least two fundamental presuppositions.[111] The first is the conviction, inspired by Aristotle, that even though they have an internal origin, character traits can be discouraged when negative and, on the contrary, nourished and cultivated when virtuous so that they can be rendered stabile and enduring in view of promoting human flourishing. Virtue is a quality of the self that is rooted, in Hume's words, in "durable principles of the mind, which extend over the whole conduct, and enter into the personal character."[112] The subject is capable of acquiring this quality by cultivating it autonomously, permanently defining the subject's entire personality. The virtuous character is, ultimately, the outcome of a choice by a subject that does not ask what the universal rules to act in a right way are; rather, the subject asks itself, in view of the parameters of a good life: How should I live my life? What kind of person should I be? The second presupposition concerns the importance conferred to the emotive sphere—which, on the contrary, is considered irrelevant, when not harmful, in Kant's deontological model—insofar as, according to the perspective of moral psychology accepted by virtue ethics, it includes within morality matters that are outside our control as long as they imply the eudaimonistic goal of the flourishing of the human being. Consequently, together with the role of luck in morality, it reintroduces the awareness of the inescapable fragility of the human condition.[113]

Virtue ethics can be appreciated, in comparison with deontological ethics, for its emphasis on personal qualities and the relevance given to the role of emotions and motivations;[114] yet, it presents some limits. First, possessing some specific virtues does not translate into their effectiveness in any situation.[115] As I have already remarked in the case of the distant other, one can be a compassionate person who is extremely sensitive to the suffering of migrants and the poor of the earth and, at the same time, be entirely indifferent toward the destiny of future generations. Second, it is not entirely clear what strategies we could adopt, beside education, to nourish virtue. Nor is it clear what might constitute the guiding principles of action from which we can infer how we ought concretely to behave (beside role modeling and letting oneself be guided by the exemplarity of virtuous actors).[116] Finally and principally, this ethics evidently reproposes the idea of a self-centered subject, which is sovereignly capable of its own self-constitution as a moral subject. This does not mean that it disregards the presence of the other, if it is true that, as Annette Baier claims in a Humean perspective, it tells us how to cultivate those character traits that not only contribute to our well-being but also make us be "good company for others."[117] Yet, in the constitution of the moral subject, virtue ethics does not seem to ascribe any active role to the other and to relationships.

We have seen that, on the contrary, this feature is the foundation of the ethics of care. Despite undeniable affinities between the two ethics (such as attention to the practices of morality and the need to cultivate them), the difference lies nevertheless in the fact that virtue ethics remains basically individualistic, as it focuses on an individual person's qualities and disposition. The ethics of care, on the contrary, accentuates the relational fabric and the context of reciprocal connections.[118]

The same relational approach characterizes another ethical paradigm, which is the object of a recent revival. It is the paradigm of *generativity*, which considers the relationship with the other as the source of self-transcending that opens the boundaries of the self-referential self and gives shape to a new imaginary of freedom.[119] In other words, on the basis of relationality, the subject is pushed no longer toward hybris and the unlimited desire of an atomistic and unrelated subject but toward what is defined as "generative freedom."[120] This freedom liberates us from ourselves and the sterile immobility of the narcissistic prison in order to reinsert us into the vital cycle of creation of the new, thereby favoring an emancipatory metamorphosis. Unlike the ascetic model but also the individualistic posture of virtue ethics, the paradigm of generativity grounds the possibility of self-transcendence and of the birth of the new on the subject's ability to think of itself within the relationship with the other and take care of such a relationship.

What is missing in both of these relational paradigms is, however, a more targeted and profound attention to the emotive dynamics understood as that which must primarily be cultivated, as it represents the place where relationships are built, with their lights and shadows, their successes and failures, their conflicts and accomplishments. To take care of one's emotions within the relationship with the other as (inter)active subject is the act that foreshadows the generation of the new, thereby involving self-transformation and world-transformation in a single and indistinguishable path.

This is what, in the spirit of an ontology of actuality and a critique of the present, we have observed with respect to the emotive dynamics concerning the two figures of the distant other, the spatially distant other and the temporally distant other. Here, even though it must overcome particularly arduous difficulties, the possibility of a paideia of the emotions measures itself against our abilities to grasp and generate the new. That is, it measures itself against our ability not only to correct pathologies and reactivate passions that have burnt out but also to favor, in the face of unprecedented events, the birth of new feelings that are fitting for the challenges of the present. Thanks to what I would like to refer to as homeopathic cure, the challenging and estranging encounter with the spatially and culturally distant other, which exposes us to fear and resentment, can also simultaneously produce an emotive shock that decenters us from our identitarian borders and dilates our imaginary, opening us up to empathic passions, compassion, and hospitality. Less paradoxical than we may at first think is then Gayatri Spivak's claim, when she asserts that the more impossible the encounter with the other appears, the more available the possibility of exiting ourselves and finding access to ethics becomes.[121] This claim is valid also with respect to the other distant in time. Even though, in this case, we cannot count on a shocking effect, nevertheless we have seen that the surging of shame for the harms produced by our power and hybris can break the wall of our intergenerational indifference and egoism, thereby pushing us to generate fear for the world and the generations that will come after us—as a first, necessary act to reimagine and generate the future. In other words, it can lead us to retrieve the essential dimension of generative action that has been removed by an obstinate emphasis on the I and the present. This is the intertemporal connection or, as it has been called, *transitivity*, that is "[t]he opening forward and backward, precisely the opening that makes us capable of receiving the legacy of those who have preceded us, of receiving the other that fecundates us somehow; but it is also an opening forward, which translates precisely in passing the tradition, life, experience through us so that it may go beyond us."[122] Relationality, even in its most impervious and unforeseeable forms, is the cradle for the possibility of metamorphosis. It is the surging and dawning place in which the I's self-reflective posture may suffice to initiate the process of awareness that promotes cultivation of emotions, thereby transforming them into fecund and cohesive energies.

Generating the Future

The subjects' psychic-anthropological metamorphosis, jointly with the birth of a new and audacious ethical consciousness, is thus the precondition for being able to confront the task to which we are currently called without delay. It is the task of living up to the unprecedented challenges of the present—first of all, the ecological challenge—that place a heavy mortgage on the future. This precondition, however, opens up a question that is not easy to answer. How can we make the process of metamorphosis go viral, break the wall of apathy, of resignation, of carelessness, and reach wider segments of the population? There is no point in denying that, unfortunately, the condition of those who currently achieve an ethical consciousness of the possible loss of the world is similar to the situation of the prisoner in Plato's cave. That is the condition of the one who, after daring to exit the cave toward the authentic light of reality, must convince the other prisoners to enact a similar conversion toward a new beginning. There is an aggravating difference, though: whereas the prisoners in Plato's cave do not know that there is an outside, another and truer reality to access, contemporary individuals know about that reality, they are informed about it; and yet, partly unconsciously, they deny it. Therefore, those who wish to persuade them to break the obscurity of denial and indifference and enact the conversion toward light must challenge the resistance, when it is not ironical detachment, of an entire collectivity that prefers to remain in the inertial darkness of the sad passions and in the guilty ignorance of truth. How to engage others—deceived by the sticky shadows of their own self-defense mechanisms—to enact the *periagoge*, the conversion? How to identify the tools that are available to us in order to nourish our collective imaginary and extend the metamorphosis to the point of making it collectively productive? How to promote positive emotions in a world that, with Harmut Rosa's expression, is increasingly less resonant?

The issue is that, as we have seen,[123] no enlightened knowledge or reiterated information coming from the outside, even though from reputable sources, will be effective on our consciousness until it succeeds in overcoming the wall of denial, thereby opening a breach in our emotive sphere; that is, until it succeeds in breaking the dam of our defense mechanisms and finally reopening access to reality. For this to happen, we perhaps need something that helps us tear down the bogus curtain of a *Truman Show* that has now reached its last performance. We need something that works like the shock of a sudden awakening and brusquely confronts us not only with the possibility but also with the necessity of a metamorphosis. In other words, we need what I would like to call an *experience of vulnerability*.

Awareness of vulnerability is, as I have often remarked, a value that has been removed by the hybris of the modern subject. Yet, awareness of vulnerability as a constitutive dimension of the human can become a resource to enact the metamorphosis that allows us to demolish the Promethean-Faustian myth of unlimited power and retrieve a perception of limits and interdependency, thereby allowing us to access again the alliance of solidarity with the living world of which we partake. This world, which contains forests, waters, animals, and rocks in addition to ourselves, is not a separate, extraneous, and inert reality, a res extensa to exploit and manipulate as we wish in order to maintain our anthropocentric supremacy and sate our unlimited appetites. Rather, it is the only dwelling place we have or, better, to which we belong while sharing it with the ensemble of other beings that populate it.

We cannot access this awareness, however, without experience, without our psyche and bodies being touched, affected, and even overwhelmed by events promising to be more effective, the more suddenly and uncontrollably they irrupt into the inertial routines of our lives, which are protective of their rhythms and satisfied with their privileges. Undeniably, there has been more than one event of this kind in recent history, which unfortunately has seen us being spectators and victims of tsunamis of different kinds—social, ecological, financial—all having a global impact. We could just point to the 2001 terroristic attack on the Twin Towers in New York City, which not only shattered the myth of the impenetrable invulnerability of the most powerful country in the world but also exposed the entire globe to the threat of Islamic terrorism. Or we could think of the 2008 economic-financial crisis, which started in the United States, then produced domino effects throughout the continents and exposed the precariousness of a development model increasingly engulfed in a true systemic crisis. Or, still, we can refer to the cyclic explosion of lethal viruses (the Aviary in 1977, Sars in 2002, Ebola in

2014, Zika in 2015) capable of disclosing the surprising weaknesses of all countries' health systems and finding even the most advanced ones to be unprepared in the face of rampant epidemics.

One could rightly object that no true awareness of vulnerability, no conversion, no new beginning seems to have emerged from these events. On the contrary, they have produced opposite outcomes, fostered not by what would be "right passions" but rather by negative and regressive ones. The terroristic attack was followed by the simultaneously immunitary and aggressive reaction of the Western world toward world countries hastily assimilated in the so-called axis of evil, and by the construction of scapegoats on which to direct collective fears and blaming, thereby producing a polarization of us versus them and a mirroring spiral of fear and resentment. The 2008 crisis marked the expansion of an increasingly blind, avid, and predatory capitalism aware of the erosion of resources and the unsustainability of a development model compelled to infinite and impossible innovation. Finally, the sequence of viral epidemics triggered, now and again, only explosions of panic and anxiety and then disappeared into the nothingness of media silence and peoples' indifference, as they prefer to delude themselves about their recovery.

Recent history seems to tell us that the experience of vulnerability does not necessarily turn into the recognition of the fragility of the human condition and the awakening of collective consciousness. It will not, I would like to suggest, until it succeeds in deeply shaking the roots of the very foundations of our life. This is perhaps the novelty of the event that has recently been upsetting the world, that is, the COVID-19 pandemic, as it possesses the requisites of a true catastrophe or, better, of a global catastrophe. In its etymology, "catastrophe" means, in fact, overturning, (tragic and mournful) reversal of the existent—much like what exactly happens on account of the coronavirus with its burden not only of suffering and death but also of paradoxical effects. As we have observed in live time, this is an event that transforms us from obsessive consumers into law-abiding users of what is strictly needed, from careless hedonists into ascetics of everydayness who are capable of cherishing even just a brief walk. It is an event that fractures our reciprocal indifference and fuels our desire for chorality; an event that replaces the solitude of atoms sucked in the formless fusionality of the crowds with solidarity and proximity, paradoxically created through bodily distance. Furthermore, it is an event that gives us back the pleasure of breathing while liberating our cities from the poison of particulate matter, and that makes us appreciate even the journey into the interiority we had sacrificed for the sake of appearances, acquisitive drives, and the phantasmagoria of commodities. Finally, the fact that, for the first time, this event originates a truly global catastrophe—no corner of the planet can in fact consider itself safe from the contagion—discloses to us our irreversible condition of interdependency. Thereby the event lays bare the hypocrisy of the regressive and muscular immunitary politics that increasingly and stubbornly abound in the world, resulting in the foolish arrogance of some leaders who, from Europe to the Americas, duel in the "virile" spectacle of a pathetic disdain for danger.

Exposed to the shock of our extreme vulnerability, which, in investing our bodies, also inflicts a wound on our lifestyles, privileges, and certainties, we have the opportunity of opening a crack in the fortress of our convictions and presumptions and try to invert the course in the quest for a place to land, as Bruno Latour would say. This could occur only if, finally mindful of the shared condition of vulnerability characterizing the human, we become convinced that we could only do it together, while we are open to an assumption of responsibility that is simultaneously singular and common and in which we are both subjects and objects. Never has our destiny been tied to the destiny of others as it currently is.

We can only wager, of course, on our ability to grasp the chance harbored in the difficult situation that is offered by the catastrophe. This wager is to be understood in the exquisitely Pascalian sense of betting everything on the fact that we can succeed even though we have no certainty or guarantee of success, because, unfortunately, we have no alternatives for defending the future. It is only based on this wager that we can try to identify possible strategies to produce a fecund change based on the resources we still have available—although they may seem modest compared with the enormity of what is at stake.

There is certainly no one single answer or resource to carry out the process toward a metamorphosis. The metamorphosis rather requires that we practice all possible strategies, be they material or symbolic, mental or political. Let us try, then, to select some of these strategies, not only because they are exemplary but also because they clearly bring us back to the role of the emotive dimension and its constructive potentialities.

First and foremost, we can think of the resource represented by the educational path and we can orient the institutions that are par excellence devoted to paideia (schools above all) toward a new pedagogical vision.

This vision ought to be based no longer (only) on learning rules, rights, and duties, and, even less, on a superficial behaviorism, but rather on what the Greeks called "care of the soul" and on the educators' ability to grow virtue—if we want to maintain this vocabulary—out of the subjects' emotive dynamics. This can occur through a kind of Socratic maieutics that stimulates active participation on the part of subjects, that lets emerge not only everyone's truth but also the ability to transform it on the basis of an open and interactive debate on the passions and sentiments.

Second, we have available the multifarious archipelago of symbolic language—from artistic performances to music, from literature to cinema—which is capable, more than other languages, to live up to the times, describe without reticence the new forms of evil, and prefigure dystopian scenarios, thereby mobilizing our emotions. In all its expressions, true art not only has the ability to shake our deepest regions and invest us with the disquieting force of the uncanny [il perturbante]; it is also, perhaps, the best antidote to the market of emotions that is skillfully fueled by the media and by an advertising industry hungry with consumerism. This market of emotions sucks us up into the opioid universe of unconscious addiction, corroding our freedom at its root. A movie, a musical event or a theatrical pièce can, on the contrary, transform us from passive spectators, intoxicated with the seductive and hammering parade of images, into "moved spectators," as Boltonski characterizes them. That is, spectators capable of perceiving the power of an image—thereby tearing apart the veil of media homologation—and of becoming attentive and conscious viewers, ready to turn into actors. The television image of a child dead on the beach, which reawakens the taboo of the untouchability of infancy, or that of an exhausted body that has been fished out of the sea by merciful hands, which evokes Christ's suffering, or movies that document horror and desolation, such as Fuocoamaro and Terraferma,[124] can awaken empathy for the different and open us to hospitality, much more than many collective petitions or politically organized demonstrations. Marina Abramović's provocative performances, which subject the body to extreme trials, can sensitize us to physical and psychological suffering, which generally we prefer to ignore, much more than any journalistic denunciation. Analogously, a book like Cormac McCarthy's The Road or a movie such as Elysium (2013) violently throw us into the dystopian universe of a nuclear or ecological catastrophe, reawakening fear for the real dangers incumbent on humanity. On the contrary, movies and documentaries such as Wim Wenders's *The Salt of the Earth* and Cyril Dion and Mélanie Laurent's *Tomorrow* or, more recently, *Woman at War* and the truly beautiful docufilm *Amaranto* (which takes a plant sacred to the Aztecs as a metaphor for the possibility of opposing the destruction of the planet) can rekindle the will to fight and the hope for the future.

Third is the function of politics, which we can perhaps understand as the resource to cultivate the positive passions, as proposed by Martha Nussbaum, who identifies an effective witness of this idea in the rhetorically exemplary message of great political individuals (such as Lincoln and Gandhi, Nehru and Mandela). This proposal is undoubtedly appealing. It is grounded on the (certainly not guaranteed) presupposition that emotions such as love and compassion represent the social glue our democracies cannot do without, if they want to build a fair and supportive [*solidale*] society.[125] Currently though, enlisting political rhetoric among the useful tools to promote positive emotions seems at least audacious, given that not only are we inexorably orphans of exemplary heroes but also that the increasingly pervasive emergence of politics with no scruples or projects is seeming to proceed in the exact opposite direction. That is the direction of fueling, if not even creating, negative emotions (such as fear and hatred, envy and resentment) in order to obtain at all cost an endogamous social cohesion, exclusively functional for managing forms of power ever more concerned with their own survival, as Canetti would say, and brutally skilled in manipulating masses and their passions.[126] It may seem trivial, but the only politics that can hope to contribute to a metamorphosis is bottom-up politics, or, in Arendt's more sophisticated terms, politics as a horizontal action of agreement, of shared commitment to the public realm, as a "miraculous" cooperation. We may perhaps see the emergence of timid and frail traces of this in the new social movements, which are increasingly globally connected and nourished—through the internet and the viral dynamics of social media (such as the Fridays for Future or the Italian Sardine)—with a new enthusiasm not only for freedom and justice but also for sharing and caring for the world. Or we may observe it in the myriad of global and local experiences of women who are irreducible, not only in terms of their resistance to domination but also for their tireless invention of alternative practices and novel lifestyles on which to wager, despite everything, in order to redesign the image of the future.

This is evidently a crucial theme, which would deserve its own new chapter. What is certain is that these phenomena confirm the need to take seriously our emotive life and take care of it by activating the already invoked principle of fighting the passions with the passions. This means contrasting negative passions with massive doses of empathic passions to be injected into the social body as potential leverages for mobilizations for justice, solidarity, and care. In sum, the passions form the emotive cement we cannot do without, if we want to produce the metamorphosis capable of stimulating and nourishing our legitimate demand for justice and our abilities for care. These are the necessary foundations for what, evoking a slogan that is perhaps a bit nostalgic but still actual, we can still call a better world.

Notes

Introduction

1. Carol Gilligan, *In a Different Voice: Psychological Theory and Women's Development* (Cambridge, MA: Harvard University Press, 1982).

2. We could refer to two opposed positions to which we will return, namely, the one that reabsorbs care into justice (Martha Nussbaum) and the one that reabsorbs justice into care (Michael Slote).

3. Essential in generating this perspective are G. E. M. Anscombe, "Modern Moral Philosophy," *Philosophy* 33, no. 124 (1958): 1–19, and Iris Murdoch, *The Sovereignty of Good* (London: Routledge, 1970). These authors inspired the philosophical debate (especially the philosophical-analytical debate) that, starting from the 1980s and, in particular, from Bernard Williams's *Moral Luck* (Cambridge: Cambridge University Press, 1981), proposes a reevaluation of emotions in the field of ethics. See the excellent critical reconstruction made by Carla Bagnoli in the introduction to the collective volume *Morality and the Emotions* (Oxford: Oxford University Press 2011). See also John M. Doris and the Moral Psychology Research Group, *The Moral Psychology Handbook* (Oxford: Oxford University Press, 2012), and Keith Oatley, *Emotions: A Brief History of Emotions* (Hoboken, NJ: Wiley-Blackwell, 2004). Also relevant is the work of Jonathan Haidt, who underlines how the first principle of moral psychology is that intuitions, based on our emotions, precede strategic reasoning in moral judgment. See Jonathan Haidt, "The New Synthesis in Moral Psychology," *Science* 316, no. 5827 (2007): 998–1002. It is interesting to note that some authors who address the problem of intergenerational justice (including Ernest Partridge and Dieter Birnbacher) refer, as we will see, to moral psychology.

4. It should be pointed out that, in contrast to the Aristotelian or cognitive traditions, it is the Humean tradition of moral sentimentalism (which, in the following reflection, will be given a priority role) that emphasizes especially the function of the passions as motivations.

156

5. Gilligan, *In a Different Voice*; Joan C. Tronto, *Moral Boundaries: A Political Argument for an Ethics of Care* (London: Routledge, 1995); Virginia Held, *The Ethics of Care: Personal, Political, and Global* (Oxford: Oxford University Press, 2006); Eva Kittay, *Love's Labor: Essays on Women, Equality and Dependency* (New York: Routledge, 1999).

6. John Rawls, *A Theory of Justice* (Cambridge, MA: Harvard University Press, 1971).

7. Martha Nussbaum, *Frontiers of Justice: Disability, Nationality, Species Membership* (Cambridge, MA: Harvard University Press, 2006).

8. Amartya Sen, *The Idea of Justice* (London: Allen Lane, 2009).

9. Emmanuel Renault, *The Experience of Injustice: A Theory of Recognition*, trans. Richard A. Lynch (New York: Columbia University Press, 2019).

10. Paul Ricoeur, "Love and Justice," in *Figuring the Sacred: Religion, Narrative, and Imagination*, trans. David Pellauer (Minneapolis: Fortress, 1995).

11. Aristotle, *Nicomachean Ethics* 1.8.1.1155a–b: "Friendship seems too to hold states together, and lawgivers to care more for it than for justice. . . . When men are friends they have no need of justice, while when they are just they need friendship as well, and the truest form of justice is thought to be a friendly quality."

12. Peter Sloterdijk, *You Must Change Your Life* (Cambridge, UK: Polity, 2014).

Chapter One

1. Jon Elster, "Sadder but Wiser? Rationality and the Emotions," *Social Science Information* 24, no. 2 (1993): 375–406. See also Jon Elster, *Strong Feelings: Emotion, Addiction, and Human Behavior* (Cambridge, MA: MIT Press, 1999).

2. Martha Nussbaum, *Upheavals of Thought: The Intelligence of Emotions* (Cambridge: Cambridge University Press, 2001).

3. I will return to this topic in chapter 7 of this volume.

4. The need to differentiate among the multiple variations of the emotional life is one of the theses of the present volume, and I return to it on many occasions. For a broader reflection on this topic, see Elena Pulcini, "Passioni," in *Enciclopedia del pensiero politico*, ed. Carlo Galli and Roberto Esposito (Rome: Laterza, 2000), and "Passioni," in *I racconti della storia*, vol. 6, ed. Franco Cardini, Mario Rosa, and Aldo Schiavone (Milan: Garzanti, 2004).

5. See Sergio Manghi, "Emozioni," in *Parole chiave: Per un nuovo lessico delle scienze sociali*, ed. Alberto Melucci (Rome: Carocci, 2000), 97–105 where he writes, "The word 'emotions' has not always existed nor has it always had the same meaning. It ends up designating an area previously defined by the word 'passions.' Yet, in the positivistic cultural milieu of the middle of the nineteenth century, the term 'passions' seemed inapt for the objectifying instances

inspiring the construction of the new social sciences. . . . From then on, the ancient root *pathos*, which variously qualified the term 'passion,' would follow a semantic vocation separate and well distinct, namely, that of suffering [*patimento*], pathetic, and pathologic."

6. Adam Smith, *The Theory of Moral Sentiments* (New York: Penguin, 2009).

7. Nussbaum, *Upheavals of Thought*, 297ff.

8. For an effective critical reconstruction of this notion, see Sergio Caruso, *Homo oeconomicus: Paradigma, critiche, revisioni* (Florence: Firenze University Press, 2012).

9. "A person thus described may be 'rational' in the limited sense of revealing no inconsistencies in his choice behavior, but if he has no use for these distinctions between quite different concepts, he must be a bit of a fool. The purely economic man is indeed close to being a social moron. Economic theory has been much preoccupied with this rational fool decked in the glory of his one all-purpose preference ordering. To make room for the different concepts related to his behavior we need a more elaborate structure." Amartya Sen, "Rational Fools: A Critique of the Behavioral Foundation of Economic Theory," *Philosophy and Public Affairs* 6, no. 4 (1977): 336.

10. Elsewhere I have defined these passions "passions of utility and passions of the I." To my mind, they sum up the fundamental emotive core of the modern individual. See Elena Pulcini, *The Individual without Passions: Modern Individualism and the Loss of the Social Bond*, trans. Karen Whittle (Washington, DC: Lexington Books, 2012).

11. This objection does not mean to deny the existence of egoism. It is not by chance that one of the most convinced theorists of empathy and sympathetic motives such as Frans de Waal confirms the existence of egoism on the ground of zoological and biological researches. See Frans de Waal, *Our Inner Ape* (New York: Riverhead Books, 2005).

12. For a criticism of the monistic and reductivistic feature of this figure and of utilitarianism based on Mauss's theory of gift, see Alain Caillé, *The Gift Paradigm: A Short Introduction to the Anti-Utilitarian Movement in the Social Sciences*, trans. Gordon Connell and François Gauthier (Chicago: Prickly Paradigm, 2020): "An anti-utilitarian theory of action, on the contrary, without ignoring the force of interests, must show that a systematic reduction to the play of interests is untenable and, ultimately, fails to account for what essentially matters to humans."

13. See Philippe Chanial, *La sociologie comme philosophie politique, et réciproquement* (Paris: La Découverte, 2011), especially chapter 3, "Théorie des sentiments moraux, le retour?"

14. Michael Slote, *Moral Sentimentalism* (Oxford: Oxford University Press, 2010); Shaun Nichols, *Sentimental Rules: On the Natural Foundations of Moral Judgment* (Oxford: Oxford University Press, 2004); and Eugenio Lecaldano, *Prima lezione di filosofia morale* (Rome: Laterza, 2010).

15. Amartya Sen, *The Idea of Justice* (Cambridge, MA: Harvard University Press, 2009); Nussbaum, *Frontiers of Justice*.

16. Antonio Damasio, *Descartes' Error: Emotion, Reason, and the Human Brain* (New York: Penguin, 1994), xvi.

17. Jonathan Haidt, "The Emotional Dog and Its Rational Tail: A Social Intuitionist Approach to Moral Judgment," *Psychological Review* 108, no. 4 (2001): 814–34.

18. Giacomo Rizzolatti and Corrado Sinigaglia, *Mirrors in the Brain: How Our Minds Share Actions and Emotions*, trans. Frances Anderson (Oxford: Oxford University Press, 2008), and see also Antonio Damasio, *Looking for Spinoza: Joy, Sorrow, and the Feeling Brain* (Orlando, FL: Harcourt, 2003).

19. Gérard Jorland, "Empathie, histoire d'un concept," in *Empathie*, ed. Alain Berthoz and Gérard Jorland (Paris: Odile Jacob, 2004), 19–49.

20. Frédérique de Vignemont and Pierre Jacob, "What Is It Like to Feel Another's Pain?," *Philosophy of Science* 79, no. 2 (2012): 296n1, remind readers that "the English word *empathy* was introduced in 1907 by the psychologist Titchener as a translation of the German *Einfühlung*."

21. Eva-Maria Engelen and Birgitt Röttger-Rössler, "Current Disciplinary and Interdisciplinary Debates on Empathy," *Emotion Review* 4, no. 1 (2012): 5.

22. Empathy is defined as "a process or activity, where to empathize with a person, A, is to vicariously experience A's internal experience." Yujia Song, "How to be a Proponent of Empathy?," *Ethical Theory and Moral Practice* 18 (2018): 438. See also Amy Coplan, "Understanding Empathy: Its Features and Effects," in *Empathy: Philosophical and Psychological Perspectives*, ed. Amy Coplan and Peter Goldie (Oxford: Oxford University Press, 2011), 3–185; Monika Betzler, "Ripensare l'importanza morale dell'empatia," in *Cura ed emozioni: Un'alleanza complessa*, ed. Elena Pulcini and Sophie Bourgault (Bologna: Il Mulino, 2018), 105–28.

23. Edith Stein, *On the Problem of Empathy*, trans. Waltraut Stein (Washington, DC: ICS Publications, 1989).

24. This aspect is rightly emphasized by Laura Boella, *Sentire l'altro: Conoscere e praticare l'empatia* (Milan: Cortina, 2006).

25. I simply want to recall here that, in its everyday usage, sympathy is "the mode of being *for* the other, in favour of the other," and that "the distinction between empathy and sympathy has been described as 'feeling *as* and feeling *for* the other'" See Grit Hein and Tania Singer, "I Feel How You Feel but Not Always: The Empathic Brain and Its Modulation," *Current Opinion in Neurobiology* 18, no. 2 (2008): 153–58.

26. David Hume, *A Treatise of Human Nature* (Oxford: Oxford University Press, 2001), 2.1.11.

27. See Eugenio Lecaldano, *Simpatia* (Milan: Cortina, 2013).

28. Hume, *Treatise*, 2.2.5. On the relational character of passions, see also Manghi, *Emozioni*, and Paul Dumouchel, "Y-a-t-il des sentiments moraux?,"

Dialogue 43, no. 3 (2004): 471–90, according to whom moral sentiments as well as all emotions are not atomistic and independent structure; rather, they always function within relationships among persons. I will return to this in chapter 7 in this volume.

29. "Whatever other passions we may be actuated by; pride, ambition, avarice, curiosity, revenge or lust; the soul or animating principle of them all is sympathy; nor wou'd they have any force, were we to abstract entirely from the thoughts and sentiments of others." See Hume, *Treatise*, 2.2.5.

30. Hume, *Treatise*, 2.1.11.

31. Smith, *Theory of Moral Sentiments*, 1.1.1.

32. Smith, *Theory of Moral Sentiments*, 1.1.1.

33. "Whatever is the passion which arises from any object in the person principally concerned, an analogous emotion springs up, at the thought of his situation, in the breast of every attentive spectator." Smith, *Theory of Moral Sentiments*, 1.1.1.

34. Smith, *Theory of Moral Sentiments*, 1.1.1.

35. Engelen and Röttger-Rössler, "Current Disciplinary," 5

36. Martin L. Hoffman, *Empathy and Moral Development: Implications for Caring and Justice* (Cambridge: Cambridge University Press, 2000), 3.

37. According to Hume, every quality of the mind is virtuous if it provides pleasure whereas it is vicious if it provides pain. Pleasure (and pain) are born of *four* different *sources*: we feel pleasure when faced with a character that is useful to others or to oneself or agreeable to others or to oneself. See Hume, *Treatise*, 3.3.1.

38. See Hume, *Treatise*, 3.3.1. See also Patricia Churchland, *Braintrust: What Neuroscience Tells Us about Morality* (Princeton, NJ: Princeton University Press, 2018), 6, according to which, Hume's naturalism (which refuses to explain morality through transcendent dimensions or an unrealistic rationality) "finds the roots of morality in how we are, what we care about, and what matters to us—in our nature."

39. Smith, *Theory of Moral Sentiments*, 1.1.3.

40. See, among others, Lecaldano, *Prima lezione di filosofia morale*; Jacqueline Taylor, *Reflecting Subjects: Passion, Sympathy, and Society in Hume's Philosophy* (Oxford: Oxford University Press, 2015); Annette Baier, "Reflexivity and Sentiment in Hume's Philosophy," in *The Oxford Handbook of Hume*, ed. Paul Russell (Oxford: Oxford University Press, 2016); and the interesting volume by Caterina Botti, *Cura e differenza: Ripensare l'etica* (Milan: LED, 2009), which considers reflective sentimentalism as a possible source of enrichment for the ethics of care.

41. "The propriety of every passion excited by objects peculiarly related to ourselves, the pitch which the spectator can go along with, must lie, it is evident, in a certain mediocrity"; Smith, *Theory of Moral Sentiments*, 1.2, introd. On the figure of the "impartial spectator," see also Smith, *Theory of Moral Sentiments*, 3.1.6.

42. Smith, *Theory of Moral Sentiments*, 1.3.1.

43. Smith, *Theory of Moral Sentiments*, 1.2.4.

44. Smith, *Theory of Moral Sentiments*, 1.1.4.

45. See for example Hume, *Treatise*, 3.3.3: "The passions are so contagious, that they pass with the greatest facility from one person to another, and produce correspondent movements in all human breasts."

46. Engelen and Röttger-Rössler, "Current Disciplinary," 4. Fundamental, on this, are Smith's clarifications when he says that, at times, on someone else's behalf we feel a passion that the other seems him or herself incapable of feeling; for example, when we blush because of someone's impudence or roughness, or when we feel angst in the face of the madness of someone who is unaware of it, or when a mother feels anxiety for her sick child. See Smith, *Theory of Moral Sentiments*, 1.1.1.

47. Hume, *Treatise*, 3.3.1.

48. "Where a character is, in every respect, fitted to be beneficial to society, the imagination passes easily from the cause to the effect, without considering that there are still some circumstances wanting to render the cause a compleat one. *General rules* create a species of probability, which sometimes influences the judgment, and always the imagination." See Hume, *Treatise*, 3.3.1.

49. Hume, *Treatise*, 3.3.1.

50. As he says with a very eloquent formulation, "Virtue in rags is still virtue." Hume, *Treatise*, 3.3.1.

51. See later in this volume, chapter 7, the section "Generative Sentiments."

52. For a general overview, see Piergiorgio Donatelli and Emidio Spinelli, eds., *Il senso della virtù* (Rome: Carocci, 2009).

53. Hume, *Treatise*, 3.3.6. [Italics added by Pulcini.]

54. "We sympathize more with persons contiguous to us, than with persons remote from us: With our acquaintance, than with strangers: With our countrymen, than with foreigners." Hume, *Treatise*, 3.3.1.

55. Sympathy "is far from being as lively as when our own interest is concern'd, or that of our particular friends; nor has it such an influence on our love and hatred: But being equally conformable to our calm and general principles, 'tis said to have an equal authority over our reason, and to command our judgment and opinion. We blame equally a bad action, which we read of in history, with one perform'd in our neighbourhood t'other day: The meaning of which is, that we know from reflexion, that the former action wou'd excite as strong sentiments of disapprobation as the latter, were it plac'd in the same position." Hume, *Treatise*, 3.3.1.

56. See Peter Singer, *The Expanding Circle: Ethics, Evolution, and Moral* (Princeton, NJ: Princeton University Press, 2011); Fonna Forman-Barzilai, *Adam Smith and the Circles of Sympathy* (Cambridge: Cambridge University Press, 2010); Nichols, *Sentimental Rules*.

57. Hume, *Treatise*, 3.3.1.

58. See later, chapter 5 of the present volume.

59. Smith, *Theory of Moral Sentiments*, 1.1.1.

60. Hume, *Treatise*, 3.3.1.

61. Hume, *Treatise*, 3.3.1.

62. Stephen Darwall, "Empathy, Sympathy, and Care," *Philosophical Studies* 89 (1998): 261–82; Benjamin M. P. Cuff, Sarah J. Brown, Laura Taylor, and Douglas J. Howat, "Empathy: A Review of the Concept," *Emotion Review* 8, no. 2 (2014): 144–53.

63. Andrea Pinotti, *Empatia: Storia di un'idea da Platone al postumano* (Rome: Laterza, 2011), 28ff.

64. Sara D. Hodges and Robert Biswas-Diener, "Balancing the Empathy Expense Account: Strategies for Regulating Empathic Response," in *Empathy in Mental Illness*, ed. Tom Farrow and Peter Woodruff (Cambridge: Cambridge University Press, 2007), 389–407.

65. Max Scheler, *Zur Phänomenologie und Theorie der Sympathiegefühle und von Liebe und Haß* (Halle: Niemeyer, 1913).

66. The importance of the distinction between I and other is emphasized by Stein, *The Problem of Empathy*.

67. See later in this volume chapter 3, "The Passions of Justice."

68. Hoffman, *Empathy and Moral Development*; Slote, *Moral Sentimentalism*; Frans de Waal, *The Age of Empathy: Nature's Lessons for a Kinder Society* (New York: Broadway Books, 2010).

69. See Karsten R. Stueber, "Variety of Empathy: Neuroscience and the Narrativist Challenge to the Contemporary Theory of Mind Debate," *Emotion Review* 4, no. 1 (2012): 55–63.

70. Hodges and Biswas-Diener, "Balancing the Empathy Expense Account."

71. See C. Daniel Batson, "These Things Called Empathy: Eight Related but Distinct Phenomena," in *The Social Neuroscience of Empathy*, ed. Jean Decety and William Ickes (Cambridge, MA: MIT Press, 2009), 3–15.

72. Engelen and Röttger-Rössler, "Current Disciplinary," 5.

73. Harry Frankfurt, *The Reasons of Love* (Princeton, NJ: Princeton University Press, 2004); Christine Korsgaard, *The Sources of Normativity* (Cambridge: Cambridge University Press, 1996); Singer, *Expanding Circle*.

74. I will return to this topic in the last chapter of the volume.

75. J. L. Goetz, D. Keltner, and E. Simon-Thomas, "Compassion. An Evolutionary Analysis and Empirical Review," *Psychological Bulletin* 136, 3 (2010): 351.

76. See Darwall, "Empathy, Sympathy, and Care"; also Nancy Eisenberg, Cindy L. Shea, Gustavo Carlo, and George P. Knight, "Empathy-Related Responding and Cognition: A 'Chicken and the Egg' Dilemma," in *Handbook of Moral Behavior and Development*, vol. 2, *Research*, ed. William Kurtines and Jacob Gewirtz (Hillsdale, NJ: Erlbaum, 1991), 65, where sympathy is defined as a

"vicarious emotional reaction based on the apprehension of another's emotional state or situation, which involves feelings of sorrow or concern for the other."

77. Hein and Singer, "I Feel How You Feel," 81.

78. Nussbaum, *Frontiers of Justice*, 91.

79. Nussbaum, *Frontiers of Justice*, 408.

80. Sen, *Idea of Justice*, 191.

81. Sen, *Idea of Justice*, 191. On the social-historical as well as theoretical reasons of the devaluing of moral sentiments, see Tronto, *Moral Boundaries*, which attributes such a devaluation to the victory of eighteenth-century universalistic morality and highlights the connection with the devaluation of care and woman subjectivity.

82. Peter Sloterdijk, *Rage and Time: A Psychopolitical Investigation*, trans. Mario Wenning (New York: Columbia University Press, 2012).

83. On shame, see Gabriella Turnaturi, *Vergogna: Metamorfosi di un'emozione* (Milan: Feltrinelli, 2012), and Lorenzo Bruni, *Vergogna: Un'emozione sociale dialettica* (Salerno: Orthotes, 2016).

84. See, for example, Jesse J. Prinz, "Is Empathy Necessary for Morality?," in *Empathy: Philosophical and Psychological Perspectives*, ed. Amy Coplan and Peter Goldie (Oxford: Oxford University Press, 2014), 211–29, who claims that morality is not made possible by empathy (which does not motivate and can be manipulated) but by other emotions independent from this psychological process, such as the feeling of guilt and rage.

85. See Michael Lewis, *Shame: The Exposed Self* (New York: Free Press, 1992).

86. Hans Jonas, *The Imperative of Responsibility: In Search of an Ethics for the Technological Age*, trans. Hans Jonas with David Herr (Chicago: University of Chicago Press, 1984). I have addressed this theme widely in Elena Pulcini, *Care of the World: Fear, Responsibility, and Justice in the Global Age*, trans. Karen Whittle (Dordrecht: Springer, 2013), and I will return to it later in this volume in chapter 6, "Global Perspectives: Care and Justice Confronting the Challenge of the Temporally *Distant Other*."

87. See chapter 3 in the present volume, "Empathy and Compassion."

88. See Lecaldano, *Simpatia*; Susan Sontag, *Regarding the Pain of Others* (New York: Picador, 2004).

89. The theme recurs in Martha Nussbaum's reflection especially starting with Nussbaum, *Upheavals of Thought*.

90. See later in this volume chapter 7, "For an Emotive Subject: Taking Care of the Passions."

91. The theme is too broad to be addressed here. I will simply indicate some meaningful references. According to Charles Larmore, *Les pratiques du moi* (Paris: PUF, 2004), the Self is constituted not (only) through cognitive relations but (mainly) through *practical relations* when it takes up a commitment

(*engagement*) toward something. It is through practical relations that we commit to doing something we believe or desire. The Self commits itself even when it simply declares to desire or love something. According to Axel Honneth, "our actions do not primarily have the character of an affectively neutral, cognitive stance toward the world but rather that of an affirmative, existentially colored style of caring comportment." Axel Honneth, *Reification: A New Look at an Old Idea* (New York: Oxford University Press, 2012), 38. See also Simon Critchley, *Infinitely Demanding: Ethics of Commitment, Politics of Resistance* (London: Verso, 2007).

92. In this sense, these are three exemplary authors for whom the theoretical reflection finds substantial unfolding in their own personal involvement in social and political practice.

93. Starting with Tronto, *Moral Boundaries*.

94. See Held, *Ethics of Care*.

95. Held, *Ethics of Care*, 4.

96. Held, *Ethics of Care*, 4.

Chapter Two

1. I have further examined this theme in Pulcini, *Care of the World*, 186ff.

2. See Lawrence Kohlberg, *Essays on Moral Development*, 2 vols. (San Francisco: Harper and Row, 1981–84).

3. Starting with a critique of Kohlberg's theory, which privileges a male model of judgment over a feminine one, Gilligan affirms that two models exist. She shows the different moral orientations of the two sexes through the responses of two children (Amy and Jake) to Heinz's dilemma, which revolves around the question of whether he should steal the drug necessary to help his gravely ill wife, by comparing the two responses (Jake: Heinz must steal the medicine; Amy: Heinz must do his best to help his wife without stealing the medicine). The male response resolves moral conflicts by appealing to an ethics of rights and justice based on universal principles, whereas the female response, which seeks first to preserve the network of relations and bonds between the involved parties, resolves the dilemma through criteria based on an ethics of responsibility and care. See Gilligan, *In a Different Voice*, 25ff.

4. One could argue that, according to the care paradigm, care of relations is equally as relevant as, if not more relevant than, the care of the other.

5. "The potential error in justice reasoning lies in its latent egocentrism, the tendency to confuse one's perspective with an objective standpoint or truth, the temptation to define others in one's own terms by putting oneself in their place. The potential error in care reasoning lies in the tendency to forget that one has terms, creating a tendency to enter into another's perspective and to see

oneself as 'selfless' by defining oneself in other's terms." Carol Gilligan, "Moral Orientation and Moral Development," in *Justice and Care: Essential Readings in Feminist Ethics*, ed. Virginia Held (Boulder, CO: Westview Press, 1987), 43. The citation is taken from Sandra Laugier, *Etica e politica dell'ordinario* (Milan: MED, 2015), 50.

6. We find confirmation of this claim in Nancy Fraser's insight concerning the plurality of the claims of justice in relation to globalization when she writes, "Given the plurality of competing frames for organizing and resolving justice conflicts, how do we know which scale of justice is truly just?" Nancy Fraser, *Scales of Justice: Reimagining Political Space in a Globalizing World* (New York: Columbia University Press, 2010), 2.

7. Virginia Held, "Care, Empathy, and Justice: Comments on Michael Slote's Moral Sentimentalism," *Analytic Philosophy* 52, no. 4 (2011): 312–18.

8. Luc Boltanski, *Love and Justice as Competences* (Cambridge, UK: Polity, 2012).

9. I refer here to Avishai Margalit, *The Decent Society* (Cambridge, MA: Harvard University Press, 1996).

10. Tronto, *Moral Boundaries*; Held, *Ethics of Care*; Kittay, *Love's Labor*; Nussbaum, *Frontiers of Justice*.

11. A legacy of the philosophers of alterity (Levinas, Ricoeur, Jonas), the theme of vulnerability is the subject of much reflection. It is a shared topic of concern for different kinds of philosophy, including feminist philosophy, in that it theoretically underscores the multiplicity of forms of alterity, some of which we will encounter in subsequent chapters. A thick and prismatic concept, vulnerability assumes a foundational role for the articulation of models, different from modern ones, that present a subject who exists in relationships with others rather than a sovereign individual, that uphold an ethics of care and responsibility as opposed to a unilateral ethics of justice, and that oppose an individualist ontology with a relational one. See *Vulnerabilità, etica, politica, diritto*, ed. Maria Giulia Bernardini, Brunella Casalini, Orsetta Giolo, Lucia Re (Rome: IF Press, 2018); Alessandra Grompi, *V come vulnerabilità* (Assisi: Cittadella, 2017).

12. We saw earlier how Gilligan justifies her thesis by examining the different responses of the two children (male and female) to Heinz's dilemma.

13. Carol Gilligan, Janie Victoria Ward, and Jill McLean Taylor, with Betty Baridge, eds., *Mapping the Moral Domain: A Contribution of Women's Thinking to Psychological Theory and Education* (Cambridge, MA: Harvard University Press, 1988), xviii.

14. Gilligan, *In a Different Voice*, 100.

15. Tronto, *Moral Boundaries*.

16. Tronto, *Moral Boundaries*, 117, 134.

17. Tronto, *Moral Boundaries*, 118.

18. Tronto, *Moral Boundaries*, 147.

19. Tronto, *Moral Boundaries*, 148.

20. Rawls, *Theory of Justice*; Jürgen Habermas, *The Theory of Communicative Action*, trans. Thomas McCarthy, 2 vols. (Cambridge, UK: Polity, 1984); Jürgen Habermas, *Moral Consciousness and Communicative Action*, trans. Christian Lenhardt and Shierry Weber Nicholsen (Cambridge, UK: Polity, 1990).

21. Tronto, *Moral Boundaries*, 152.

22. Tronto, *Moral Boundaries*, 214.

23. Held, *Ethics of Care*.

24. In other words, we need to remove care from devaluing, patriarchal male thought, proposing instead a post patriarchal conception that clearly presupposes the autonomy and dignity of women. See Held, *Ethics of Care*, 64.

25. "Second, in the epistemological process of trying to understand what morality would recommend and what it would be morally best for us to do and to be, the ethics of care values emotion rather than rejects it. Not all emotion is valued, of course, but in contrast with the dominant rationalist approaches, such emotions as sympathy, empathy, sensitivity, and responsiveness are seen as the kind of moral emotions that need to be cultivated not only to help in the implementation of the dictates of reason but to better ascertain what morality recommends." Held, *Ethics of Care*, 10.

26. Held, *Ethics of Care*, 66. I will develop this theme in chapters 5 and 6.

27. Held, *Ethics of Care*, 63–64.

28. Annette Baier, "The Need for More than Justice," *Canadian Journal of Philosophy* 13 (2013): 41–56.

29. "Gilligan saw these as alternative interpretations that could be applied to given moral problems, yielding different ways of construing what the moral problem was and how it should be handled. . . . But with respect to a given problem, this suggestion leaves us with alternative interpretations but no advice on choosing between them. Why should we see an issue as one of justice primarily or as one primarily of care?" Held, *Ethics of Care*, 62.

30. For example, Nel Noddings, *Caring: A Feminine Approach to Ethics and Moral Education* (Berkeley: University of California Press, 1986). By contrast, Diemut Bubeck calls us to be on guard against an excessive emphasis on care, arguing that, as long as it is understood as the explicit work of women, it runs the risk of being exploited, and this can be avoided only by maintaining a strong ethics of justice. See Diemut Bubeck, *Care, Gender, and Justice* (Oxford: Clarendon Press, 1995).

31. See Held, *Ethics of Care*, 67.

32. Held, *Ethics of Care*, 15.

33. Held, *Ethics of Care*, 15–16.

34. "We need new images for the relations between justice and care, rejecting the impulse toward reductionism." Held, *Ethics of Care*, 73.

35. Held, *Ethics of Care*, 17.

36. Held, *Ethics of Care*, 69.

37. Held, *Ethics of Care*, 71.

38. Charles R. Beitz, *Political Theory and International Relations* (Princeton, NJ: Princeton University Press, 1979); Thomas Pogge, *World Poverty and Human Rights: Cosmopolitan Responsibilities and Reforms* (Cambridge, UK: Polity, 2008).

39. See chapter 5 in this volume.

40. Held specifically refers to John Keane, *Global Civil Society?* (Cambridge: Cambridge University Press, 2003).

41. Relevant here is Sandra Laugier's question: "The question is not one of choosing between care and justice or of discovering the novelty about care reasoning; rather, it is about understanding how we could have lost this voice." See Sandra Laugier, "L'etica di Amy: La cura come cambio di paradigma," *Iride* 24, no. 2 (2011): 339.

42. As already mentioned, I use interchangeably the terms "emotion" and "passion."

43. Nussbaum, *Frontiers of Justice*.

44. Martha Nussbaum, *Women and Human Development: The Capabilities Approach* (Cambridge: Cambridge University Press, 2000).

45. Nussbaum, *Frontiers of Justice*, 70.

46. Kittay, *Love's Labor*, xiii.

47. Kittay, *Love's Labor*.

48. Kittay, *Love's Labor*, 2.

49. Nussbaum, *Frontiers of Justice*, 27–28.

50. Nussbaum, *Frontiers of Justice*, 156–57.

51. Nussbaum, *Frontiers of Justice*, 408.

52. Nussbaum, *Frontiers of Justice*, 409–10. Amartya Sen too maintains the presence of a moral component in the thought of Rawls, which ultimately distinguishes the latter from rational choice models. He writes, "Rawls makes another basic contribution in pointing to 'the moral powers' that people have, related to their 'capacity for a sense of justice' and 'for a conception of the good.'" Sen, *The Idea of Justice*, 63.

53. Nussbaum, *Frontiers of Justice*, 82.

54. Nussbaum, *Frontiers of Justice*, 89.

55. Nussbaum, *Frontiers of Justice*, 273.

56. Nussbaum, *Frontiers of Justice*, 324.

57. "Why focus only on the more extreme dependencies? Dependency is found not only in the case of a young child who is dependent on a mothering person. A boss is dependent on his or her secretary. Urban populations are dependent on agricultural communities. Persons on farms are dependent on electrical workers. Professors are dependent on janitors, and janitors are dependent on engineers. And so on. We are all interdependent. My point is that this interdependence begins with dependence." Kittay, *Love's Labor*, xii.

58. Kittay, *Love's Labor*, 25.
59. Kittay, *Love's Labor*.
60. Nussbaum, *Frontiers of Justice*, ch. 7.
61. Michael Slote, *The Ethics of Care and Empathy* (New York: Routledge, 2007).
62. Michael Slote, "Hume e l'etica della cura," *Iride* 25, no. 67 (2012): 557–71.

Chapter Three

1. Nussbaum, *Upheavals of Thought*, 301.
2. Nussbaum, *Upheavals of Thought*, 302.
3. See what was said earlier in this volume in chapter 1, in the section "From Empathy to Moral Sentiments, from Sentiments to Engagement."
4. Nussbaum, *Upheavals of Thought*, 319.
5. "So, it [the capabilities approach] adopts a thoroughly anti-Stoic picture of the world, according to which human beings are both dignified and needy, and in which dignity and neediness interact in complex ways." Nussbaum, *Upheavals of Thought*, 319, 405.
6. Nussbaum, *Upheavals of Thought*, 342ff.
7. Nussbaum, *Upheavals of Thought*, 310.
8. Nussbaum, *Upheavals of Thought*, 404–5.
9. Nussbaum, *Upheavals of Thought*, 399.
10. Bernard Mandeville, "An Essay on Charity and Charity Schools," in *The Fable of the Bees, or Private Vices, Public Benefits* (London: Ostell, 1806), 157.
11. Friedrich Nietzsche, *Genealogy of Morals*, trans. Walter Kaufman (New York: Random House, 1967).
12. Simone Weil, *Gravity and Grace*, trans. Emma Crawford and Mario von der Ruhr (London: Routledge, 2002). On these themes, see the acute interpretation by Sophie Bourgault, "Cura come attenzione," in *Cura ed emozioni: Un'alleanza complessa*, ed. Elena Pulcini and Sophie Bourgault (Bologna: Il Mulino, 2018), 209–28. For an example of valorization of pity, see Emmanuel Housset, *L'intelligence de la pitié: Phénoménologie de la communauté* (Paris: Cerf, 2003), who considers pity a sentiment provoked by the other's suffering that grasps the Self from the outside, causing the Self's decentering and its opening to the other and the world, thereby opening the way to ethics. On this, see Inge van Nistelrooij, "Coesistenza affettiva: La pietà come connessione tra emozione e cono-scenza etica," in *Cura ed emozioni*, 129–52.
13. I will return to the limits of compassion in chapter 5 of this volume.
14. Hannah Arendt, *On Revolution* (New York: Penguin, 1963).
15. Arendt, *On Revolution*, 89.

16. Arendt, *On Revolution*, 89.

17. Nussbaum, *Upheavals of Thought*, 426ff.

18. See Paolo Costa, "Martha Nussbaum: La compassione entro i limiti della ragione," *La società degli individui* 18 (2003): 131–48

19. Nussbaum, *Upheavals of Thought*, 399.

20. For a critical reconstruction of the complexity of modern thought regarding the theme of compassion, see Antonio Prete, *Compassione: Storia di un sentimento* (Turin: Bollati Boringheri, 2013). On the connection between care and justice, particularly convincing is the interpretation by Ferruccio Andolfi, "Due modi di universalismo etico: Giustizia e compassione," *La società degli individui* 18 (2003): 7–20, who claims that the perspective that opposes justice and compassion can be overcome as long as one considers compassion appropriately as "a preliminary understanding, which marks the context within which all subsequent possible doing, including that of justice, is rendered possible." Andolfi, "Due modi di universalismo etico," 19.

21. See chapters 5 and 6 in this volume.

22. Sontag, *Regarding the Pain of Others*.

23. Sloterdijk, *Rage and Time*.

24. Sen, *Idea of Justice*.

25. Sen, *Idea of Justice*, 410.

26. Rawls's merits consist, according to Sen, in his vision of justice as fairness, in the recognition of the moral faculties of the individuals and their ability to have a sense of justice, in the primacy of freedom. See Sen, *Idea of Justice*, 53ff.

27. On the theory of social choice, see Sen, *Idea of Justice*, 87ff.

28. Sen, *Idea of Justice*, 398.

29. With respect to this, Sen refers to the traditional distinction in Indian jurisprudence between justice founded on structure (*niti*) and justice founded precisely on concrete realizations (*nyaya*). See Sen, *Idea of Justice*, xv.

30. Sen, *Idea of Justice*, 6.

31. Sen, *Idea of Justice*, vii.

32. In this case too, Sen's privileged reference is Adam Smith and the English tradition. See Sen, *Idea of Justice*, 44ff.

33. Sen, *Idea of Justice*, 414.

34. "As Adam Smith noted, we do have many different motivations, taking us well beyond the single-minded pursuit of our interest. There is nothing contrary to reason in our willingness to do things that are not entirely self-serving. Some of these motivations, like 'humanity, justice, generosity and public spirit,' may even be very productive for society, as Smith noted." Sen, *Idea of Justice*, 191.

35. Sen, *Idea of Justice*, 388.

36. Sen, *Idea of Justice*, 49.

37. Sen, *Idea of Justice*, 390ff.

38. One could hypothesize that this comes from presupposing, in both cases, the presence of that essential figure for ethical judgement constituted, in Sen's Smithian perspective, by the "impartial spectator."

39. "If one tries to remove the misery of others only because—and only to the extent that—it affects one's own welfare, this does not signify a departure from self-love as the only accepted reason for action. But if one is committed, say, to doing what can be done to remove the misery of others—whether or not one's own welfare is affected by it, and not merely to the extent to which one's own welfare is so influenced—then that *is* a clear departure from self-interested behavior." Sen, *Idea of Justice*, 189.

40. Renault, *Experience of Injustice*.

41. Renault reports the absence, in both Rawls and Habermas, of a diagnostic analysis of the situations that generate injustice. This consequently yields to a static conception of justice that in fact ignores the pathologies of the social and prevents seeing justice as a dynamic of transformation of injustice.

42. On the theme of justice as negation of injustice, see Leonard Mazzone, *Una teoria negativa della giustizia: Per un'etica del conflitto contro i mali comuni* (Milan: Mimesis, 2014).

43. See Axel Honneth, *The Struggle for Recognition*, trans. Joel Anderson (Cambridge, MA: MIT Press, 1996).

44. By proposing the concept of "experience of injustice" as that which sums up all forms of injustice (whether of distributive or identitarian origin), Renault aims at overcoming the opposition between "redistribution" and "recognition" that has spurred the debate between Axel Honneth and Nancy Fraser. See Nancy Fraser and Axel Honneth, *Redistribution or Recognition? A Political-Philosophical Exchange* (London: Verso, 2003).

45. Emmanuel Renault, *L'expérience de l'injustice* (Paris: La Découverte, 2004), 126. [Translators' note: As specified in the preface to the English translation, the section "La normativité de la reconnaissance," which constitutes the last section of the chapter "Les apories de la justice sociale" and from which the quote is taken, does not appear in the English translation of Renault's work.]

46. "Different forms of the feeling of injustice . . . must be interpreted as subjective experiences of the denial of recognition—they are explained as different forms of social disrespect or of the denial of socially established recognition." Renault, *Experience of Injustice*, 26.

47. See Renault, *Experience of Injustice*, chs. 4 ("Identity as the Experience of Injustice") and 5 ("A Defense of Identity Politics").

48. Renault, *Experience of Injustice*, 12.

49. See Renault, *Experience of Injustice*, ch. 6 ("Social Critique as a Voice for Suffering").

50. Renault, *Experience of Injustice*, 13.

51. I simply remark that taking charge of the invisible forms of injustice and of the social and psychic suffering of those who have no voice or awareness of injustice is one of the most interesting aspects of Renault's analysis. I do not linger on this, because what I am interested in underlining here is the importance of the sentiment of injustice.

52. There are forms of injustice that are not perceived as such by those who undergo them in order not to incur the suffering produced by the recognition of the injustice (as happens in some forms of subordinate work). Or, on the opposite, there are situations wrongly perceived as unjust by some who, in truth, are motivated more by envy than by injustice, as we shall see later.

53. Noticing the lack of this aspect in Honneth, Marcus Ohlström claims that "the need critically to ascertain our value structures is therefore, at least partly, a theoretical or prepolitical necessity. This means that a theory adequate to justice cannot be limited to tracing the moral grammar of social conflicts and thus letting the conflicts be played out by the actors themselves. A theory adequate to justice must go beyond this point. It must be capable of guiding political praxis and indicating the direction toward the just, avoiding the incorrect, with no concern for the beliefs considered true by dominant or other social groups." See Marcus Ohlström, "Sulle basi motivazionali delle lotte sociali: Honneth versus Fraser," *Iride* 23, no. 60 (2010): 448–52.

54. See Nietzsche, *Genealogy of Morals*.

55. Friedrich von Hayek, *Law, Legislation and Liberty: A New Statement of the Liberal Principles of Justice and Political Economy*, 3 vols. (Chicago: University of Chicago Press, 1973–79).

56. Helmut Schoeck, *Envy: A Theory of Social Behaviour* (Indianapolis: Liberty Fund, 1987)

57. This is unexpected, as Rawls is not generally interested in a critical approach that starts with an analysis of the passions.

58. Exemplary is the story told by Slavoj Žižek about a Slovenian farmer who, in front of the alternative proposed by a witch—she can either give a cow to him and two to his neighbor or take one cow away from him and two from his neighbor—unhesitatingly chooses the second option. See Slavoj Žižek, *Violence: Six Sideways Reflections* (New York: Picador, 2008). There is also a more morbid version of the story, in which the witch tells the farmer, "I will do to you whatever you want, but I warn you, I will do it to your neighbor twice"; and the farmer replies: "Take one of my eyes!" In other words, we are ready to inflict self-harm as long as we can prevent the other from benefitting from possession of something. What emerges here is a nihilistic vocation that Nietzsche calls "the height of envy," which drives us to self-sacrifice in order not to grant anything to the other. See Friedrich Nietzsche, *The Dawn of Day*, trans. J. M. Kennedy (Mineola, NY: Dover, 2007), aphorism 304. Perhaps Nietzsche gives us the key to understanding also the source of that exquisitely contemporary

passion that, according to Mirko Alagna's interesting thesis, coagulates within itself a toxic mix of rancor, fear, resentment, and frustration; that is, the "growl" inspired by the terror of being caught by others rather than by the desire to reach them. See Mirko Alagna, "Look Down in Anger: L'epoca del ringhio," *Lo Sguardo* 27 (2018): 297–315.

59. "Therefore, for reasons both of simplicity and moral theory, I have assumed an absence of envy and a lack of knowledge of the special psychologies. Nevertheless these inclinations do exist and in some way they must be reckoned with." Rawls, *Theory of Justice*, 465.

60. Rawls, *Theory of Justice*, 466.

61. Among others, Jean-Pierre Dupuy blames Rawls for reducing the individuals that are protagonists of the pact of cooperation to evanescent ectoplasms, void of any emotive dimension. See Jean-Pierre Dupuy, *Le sacrifice et l'envie: Le libéralisme aux prises avec la justice sociale* (Paris: Calmann-Levy, Paris 1992). Žižek denounces the paradox intrinsic in the idea of just society: "What Rawls doesn't see is how a society of this kind would create conditions for an uncontrolled explosion of resentment: in it, I would know that my lower status is fully 'justified,' and would thus be deprived of excusing my failure as the result of social injustice." See Žižek, *Violence*, 88.

62. Nietzsche, *Genealogy of Morals*, 76.

63. Nietzsche claims that, when there is justice, "the eye is trained to an ever more *impersonal* evaluation of the deed, and this applies even to the eye of the injured person himself." Nietzsche, *Genealogy of Morals*, 76.

64. This theme is increasingly present in contemporary reflections. See Martha Nussbaum, *Hiding from Humanity: Disgust, Shame, and the Law* (Princeton, NJ: Princeton University Press, 2004), which opposes indignation to disgust; Gabriella Turnaturi, *Vergogna: Metamorfosi di un'emozione* (Milan: Feltrinelli, 2012), which addresses the link between shame and indignation; and Livio Pepino and Marco Revelli, *Grammatica dell'indignazione* (Turin: Edizioni Gruppo Abele, 2014), which highlights the risks and ambivalences of indignation within the current contexts.

65. John Rawls, "The Sense of Justice," *Philosophical Review* 72, no. 3 (1963): 299.

66. This reaction, however, presents an intrinsically normative push capable of transforming the existent in an emancipatory direction, as we have seen in Renault.

67. This remark can also be applied to Salvatore Veca at points where he seems to share with Rawls a positive and moral view of resentment. See Salvatore Veca, *La bellezza e gli oppressi: Dieci lezioni sull'idea di giustizia* (Milan: Feltrinelli, 2002).

68. See Nietzsche, *Genealogy of Morals*; Max Scheler, *Ressentiment*, trans. Louis Coser (Milwakee: Marquette University Press, 1994).

69. Scheler, *Ressentiment*, 4.

70. Scheler, *Ressentiment*, 6.

71. A rancorous and poisoning passion, resentment can result in depression and even self-harm. Scheler, *Ressentiment*, 20.

72. René Descartes, *Passions of the Soul*, trans. Stephen Voss (Indianapolis: Hackett, 1989), part 3, sec. 182.

73. Aristotle, *Nicomachean Ethics* 1108b1–7.

74. Sloterdjik, *Rage and Time*.

75. See Elena Pulcini, *Invidia: La passione triste* (Bologna: Il Mulino, 2011).

76. Lecaldano remarks that for Adam Smith too, in *A Theory of Moral Sentiments*, justice has to do with the sentiments of indignation (and resentment) of the impartial spectator in front of an unjust condemnation (like Zola who defends Dreyfus). see Eugenio Lecaldano, *Prima lezione di filosofia morale*.

77. Aristotle, *Rhetoric* 1378a.

78. On rage, see Remo Bodei, *Ira: La passione furente* (Bologna: Il Mulino, 2010), especially chapter 5, "Giusta ira [Just Rage]." On the chiaroscuro aspects of rage, see Paola Giacomoni, *Ardore: Quattro prospettive sull'ira da Achille agli indignados* (Rome: Carocci, 2015).

79. See Nussbaum, *Upheavals of Thought*, 394.

80. Stéphane Hessel, *Indignez-vous!* (Montpellier: Indigène, 2010).

81. I will return on this topic in chapter 5 of this volume.

82. "Hegel was convinced that a struggle among subjects for the mutual recognition of their identity generated inner-societal pressure toward the practical, political establishment of institutions that would guarantee freedom. It is individuals' claim to the intersubjective recognition of their identity that is built into social life from the very beginning as a moral tension, transcends the level of social progress institutionalized so far, and so gradually leads—via the negative path of recurring stages of conflict—to a state of communicatively lived freedom." Honneth, *Struggle for Recognition*, 5.

83. Chantal Mouffe, *On the Political* (London: Routledge, 2005).

84. Marcel Mauss, *The Gift: Forms and Functions of Exchange in Archaic Societies*, trans. W. D. Halls (London: Routledge, 1990).

85. Miguel Benasayag and Angélique Del Rey, *Éloge du conflit* (Paris: La Decouverte, 2007).

86. Essential for a theory of conflict that underlines not only the complexity but also the different quality is the reflection by Alessandro Pizzorno, who, through a confrontation with some classics such as Machiavelli, Hobbes, Marx, and Hegel, differentiates three fundamental variations: conflicts of interest, of recognition, and of ideologies. See especially Alessandro Pizzorno, *Le radici della politica assoluta e altri saggi* (Milan: Feltrinellli, 1993).

87. Danilo Martuccelli, "La partecipazione con riserva: Al di qua del tema della critica," *Quaderni di teoria sociale* 1 (2015): 11–34.

88. Alain Touraine, *Défense de la modernité* (Paris: Seuil, 2018).

89. The exception is, according to Touraine, the authentically emancipatory and global movement currently represented by the women's fight for their rights and dignity.

90. Sen, *Idea of Justice*, 390.

91. Sen, *Idea of Justice*, 46.

92. "A sense of injustice could serve as a signal that moves us, but a signal does demand critical examination, and there has to be some scrutiny of the soundness of a conclusion based mainly on signals. Adam Smith's conviction of the importance of moral sentiments did not stop him from seeking a 'theory of moral sentiments,' nor from insisting that a sense of wrongdoing be critically examined through reasoned scrutiny to see whether it can be the basis of a sustainable condemnation." Sen, *Idea of Justice*, viii.

93. Sen, *Idea of Justice*, 402–3.

Chapter Four

1. I claim here that indignation is not only felt on the part of the person subjected to injustice but also by those who witness it. One can rebel and act with social contempt toward intolerable situations.

2. Stein, *The Problem of Empathy*.

3. Boella, *Sentire l'altro*, 22.

4. Slote, *Ethics of Care and Empathy*, 4.

5. As mentioned previously, I disagree with Slote when he claims that a "[c]are ethics can and should offer a comprehensive account of individual and political morality." Slote, *Ethics of Care and Empathy*, xiii. I also disagree with his claim that care ethics comprehensively includes an ethics of justice.

6. Engelen and Röttger-Rössler, "Current," 5.

7. Hoffman, *Empathy and Moral Development*, 3.

8. Eugenio Lecaldano, *Simpatia*; Nussbaum, *Upheavals of Thought*.

9. Max Scheler, *The Nature of Sympathy*, trans. Peter Heath (Piscataway, NJ: Transaction, 2007), 47.

10. Martha Nussbaum is right to argue that, though empathy is a necessary condition for the self to extend itself, one must distinguish compassion from empathy. The latter is a mental activity that is important for compassion in that it promotes the extension of the self, but it is morally neutral for it is simply an imaginary reconstruction of the experience of another person. This means, then, that we can be indifferently empathic, for example, to joyous or sad experiences. We also can have a good understanding for the suffering of another without feeling any compassion.

11. Held, *Ethics of Care*, 10. See also chapter 2, note 26, in the present volume.

12. Patricia Paperman, *Care et sentiments* (Paris: PUF, 2013); Patricia Paperman and Sandra Laugier, eds., *Le souci des autres: Éthique et politique du care* (Paris: EHESS, 2006).

13. Tronto, *Moral Boundaries*, 111–24.

14. On the multiplicity of relations of care (within the contexts of family, friends, neighbors, and strangers), see Marian Barnes, *Care in Everyday Life: An Ethic of Care in Practice* (Bristol: Policy, 2012).

15. Simone Weil, "Lettre à Joë Bousquet (1942)," in Simone Weil and Joë Bousquet, *Correspondance 1942: "Quel est donc ton tourment?,"* ed. Florence de Lussy and Michel Narcy (Paris: Editions Claire Paulhan, 2019), 22.

16. "Attention consists of suspending our thought, leaving it detached, empty, and ready to be penetrated by the object. . . . Above all our thought should be empty, waiting, not seeking anything, but ready to receive in its naked truth the object that is to penetrate it." Simone Weil, *Waiting for God*, trans. Emma Craufurd (New York: Harper and Row, 1973), 111–12.

17. On this theme, see Sophie Bourgault, "Cura come attenzione." Here, Bourgault highlights the affinity of Simone Weil's idea of attention with Iris Murdoch's "loving attention." See Iris Murdoch, *Existentialists and Mystics: Writings on Philosophy and Literature* (New York: Penguin, 1997). See also Marie Garrau, *Care et attention* (Paris: PUF, 2014).

18. A fundamental concept that often appears in Simone Weil's thought, from *Gravity and Grace* to her *Notebooks*. It is foundational for her idea of attention: "In such a work all that I call 'I' has to be passive. Attention alone—that attention which is so full that the 'I' disappears—is required of me. I have to deprive all that I call 'I' of the light of my attention and turn it on to that which cannot be conceived." Simone Weil, *Gravity and Grace*, trans. Emma Craufurd and Mario von der Ruhr (London: Routledge, 2002), 118.

19. Anthony Giddens, *The Transformation of Intimacy: Sexuality, Love and Eroticism in Modern Societies* (Redwood, CA: Stanford University Press, 1993).

20. Nussbaum, *Upheavals of Thought* and *Frontiers of Justice*.

21. I refer here to one of the most interesting definitions of love, given by Georg Simmel, who states that it is much like the synthesis of two of his archetypical images: love is a special form of interaction that binds two subjects who are ready to expose themselves to one another for the sake of the relationship without either forgetting oneself or negating the other. Georg Simmel, "Über die Liebe (Fragment)" [On Love (A Fragment)], in *Gesamtausgabe*, vol. 20 (Frankfurt am Main: Suhrkamp, 2004). For more on the overcoming of both egoism and altruism, see C. S. Lewis, *The Four Loves* (New York: Harper-Collins, 2012); Ricoeur, "Love and Justice."

22. Frankfurt, *The Reasons of Love*.

23. Gilligan, *In a Different Voice*, 35.

24. Care carried out in a family context implies the "work" of care, but this labor goes unpaid and is different from paid, professional work, upon which I seek to build a second model of care.

25. Michael Hardt and Antonio Negri, *Empire* (Cambridge, MA: Harvard University Press, 2000).

26. Arlie Russel Hochschild, *The Managed Heart: Commercialization of Human Feeling* (Berkeley: University of California Press, 2012).

27. Michael Hardt and Antonio Negri, *Multitude: War and Democracy in the Age of Empire* (London: Penguin, 2004), 146; Arlie Russel Hochschild, "The Nanny Chain," *American Prospect*, December 19, 2001, https://prospect.org/features/nanny-chain/.

28. Paula England, "Emerging Theories of Care Work," *Annual Review of Sociology* 31 (2005): 381–99.

29. Vivian A. Zelizer, "Caring Everywhere," in *Intimate Labors: Cultures, Technologies, and the Politics of Care*, ed. Eileen Borris and Rachel Salazar Parreñas (Redwood, CA: Stanford University Press, 2010), 267–79; Julie A. Nelson, "Of Markets and Martyrs: Is It OK to Pay Well for Care?," *Feminist Economics* 5, no. 3 (1999): 43–59.

30. Nancy Folbre, *The Invisible Heart: Economics and Family Values* (New York: New Press, 2001).

31. England, "Emerging Theories of Care Work," 381.

32. England, "Emerging Theories of Care Work," 395.

33. Here, the work on nursing care, health care, and care of the aged is relevant, especially work aimed at professionals and educators, for example, the blog *Practical Ethics*, of Oxford University, "Is Compassion a Necessary Component of Healthcare," September 25, 2013, http://blog.practicalethics.ox.ac.uk/2013/09/is-compassion-a-necessary-component-of-healthcare/. There is also the *Journal of Compassionate Health Care* (http://jcompassionatehc.com). By visiting the websites of various care associations and institutions, one quickly notices that compassionate care is fundamental for individuals seeking to work in the aforementioned sectors. See also works by various care theorists: Carlo Leger, Chris Gastmans, and Marian Verkerk, eds., *Care, Compassion, and Recognition: An Ethical Discussion* (Leuven: Peeters, 2010); and, in Italian and besides the works that address theories of mindfulness, Luigi Alici, *Prossimità difficile: La cura tra compassione e competenza* (Rome: Aracne, 2012).

34. Nussbaum, *Upheavals of Thought*, 395ff. For Nussbaum, compassion essentially is the emotion that inspires justice.

35. Paul Stenner, "Rights and Emotions, or: On the Importance of Having the Right Emotions," *History and Philosophy of Psychology* 7, no. 1 (2005): 11–21.

36. Kittay, *Love's Labor*.

37. On degenerative forms of care, see Claudia Card, "Caring and Evil," *Hypatia* 5, no. 1 (1990): 101–8.

38. Here, we find a negative use of the term vulnerability, whose sense lies in contrast to the positive meaning I and other contemporary theorists are developing and employing.

39. Arlie Russel Hochschild, "The Nanny Chain," and *The Commercialization of Intimate Life: Notes from Home and Work* (Berkeley: University of California Press, 2003).

40. Eva Kittay, "The Global Heart Transplant and Caring across National Boundaries," *Southern Journal of Philosophy* 46 (2008): 138–65.

41. Arlie Russel Hochschild, "The Nanny Chain." See also Barbara Ehrenreich and Arlie Russel Hochschild, *Global Women: Nannies, Maids, and Sex Workers* (London: Granta, 2002); Mary K. Zimmerman, Jacquelyn S. Litt, and Christine E. Bose, eds., *Global Dimension of Gender and Carework* (Redwood, CA: Stanford University Press, 2006).

42. Brunella Casalini, "Il *care* tra lavoro affettivo e lavoro di riproduzione sociale," *La società degli individui* 46 (2012): 44–61.

43. See Kittay, *Love's Labor*; Barnes, *Care in Everyday Life*.

44. See Pulcini, *Care of the World* and *The Individual without Passions*. See also William M. Reddy, "Historical Research on the Self and Emotions," *Emotion Review* 1, no. 4 (2009): 302–15.

45. For a discussion of negative passions or emotions, in addition to the one found in the field of disability studies, which often cites the work of Eva Feder Kittay, see Christine Tappolet, Fabrice Teroni, and Anita Konzelmann Ziv, eds., *Shadows of the Soul: Philosophical Perspectives on Negative Emotions* (London: Routledge, 2018).

Chapter Five

1. Friedrich Nietzsche, "Of Love of One's Neighbour," in *Thus Spoke Zarathustra*, trans. R. J. Hollingdale (London: Penguin, 1961), 87.

2. I want to underline that, already a few years ago, gift theorists such as Jacques Godbout, *L'esprit du don* (Paris: La Découverte, 1992) and Alain Caillé, *Anthropologie du don: Le tiers paradigme* (Paris: La Découverte, 2007), had shown the relevance of the unknown other within contemporary society (for example, those to whom we donate our blood, organs, or even simply our work such as when volunteering). This figure, however, does not concern distance—both spatial and temporal—on which I want instead to focus in this and the next chapter.

3. See Jean-Luc Nancy, *The Creation of the World, or Globalization*, trans. F. Raffoul and D. Pettigrew (Albany: State University of New York Press, 2007).

4. David Harvey, *The Condition of Postmodernity: An Enquiry into the Origins of Cultural Change* (London: Blackwell, 1989).

5. For a broader analysis of these themes, see Pulcini, *Care of the World*.

6. On the "significant other," see George Herbert Mead, *Mind, Self, and Society* (Chicago: University of Chicago Press, 2015).

7. On this, see Hartmut Rosa, *Alienation and Acceleration: Towards a Critical Theory of Late-Modern Temporality* (Copenhagen: NSU Press, 2010).

8. See chapter 1 in this volume.

9. Singer, *Expanding Circle*, 120.

10. If not, sympathy/empathy ends up being in conflict with justice and its impartiality.

11. See Lecaldano, *Simpatia*, 169–77.

12. See Frans de Waal, *Primates and Philosophers: How Morality Evolved* (Princeton, NJ: Princeton University Press, 2006).

13. See the debate on de Waal by various authors, including Peter Singer and Christine Korsgaard.

14. Jeremy Rifkin, *The Empathic Civilisation: The Race to Global Consciousness in a World in Crisis* (Cambridge, UK: Polity, 2009).

15. The expression is by Garrett Hardin, "The Tragedy of the Commons," *Science* 162, no. 3859 (1968): 1243–48. A classic text on the topic of the commons is, by now, Elinor Ostrom, *Governing the Commons: The Evolution of Institutions for Collective Action* (Cambridge: Cambridge University Press, 1999).

16. Rifkin, *Empathic Civilisation*, 42.

17. See Peter Singer, *One World: The Ethics of Globalization* (New Haven, CT: Yale University Press, 2002).

18. The notion comes from John Urry, *Consuming Places* (London: Routledge, 1995). See also John Urry and Bronislaw Szerszynsky, "Cultures of Cosmopolitanism," *Sociological Review* 50, no. 4 (2002): 461–81; Scott Lash, *Another Modernity: A Different Rationality* (Oxford: Blackwell, 1999); John Tomlison, *Globalization and Culture* (Chicago: University of Chicago Press, 1999). On these themes and authors not yet widely known in Italy, see Luca Serafini, *Etica dell'estetica: Narcisismo dell'io e apertura agli altri nel pensiero postmoderno* (Macerata: Quodlibet, 2017).

19. See Tomlison, *Globalization and Culture*.

20. Peter Singer, *The Life You Can Save: How to Do Your Part to End World Poverty* (New York: Random House, 2009).

21. On denial, on which I will return later, especially in relation to the absence of an adequate answer to the environmental crisis and the destiny of the other distant in time, see Pulcini, *Care of the World*, part 3.

22. Michael Slote, *Moral Sentimentalism*, 52, 22, 107.

23. See chapter 1 in this volume.

24. Manuel Castells, *Networks of Outrage and Hope: Social Movements in the Internet Age* (Cambridge, UK: Polity, 2012).

25. The importance of the Occupy movements in terms of their ability "to create a vastly more energetic and critical form of civil power" is highlighted

by Jeffrey Alexander, "The Arc of Civil Liberation: Obama-Tahrir-Occupy," *Philosophy and Social Criticism* 39, no. 4–5 (2013): 341–47.

26. See especially the chapter "Changing the World in the Network Society" in Castells, *Networks of Outrage and Hope*, 246–71, from which the following quotations come.

27. Touraine, *Défense de la modernité*.

28. Nussbaum, *Upheavals of Thought*.

29. Luc Boltanski, *Distant Suffering: Morality, Media and Politics*, trans. Graham D. Burchell (Cambridge: Cambridge University Press, 1999). Unlike Nussbaum, Boltanski regards pity not as one of the passions capable of integrating the limits of justice from the inside but rather as what, on the contrary, functions outside the abstract parameters of justice (inspired by the pure criterion of equivalence) and acts as a separate and complementary perspective.

30. "Sentimentality, notoriously, is entirely compatible with a taste for brutality and worse. (Recall the canonical example of the Auschwitz commandant returning home in the evening, embracing his wife and children, and sitting at the piano to play some Schubert before dinner.) People don't become inured to what they are shown—if that's the right way to describe what happens—because of the *quantity* of images dumped on them. It is passivity that dulls feeling." Sontag, *Regarding the Pain of Others*, 79.

31. See Charles R. Figley, *Compassion Fatigue: Coping with Secondary Traumatic Stress Disorder in Those Who Treat the Traumatized* (London: Routledge, 1995).

32. See Boltanski, *Distant Suffering*, xv–xvi.

33. As Antonio Prete reminds us, "compassion is sharing the other's suffering, suffering with the other." Prete, *Compassione: Storia di un sentimento*, 50

34. This is the perspective of, among others, Emmanuel Housset, *L'intelligence de la pitié: Phénoménologie de la communauté* (Paris: Cerf, 2003). Even though maintaining the term "pity," Housset theorizes the possibility that it may be expanded as he connects it to a decentering of the Self that opens to the other in an unlimited way up to including the unknown other. On this, see van Nistelrooij, "Coesistenza affettiva," 149.

35. See Etti Hillesum, *An Interrupted Life: The Diaries of Etty Hillesum 1941–1943* (New York: Pantheon, 1983).

36. See Georg Simmel, "Exkurs über den Fremden," in *Soziologie: Untersuchungen über die Formen der Vergesellschaftung* (Berlin: Duncker und Humblot, 1968).

37. On the effectiveness of Freud's distinction between fear and anxiety for a diagnosis of the perception of global challenges, see Pulcini, *Care of the World*, part 2.

38. See Pulcini, *Care of the Wold*.

39. On the passage from boundary to *limes*, see Roberto Escobar, *Metamorfosi della paura* (Bologna: Il Mulino, 2007), 148.

40. On the pair *hospes/hostis*, see Émile Benveniste, *Le vocabulaire des institutions indo-européennes* (Paris: Minuit, 1969), where we are reminded that, in ancient Rome, the term *hostis* meant the "stranger" to whom the same rights are recognized as to Roman citizens and only later it takes up the negative connotation of "enemy." At that point, it becomes necessary to use a new term, *hospes*, to name precisely the concept of hospitality. See also Umberto Curi, *Straniero* (Milan: Cortina, 2010).

41. Arjun Appadurai, *Sicuri da morire: La violenza nell'epoca della globalizzazione* (Rome: Meltemi, 2005).

42. Zygmunt Bauman, *Community: Seeking Safety in an Insecure World* (Cambridge, UK: Polity, 2001).

43. Here the "us, we" becomes the dangerous pronoun discussed by Richard Sennett, *The Corrosion of Character: The Personal Consequences of Work in the New Capitalism* (New York: Norton, 1998)

44. See Elena Pulcini, "Oltre la paura e il risentimento: l'ospitalità nell'età globale," in *Nuove frontiere della cittadinanza*, ed. F. Bignami and F. Merlini (Lugano: Quaderni dell'IUFFP, 2018), 31–41.

45. Sloterdijk, *Rage and Time*, 69.

46. On just anger, which evokes an Aristotelian distinction, see Bodei, *Ira*.

47. Judith Butler, *Giving an Account of Oneself* (New York: Routledge, 2004).

48. See Amartya Sen, *Identity and Violence: The Illusion of Destiny* (New York: Norton, 2006).

49. Jean-Luc Nancy, "L'Intrus," trans. Susan Hanson, *New Centennial Review* 2, no. 3 (2002): 1–14.

50. James Clifford, "Prendere sul serio la politica dell'identità," in *Aut Aut* 312 (2002): 97ff.

51. Nancy, "L'Intrus," 2.

52. See Jacques Derrida, *Of Hospitality: Anne Dufourmantelle Invites Jacques Derrida to Respond* (Redwood, CA: Stanford University Press, 2000), 27.

53. Derrida, *Of Hospitality*, 25.

54. Derrida, *Of Hospitality*, 25.

55. "Does hospitality consist in interrogating the new arrival? Does it begin with the question addressed to the newcomer . . . what is your name?" Derrida, *Of Hospitality*, 27.

56. "The law of absolute hospitality commands a break with hospitality by right, with law or justice as rights. Just hospitality breaks with hospitality by right." Derrida, *Of Hospitality*, 25.

57. Derrida, *Of Hospitality*, 29.

58. In other words, we should retrieve the originary meaning of the term *hospes* that we find in Latin-based languages, that is, the hospes as the host and the guest. This word contains and preserves within itself the intrinsic value of reciprocity and mutual recognition.

59. On the perverted gift, see Jean Starobinski, *Largesse* (Paris: Gallimard, 2007).

60. Weil, *Gravity and Grace*, 68. A passion that seems currently to have scarce appeal within the social context and the theoretical reflection (given the corrosion of the spaces of gratuitousness), gratitude nevertheless benefits of a variety of eminent approaches (psychological, philosophical, sociological, etc.). I limit myself to make reference to Melanie Klein, *Envy and Gratitude: A Study of Unconscious Sources* (London: Tavistock, 1957), Georg Simmel, "Faithfulness and Gratitude," in *The Sociology of Georg Simmel*, ed. Kurt H. Wolff (New York: Free Press, 1950), and Hillesum, *An Interrupted Life*.

61. Mauss opposes the formula of the exchange (to give in order to receive) with the well-known formula of the gift (to give—to receive—to return), in which each of the three moments is necessary to complete the cycle of the gift. See Mauss, *The Gift*, and Jacques T. Godbout, in collaboration with Alain C. Caillé, *The World of the Gift* (Montreal: McGill-Queen's University Press, 1998).

62. One of the central themes of the theorists of the gift following Mauss is the idea that the break of the cycle of the gift can generate a rebirth of violence and conflict. Among others, see Godbout, *World of the Gift*.

63. Mouffe, *On the Political*.

64. See Vincenzo Sorrentino, *Aiutarli a casa nostra: Per un'Europa della compassione* (Rome: Castelvecchi, 2018).

65. See Umberto Curi, ed., *Vergogna ed esclusione: L'Europa di fronte alla sfida dell'emigrazione* (Rome: Castelvecchi, 2019).

66. Sontag, *Regarding the Pain of Others*, 80.

67. "The imaginary proximity to the suffering inflicted on others that is granted by images suggests a link between the faraway sufferers—seen close-up on the television screen—and the privileged viewer that is simply untrue, that is yet one more mystification of our real relations to power." Sontag, *Regarding the Pain of Others*, 80.

68. This does not mean that Derrida denies the function of justice, as the following claims attest: "Just hospitality breaks with hospitality by right; not that it condemns or is opposed to it, and it can on the contrary set and maintain it in a perpetual progressive movement; but it is as strangely heterogeneous to it as justice is heterogeneous to the law to which it is yet so close, from which in truth it is indissociable." Derrida, *Of Hospitality*, 25–27.

69. One could also say that hospitality cannot do without the gift of justice. On justice as gift, see Leonard Mazzone, "Per un diritto internazionale alla fuga: Diritto d'asilo e dovere di ospitalità," *La società degli individui* 61 (2018): 31–46.

70. Among these critics is, as we have already seen, Slote, *The Ethics of Care and Empathy*.

71. Fiona Robinson, "Globalizing Care: Ethics, Feminist Theory, and International Relations," *Alternatives: Global, Local, Political* 22, no. 1 (1997): 113–33.

72. Better stated, this is possible when those who can be recognized in the figure of the "internal stranger" are not confined in the extreme outskirts of towns or anyway displaced with respect to a center that we try to preserve from the danger of contamination, thereby ending up creating what I would call potentially explosive "*islands of alterity*."

73. In the best of cases, we respond to this distractedly, not with commitment to justice and gifts but with occasional "donations" that in fact exonerate us from real commitment and involvement.

Chapter Six

1. This expression, "ça me regarde," occurs in many of Jacques Derrida's works, from *The Gift of Death* to *Specters of Marx* and *Echographies of Television*. It refers both to an Other who looks at me and to what concerns me. On the topic and nuances of the other in Derrida, see Kas Saghafi, *Apparitions of Derrida's Other* (New York: Fordham University Press, 2010).

2. Among the increasingly frequent contributions on the topic of the *future*, I refer to Daniel Innerarity, *The Future and Its Enemies: In Defense of Political Hope*, trans. Sandra Kingery (Redwood, CA: Stanford University Press, 2012); Marc Augé, *Où est passé l'avenir?* (Paris: Editions du Panama, 2008); Paolo Jedlowski, *Memorie del futuro* (Rome: Carocci, 2017); Vincenzo Pellegrino, *Futuri possibili* (Verona: Ombre corte, 2019).

3. This topic has received increasing attention within the area of moral reflections on responsibility and intergenerational justice. See, among others, Ernest Partridge, "Why Care about the Future?," in *Responsibilities to Future Generations: Environmental Ethics*, ed. Ernest Partridge (Amherst, NY: Prometheus, 1981), 203–20; Dieter Birnbacher, "What Motivates Us to Care for the (Distant) Future?," in *Intergenerational Justice*, ed. Axel Gosseries and Lukas H. Meyer (Oxford: Oxford University Press, 2009), 273–300; John Passmore, *Man's Responsibility for Nature* (New York: Scribner, 1974); Michel Bourban, "Climate Change, Human Rights and the Problem of Motivation," *De Ethica* 1, no. 1 (2014): 37–52.

4. See Giuliano Pontara, *Etica e generazioni future* (Rome: Laterza, 1995), chs. 9–10.

5. On "global risk," see the classic works by Ulrich Beck, *Risk Society: Towards a New Modernity*, trans. Mark Ritter (London: Sage, 1992) and *World Risk Society* (Cambridge, UK: Polity, 1999).

6. See, for example, Wilfred Beckerman, "The Impossibility of a Theory of Intergenerational Justice," in *Handbook of Intergenerational Justice*, ed. Joerg Chet Tremmel (Cheltenham: Edward Elgar, 2006), 53–71.

7. Pontara, *Etica e generazioni future*, 26ff.

8. "Now, in fact, men quite often do make heroic sacrifices. They make them out of love. It is as lovers that they make sacrifices for the future more extensive than any a Benthamite calculus would be rational. . . . There is, then, no novelty in a concern for posterity, when posterity is thought of not abstractly—as 'the future of mankind'—but as a world inhabited by individuals we love or feel a special interest in." Passmore, *Man's Responsibility for Nature*, 87–89.

9. A similar position is expressed by Martin P. Golding, "Obligations to Future Generations," *Monist* 56, no. 1 (1972): 85–99, who considers, as the only foundation of responsibility, one's belonging to the same moral community bound by the same conception of the good; within an intergenerational context, he therefore regards moral obligations as possible only toward the nearest generations.

10. R. I. Sikora and Brian Barry, eds. *Obligations to Future Generations* (Philadelphia: Temple University Press, 1978); Tremmel, *Handbook of Intergenerational Justice*; Stephen M. Gardiner, Simon Caney, Dale Jamieson, and Henry Shue, *Climate Ethics: Essential Readings* (Oxford: Oxford University Press, 2010).

11. Among recent works, see Bruno Latour, *Down to Earth: Politics in the New Climatic Regime*, trans. Catherine Porter (Cambridge, UK: Polity, 2018); Anthony Giddens, *The Politics of Climate Change* (Cambridge, UK: Polity, 2009); Amitav Gosh, *The Great Derangement: Climate Change and the Unthinkable* (Chicago: University of Chicago Press, 2016); Gianfranco Pellegrino and Marcello Di Paola, *Nell'antropocene* (Rome: DeriveApprodi, 2018).

12. Francis, *Laudato Si': Encyclical Letter of the Holy Father Francis on Care for our Common Home* (Rome: Vatican Press, 2015).

13. "The thesis of full responsibility can be formulated, more or less, as follows: we are morally responsible for all consequences that our actions have on future generations." Pontara, *Etica e generazioni future*, 55.

14. Dale Jamieson clearly points out the unprecedented difficulties inherent in the moral challenges of our times: "Most of what normally accompanies moral problems is now fading. . . . It is difficult to identify agents, victims, and the causal link connecting them; for this reason, it is now difficult to ascribe responsibilities, to direct one's blame, and so on." Dale Jamieson, "Le sfide morali e politiche del cambiamento climatico," *La società degli individui* 39, no. 3 (2010): 37.

15. Derek Parfit, *Reasons and Persons* (Oxford: Clarendon Press, 1984).

16. For an excellent critical reconstruction of the various paradigms of intergenerational justice, see Ferdinando G. Menga, "Per una giustizia iperbolica e intempestiva: Riflessioni sulla responsabilità intergenerazionale in prospettiva fenomenologica," *D&Q* 14 (2014): 711–93, *Lo scandalo del futuro: Per una giustizia intergenerazionale* (Rome: Edizioni di Storia e Letteratura, 2017). See also Avner de-Shalit, *Why Posterity Matters: Environmental Policies and Future Generations* (London: Routledge, 1995).

17. The issue is addressed explicitly in Rawls, *Theory of Justice*.

18. Rawls, *Theory of Justice*, 262.

19. He does so after having analyzed and verified the inefficacy of various answers. On this topic, see Pontara, *Etica e generazioni future*, 81–88.

20. Rawls, *Theory of Justice*, 111.

21. For an accurate account of the various criticisms to Rawls, see Menga, "Per una giustizia iperbolica e intempestiva."

22. Brian Barry, *Theories of Justice* (Berkeley: University of California Press, 1989).

23. Jeremy Bentham, *Introduction to the Principles of Morals and Legislation* (London: T. Payne and Son, 1789).

24. Henry Sidgwick, *The Methods of Ethics* (London: Macmillan, 1907).

25. Axel Gosseries, "Theories of Intergenerational Justice: A Synopsis," *Surveys and Perspectives Integrating Environment and Society* 1, no. 1 (2008): 65.

26. "If you are a utilitarian, savings (in generational terms) are not just authorised; they are required since the goal is to maximize the size of the intergenerational welfare pie." Gosseries, "Theories of Intergenerational Justice," 65.

27. Rawls, *Theory of Justice*, 258.

28. Parfit, *Reasons and Persons*, part 4.

29. On this topic, see Sergio Filippo Magni, "Responsabilità e giustizia verso le generazioni future," *Cosmopolis* 1, no. 1 (2007): 269–76.

30. Parfit, *Reasons and Persons*, 388.

31. de-Shalit, *Why Posterity Matters*.

32. "If these obligations to very remote future generations clash with certain obligations to contemporaries, and especially to the worst off among our contemporaries, it is reasonable to argue that in some cases our obligations to contemporaries have some priority." de-Shalit, *Why Posterity Matters*, 11.

33. "To people of the very remote future we have a strong 'negative' obligation—namely, to avoid causing them enormous harm." de-Shalit, *Why Posterity Matters*, 13.

34. "When these obligations to very remote future generations do not contradict obligations to contemporary, we have no excuse not to fulfill them." de-Shalit, *Why Posterity Matters*, 11.

35. I will return later on the notion of "indirect motivation," which I derive from Birnbacher, "What Motivates Us to Care for the (Distant) Future?"

36. de-Shalit, *Why Posterity Matters*, 15.

37. Michael Sandel, *Liberalism and the Limits of Justice* (Cambridge: Cambridge University Press, 1982).

38. Beck, *Risk Society*.

39. de-Shalit, *Why Posterity Matters*, 35ff.

40. de-Shalit, *Why Posterity Matters*, 40.

41. de-Shalit, *Why Posterity Matters*, 31. The reference is especially to Passmore, *Man's Responsibility for Nature*.

42. de Shalit, *Why Posterity Matters*, 33.

43. "The bomb has succeeded in accomplishing what religions and philosophies, empires and revolutions have not managed to do, namely: truly turning us into *a single* humankind." Anders, *L'uomo è antiquato* (Turin: Bollati Boringhieri, 2003), 1:314.

44. Beck, *Risk Society*.

45. Nowadays, this recognition must foreshadow politics of rebalancing that are capable of a fair distribution of greenhouse gas effects and contrast the export to poor countries of toxic wastes produced by the industrialized countries. This topic has not yet been adequately explored; it has been recently raised by Pope Francis, *Laudato Si'*. See also Amy Larkin, *Environmental Debt: The Hidden Costs of a Changing Global Economy* (London: Palgrave Macmillan, 2013); Romano Trabucchi, *Limite e responsabilità: Il consumismo, il debito ecologico e le generazioni future* (Brescia: Ati Editore, 2016); Miguel Ortega Cerdá and Daniela Russi, *Debito ecologico: Chi deve a chi?* (Bologna: EMI, 2003).

46. de-Shalit, *Why Posterity Matters*, 11.

47. Emmanuel Levinas, *Otherwise than Being, or Beyond Essence*, trans. Alphonso Lingis (The Hague: Martin Nijohff, 1981); Paul Ricoeur, "Le sfide e le speranze del nostro comune futuro," in *Persona, comunità e istituzioni: Dialettica tra giustizia e amore*, ed. A. Danese (Fiesole: Cultura della pace, 1994), 107–22; Jonas, *Imperative of Responsibility*.

48. For a broader treatment of the topics addressed in the following pages, see Pulcini, *Care of the World*, part 3.

49. Anders, *L'uomo è antiquato*. On this topic, besides Pulcini, *Care of the World*, see also Elena Pulcini, "The Responsible Subject in the Global Age," *Science and Engineering Ethics* 16, no. 3 (2009): 447–61.

50. "A silent plea for sparing its integrity seems to issue from the threatened plenitude of the living world." Jonas, *Imperative of Responsibility*, 8

51. "The ontology has changed. Ours is not that of eternity but of time." Jonas, *Imperative of Responsibility*, 125.

52. Jonas, *Imperative of Responsibility*, 87.

53. "[The ethics of responsibility] is not void of hope, but gives also fear its rightful place. Its heart is veneration for the image of man, turning into trembling concern for its vulnerability." Jonas, *Imperative of Responsibility*, 201.

54. See, for example, Bernhard Waldenfels, *Schattenrisse der Moral* (Frankfurt: Suhrkamp, 2006), 333: "A genuine ethics for the future undoubtedly depends on our taking into consideration the appeals and requests of future generations and populations even before their representatives are able to claim their rights and demands. What is here required is, therefore, a radical form of substitution, which presupposes that *all individuals let themselves be appealed* beyond their death *by an extraneous future*."

55. The answer Jonas gives to the following question he poses is, in fact, affirmative: "Our question is: Ought there to be man? To ask it correctly we

must first answer the question of what it means to say of something whatsoever that it ought to be. This naturally leads us back to the question of whether there *ought* to be anything at all—rather than nothing." Jonas, *Imperative of Responsibility*, 46.

56. As I have emphasized in Pulcini, *Care of the World*, part 3, ch. 2, the transition from answering the other's vulnerability to the subject's awareness of its own vulnerability is fundamental to be able to think of an ethics of responsibility beyond an altruistic, duty-based configuration.

57. Levinas, *Otherwise than Being*.

58. "But this death, if it is a death, is only the death of a certain kind of subject, one that was never possible to begin with, the death of a fantasy of impossible mastery, and so a loss of what one never had. In other words, it is a necessary grief." Butler, *Giving an Account of Oneself*, 65.

59. "The *primat* or impress of the Other is primary, inaugurative, and there is no formation of a 'me' outside of this originally passive impingement and the responsiveness formed in the crucible of that passivity." Butler, *Giving an Account of Oneself*, 97.

60. Butler, *Giving an Account of Oneself*, 107.

61. Butler, *Giving an Account of Oneself*, 100. See also Judith Butler, *Precarious Life: The Powers of Mourning and Violence* (London: Verso, 2004), 44ff.

62. Butler, *Precarious Life*, 28.

63. "To foreclose that vulnerability, to banish it, to make ourselves secure at the expense of every other human consideration is to eradicate one of the most important resources from which we must take our bearings and find our way." Butler, *Precarious Life*, 30. As Olivia Guaraldo argues, this resource allows us also to rethink the paradigm of the political, subtract it to its traditionally unbreakable link with violence, and found it instead on the experience of loss and shared vulnerability. See Olivia Guaraldo, *Comunità e vulnerabilità: Per una critica politica della violenza* (Pisa: ETS, 2012).

64. Paul Ricoeur, "Le sfide e le speranze del nostro comune futuro," in *Persona, comunità e istituzioni. Dialettica tra giustizia e amore*, ed. Attilio Danese (San Domenico di Fiesole: Edizioni Cultura della Pace, 1994), 107–21.

65. Ricoeur, "Le sfide e le speranze del nostro comune futuro."

66. "Capacity" is, in Ricoeur, the endowment of the *homme capable* that he defines as "the fundamental concept of [his] ontology," from *Oneself as Another*, trans. Kathleen Blamey (Chicago: University of Chicago Press, 1995) to *The Course of Recognition*, trans. David Pellauer (Cambridge, MA: Harvard University Press, 2007). See Paul Ricoeur, "Per una ontologia indiretta. L'essere, il vero, il giusto (e/o il buono)," *Aquinas* 3 (1995): 494. The self is simultaneously agent and sufferer, and the self's ability to speak, act, tell stories, and answer for its own actions is also characterized by precariousness and uncertainty, "always threatened and exposed to suffering." In other words, this endowment belongs to a self that does not belong to itself, as Descartes would have it; rather, the

self decenters itself and becomes self-conscious through its own self-recognition in the multiple traces of the other.

67. Ricoeur, "Love and Justice," 323–24.

68. David Graeber, *Debt: The First 5000 Years* (New York: Melville House, 2014).

69. Roberto Esposito, *Two: The Machine of Political Theology and the Place of Thought*, trans. Zakiya Hanafi (New York: Fordham University Press, 2015).

70. Roberto Esposito, *Communitas: The Origin and Destiny of Community*, trans. Timothy Campbell (Redwood, CA: Stanford University Press, 2009), 7.

71. Esposito, *Communitas*, 5.

72. Esposito, *Communitas*, 13.

73. See also the interesting reference to the notion of debt by an author completely alien to gift theory such as Franco Crespi, *Imparare ad esistere: Nuovi fondamenti della solidarietà sociale* (Rome: Donzelli, 1994), 83ff.

74. Jean-Luc Marion, *Being Given: Toward a Phenomenology of Givenness*, trans. Jeffrey L. Kosky (Redwood, CA: Stanford University Press, 2002).

75. Jacques Lacan, "The Function and Field of Speech and Language in Psychonalysis," in *Écrits: A Selection*, trans. Bruce Finsk (New York: Norton, 2002), 197–268.

76. On the gift of birth, see also Godbout, *World of the Gift*, 39.

77. On the distinction between justice/equivalence and gift/love/agape, see also the important study by Boltanski, *Love and Justice as Competences*.

78. See Pulcini, *The Individual without Passions*, 147ff.

79. Paul Ricoeur, *Freedom and Nature: The Voluntary and the Involuntary*, trans. Erazim V. Kohák (Evanston, IL: Northwestern University Press, 1966), 434.

80. Jacques Godbout, "L'état d'endettement mutuel," *Revue du MAUSS* 4, no. 2 (1994): 205–20.

81. Luigino Bruni, *Reciprocità: Dinamiche di cooperazione, economia e società civile* (Milan: Mondadori, 2006).

82. Marcel Mauss, *The Gift: Forms and Structures of Exchange in Archaic Societies*, trans. Ian Gunnison (London: Cohen and West, 1966), 63.

83. Godbout, *World of the Gift*, 133.

84. On the importance of trust for the construction of the social bond, on which the theorists of gift insist, see also Anthony Giddens, *The Consequences of Modernity* (Redwood, CA: Stanford University Press, 1991); Luis Roniger, *La fiducia nelle società moderne: Un approccio comparativo* (Messina: Rubbettino, 1992); *Le strategie della fiducia: Indagini sulla razionalità della cooperazione*, ed. D. Gambetta (Turin: Einaudi, Torino 1989). See also Martin Hollis, *Trust within Reason* (Cambridge: Cambridge University Press, 1998); Luca Alici, *Fidarsi: Alle radici del legame sociale* (Trieste: Meudon, 2012). Among some classic works, see Jacques Derrida, *Politics of Friendship*, trans. George Collins (London: Verso, 2006); Georg Simmel, *The Philosophy of Money*, trans. Tom Bottomore and David Frisby (London: Routledge, 1978), 177ff.

85. Jacques Godbout, "Les 'bonnes raisons' de donner," *Anthropologie et Sociétés* 19, no. 1–2 (1995): 45–56.

86. Marcel Mauss, "La cohésion sociale dans les sociétés polysegmentaires" (1931), in *Oeuvres* (Paris: Minuit, 1969), 3:11–26; Marcel Henáff, "Mauss et l'invention de la réciprocité," *Revue du MAUSS* 36, no. 2 (2010): 71–86.

87. Henáff, "Mauss et l'invention de la réciprocité," 84.

88. Henáff, "Mauss et l'invention de la réciprocité," 84.

89. Henáff proposes a notion pregnant with interesting possibilities of development: "The logic of this indirect alternative reciprocity can be understood as rich with a morality of respect for things that will be born. Myths tell us, warns us about this. We can find this wisdom in ancient doxographies such as the one in Anaximander's fragment 9, which describes beings as they yield place to one another in turn and render one another justice 'according to the order of time.'" Henáff, "Mauss et l'invention de la réciprocité," 85.

90. Gosseries, *Theories of Intergenerational Justice*.

91. Annette C. Baier, "The Rights of Past and Future Persons," in *Responsibilities to Future Generations*, ed. Ernest Partridge (Buffalo, NY: Prometheus, 1981), 173.

92. Brian Barry, "Justice between Generations," in *Law, Morality and Society*, ed. P. M. S. Hacker and J. Raz (Oxford: Clarendon Press, 1977), 284. On the theories of "indirect reciprocity," see also Lawrence C. Becker, *Reciprocity* (Chicago: University of Chicago Press, 1990); Axel P. Gosseries, "Three Models of Intergenerational Reciprocity," *Intergenerational Justice*, 119–46.

93. Francis, *Laudato Si'*, 4.5.159. Very much aligned and even more radical is the Native American saying, referenced by Gosseries, "Theories of Intergenerational Justice," 62: "Treat the Earth well: it was not given to you by your parents, it was loaned to you by your children."

94. On this point, it would be helpful to integrate Butler's *Giving an Account of Oneself*, which is not void of an essentialism of the human, with Butler's *Precarious Life*, which links the notion of vulnerability to events and challenges of the global world.

95. Jonas, *Imperative of Responsibility*, ix–x.

96. Jonas, *Imperative of Responsibility*, ix.

97. Beck, *Risk Society*.

98. "Our ability to see or our blindness depend on whether the object 'concerns us' or not; we only see what concerns us. We have not yet said anything with this. On the contrary, the problem starts here. Ultimately, we do not possess an absolute value to decide what concerns us and what does not." Anders, *L'uomo è antiquato*, 1:293.

99. Anders, *L'uomo è antiquato*, 1:292.

100. Baier, "The Rights of Past and Future Persons," 176.

101. Birnbacher, "What Motivates Us to Care for the (Distant) Future?"

102. According to Birnbacher, there are three kinds of motives to act morally: *moral* motives, when one acts because one is morally required by conscience or by a sense of duty; *quasi-moral* motives, when one acts out of altruistic motives such as love, compassion, generosity, which are themselves genuinely moral without depending on a specific moral system (see Hume or Schopenhauer); and *non-moral* motives, which include self-centered and non-self-centered motivations, such as desire for self-respect, social integration, and recognition. See Birnbacher, "What Motivates Us to Care for the (Distant) Future?"

103. Birnbacher, "What Motivates Us to Care for the (Distant) Future?," 14.

104. Shaun Nichols, *Sentimental Rules: On the Natural Foundations of Moral Judgment* (Oxford: Oxford University Press, 2004).

105. Lecaldano, *Simpatia*.

106. Hume, *Treatise of Human Nature*, 3.6.618.

107. This aspect is well grasped by Jonas Olson, "The Ethics of Care and Empathy by M. Slote," *Analysis* 69, no. 1 (2009): 192: "It is an equally notorious fact that we tend to care more about the temporally near than the temporally distant. This raises the problem of our moral obligations to future generations. Slote mentions the problem in a footnote but, after pointing out that the notion of empathy is 'potentially useful' in regard to it, he sets it aside (39, n. 18). Exactly what the usefulness of empathy to this problem is remains unclear. This actualizes a more general question. Slote evidently thinks we ought to care more about the distant needy than we currently tend to do. But whence this requirement to expand our empathic care?"

108. This term is introduced by the Nobel Prize in Chemistry Paul J. Crutzen in 2000 and has been attracting an increasing amount of reflections. Among them are Pellegrino and Di Paola, *Nell'Antropocene*; J. R. McNeill and Peter Engelke, *The Great Acceleration: An Environmental History of the Anthropocene since 1945* (Cambridge, MA: Harvard University Press, 2016); Jason W. Moore, ed., *Anthropocene or Capitalocene?* (Oakland, CA: PM Press, 2016). See also the special issues devoted to this topic by various journals such as *Lo Sguardo* 22, no. 3 (2016); *La società degli individui* 65, no. 2 (2019); and *Micromega* 2 (2020).

109. See Dale Jamieson, *Ethics and Environment* (Cambridge: Cambridge University Press, 2008) and "Ethics, Public Policies, and Global Warming," in *Morality's Progress: Essays on Humans, Other Animals, and the Rest of Nature* (Oxford: Oxford University Press, 1992). See also Eugenio Lecaldano, "Una nuova concezione della responsabilità morale per affrontare le questioni dell'etica pratica del XXI secolo," *Lo Sguardo* 8, no. 1 (2012): 31–46.

110. Birnbacher, "What Motivates Us to Care for the (Distant) Future?," 20; de-Shalit, *Why Posterity Matters*, 15.

111. On the good use of shame, see Gabriella Turnaturi, *Vergogna: Metamorfosi di un'emozione* (Milan: Feltrinelli, 2012).

112. Thomas Hobbes, *Leviathan*; Jonas, *Imperative of Responsibility*.

113. See chapter 7 in the present volume.

114. Thomas Hobbes, *De Cive or the Citizen*, ed. Sterling P. Lamprecht (New York: Appletong-Century-Croft, 1949), section 32, p. 58. See also an analogous statement in Hobbes's *De Cive* (1658): "Appetite seizeth upon a present good without foreseeing the greater evils that necessarily attach to it." Thomas Hobbes, *Man and Citizen*, ed. Bernard Gert (Gloucester, MA: Peter Smith, 1978), 55. On these themes, see Dimitei D'Andrea, *Prometeo e Ulisse: Natura umana e ordine politico in Thomas Hobbes* (Rome: Carrocci, 1997), 193–94.

115. Jonas, *Imperative of Responsibility*, 28.

116. "If today one were to look for anxiety (*Angst*), real anxiety, in Vienna, Paris, London, New York—where the expression Age of Anxiety is still current—the find would be extremely modest. One would indeed find a whole host of occurrences of the word 'anxiety' in many publications. . . . Nowadays, anxiety has become merchandise; yet only few speak *through* anxiety." Anders, *L'uomo è antiquato*, 1:274.

117. Anders, *L'uomo è antiquato*.

118. Stanley Cohen, *States of Denial: Knowing about Atrocities and Suffering* (Cambridge, UK: Polity, 2001), 1: "People, organizations, governments or whole societies are presented with information that is too disturbing, threatening or anomalous to be fully absorbed or openly acknowledged. The information is therefore somehow repressed, disavowed, pushed aside or reinterpreted. Or else the information 'registers' well enough, but its implications—cognitive, emotional or moral—are evaded, neutralized or rationalized away."

119. Anders claims, "One cannot deny that 'we know' what the consequences of an atomic war would be. Yet we only know that. And this 'only' indicates that our 'knowledge' remains extremely close to not knowing or, at least, not understanding." Anders, *L'uomo è antiquato*, 1:279. As additional confirmation of the interest that the topic of ecological crisis is currently provoking in literature and art, it is interesting to read Jonathan Safran Foer, who, similarly to Anders, underlines the gap between knowing and feeling: "We are aware of the existential stakes and the urgency, but even when we know that a war for our survival is raging, we don't feel immersed in it. That distance between awareness and feeling can make it very difficult for even thoughtful and politically engaged people—people who *want* to act—to act." Jonathan Safran Foer, *We Are the Weather: Saving the Planet Begins at Breakfast* (New York: Farrar, Straus and Giroux, 2019), 13.

120. Anders, *L'uomo è antiquato*, 1:278.

121. Gosh, *The Great Derangement*.

122. Anders, *L'uomo è antiquato*, 1:291.

123. I will return to the role of imagination in chapter 7.

124. Anders, *L'uomo è antiquato*. See also Günther Anders, *Der Mann auf der Brücke: Tagebuch aus Hiroshima und Nagasaki* (Munich: Beck, 1963).

125. Jonas, *Imperative of Responsibility*, 28.

126. By beginning his *Imperative of Responsibility* with a passage from Sophocles's *Antigone*, Jonas seems to want to indicate, through the chorus' words, a different relationship with nature; human beings can certainly avail themselves of nature, as the Greeks already did through *techne*, but without exceeding the limit that allows one to preserve nature's balance and cyclical regeneration. But Prometheus's attitude is different and is precisely the symbol of a break of bonds and a trespassing of natural limits; ultimately, in the name of an unbound hubris, such an attitude ends up jeopardizing the very same life of humanity.

127. Anders, *L'uomo è antiquato*, 1:252.

128. Jonas, *Imperative of Responsibility*, 27.

129. Birnbacher, "What Motivates Us to Care for the (Distant) Future?," 17.

130. Dirk Willem Potsma, *Why Care for Nature? In Search of an Ethical Framework for Environmental Responsibility and Education* (Berlin: Springer, 2010).

131. See Partridge, *Responsibilities to Future Generations*.

132. Serge Latouche, "Will Our Children Hold Us Responsible?," *Revue du MAUSS* 42, no. 2 (2013): 281.

133. Dale Jamieson and Bonnie Nazdam, *Love in the Anthropocene* (New York: OR Books, 2015).

134. Jamieson and Nazdam, *Love in the Anthropocene*, 103.

135. Jamieson and Nazdam, *Love in the Anthropocene*, 113.

136. From an Indian colleague of mine I learned that, in Rajasthan (Jodhpur), there is an indigenous community called Bishnoi for whom religion means compassion toward the environment.

137. Beauty here would be understood certainly not as "cosmetics," as Adorno would say, which increasingly permeates the postmodern world and its emphasis on the desire to appear and, more recently, to please. On this, see Gilles Lipotevsky, *Plaîre et toucher: Essai sur la société de seduction* (Paris: Gallimard, 2017).

138. James Hillman, "The Practice of Beauty," in *Uncontrollable Beauty: Toward a New Aesthetics*, ed. Bill Beckley with David Shapiro (New York: Allworth, 1998), 264.

139. See Vincenzo Sorrentino, "Esistenza, cura ed emozioni," in *Cura ed emozioni: Un'alleanza complessa*, ed. Elena Pulcini and Sophie Bourgault (Bologna: Il Mulino, 2018), 236 ff.

140. Hillman, "Practice of Beauty," 264.

141. "The denied aesthetic response, this ignorance of the psyche's aesthetic impulse, is also an arrogant insult to the world's presence. To walk right by an ill-designed building, be served and accept poorly prepared food, put on your body a badly cut and badly sown jacket, to say nothing of not hearing the birds, not noticing the twilight, is to ignore the world." James Hillman,

"Aesthetic Response as Political Action," in *City and Soul* (Thompson, CT: Spring, 2006), 144.

142. "For love to return to the world, beauty must first return, else we love the world only as a moral beauty: clean it up, preserve its nature, exploit it less." Hillman, "Practice of Beauty," 264.

143. Tzvetan Todorov, "La beauté sauvera le monde," *Etudes theologiques et religieuses* 82, no. 3 (2007): 331–35.

144. From the interview with Tzvetan Todorov by Franco Marcoaldi, "Beauty Will Save the World," *La Repubblica*, June 28, 2012.

145. I will return to this topic in chapter 7.

146. Partridge had already proposed the notion of "self-transcendence" in a 1980 text. See Partridge, "Why Care about the Future?"

147. This is a difficult but not impossible operation, according to Partridge: "Recall that *capacity* is a condition of moral responsibility, and that the arena of moral activity is found between the extremes of *impossibility* and *inevitability*." Ernest Partridge, "Future Generations," in *A Companion to Environmental Philosophy*, ed. Dale Jamieson (Oxford: Blackwell, 2001), 384.

148. Hannah Arendt, *The Human Condition* (Chicago: University of Chicago Press, 1958), 237.

149. Nietzsche considers the ability to make promises as the highest point of the freedom of a "*sovereign individual* . . . in short, the man who has his own independent, protracted will and *the right to make promises*." Nietzsche, *Genealogy of Morals*, 59.

150. Arendt, *Human Condition*, 237.

151. According to Arendt, "despite his modern prejudice to see the source of all power in the will to power of the isolated individual," Nietzsche's merit lies in his identifying the faculty of making promises (the "memory of the will," as Nietzsche called it) as the true distinction separating human from animal life. See Arendt, *Human Condition*, 245.

152. Ricoeur, *Oneself as Another*, 155.

153. Ricoeur, *Oneself as Another*, 181.

154. Ricoeur, *Course of Recognition*, 129.

155. Ricoeur, *Course of Recognition*, 133.

156. Jacques Derrida, *Memoires for Paul de Man* (New York: Columbia University Press, 1989), 150.

157. See Jean Birnbaum, ed., *Qui tient promesse* (Paris: Gallimard, 2015).

158. Arendt, *Human Condition*, 244.

159. Birnbacher, "What Motivates Us to Care for the (Distant) Future?," secs. 6–7.

160. Birnbacher, "What Motivates Us to Care for the (Distant) Future?"

161. Maurice Hamington and Maureen Sander-Staudt, "Introduction: Care Ethics and Business Ethics," in *Applying Care Ethics to Business*, ed. Maurice Hamington and Maureen Sander-Staudt (Berlin: Springer, 2011), xi. Also, "Care ethics is concerned about sustainability because much of care is focused on maintaining life and this includes being responsible for the well-being of future generations." Hamington and Sander-Staudt, "Introduction: Care Ethics and Business Ethics," ix.

162. This obviously does not mean that care for the other distant in space ought not to have a preventive dimension (such as in the case of adequate policies of welcome and integration of the others), which is severely lacking at the institutional level. Yet this is only *ex post*, that is, it is after the event (as in the case of a migrants' landing or a refugees' exodus) that it can be practiced by individual subjects.

163. Piergiorgio Donatelli, "Forme di vita e modi di vivere/Forms of Life and Ways of Being," *Iride* 29, no. 77 (2016): 81. This synthetic and fundamental definition of a form of life emphasizes first of all the foundation shared by the philosophies of life forms in order to distinguish them from both normative and naturalistic ethics. Within a similar theoretical context, Sandra Laugier defines a life form, in a Wittgensteinian sense, as "a natural and social complex of forms of expression and connections with others." Sandra Laugier, *Etica e politica dell'ordinario* (Milan: LED, 2015), 48.

164. For an overview of the concept within the field of critical theory, see Stefano Petrucciani, "È possibile una teoria critica delle forme di vita?," *Iride* 29, no. 77 (2016): 137–54.

165. Rahel Jaeggi, *Critique of Forms of Life* (Cambridge, MA: Harvard University Press, 2018). As is aptly synthesized by Leonard Mazzone, "with the notion of form of life, Jaeggi means a set of social practices that shapes subject's vital relations with the natural, intersubjective, and reflexive world." Leonard Mazzone, "Perché dovremmo vivere altrimenti? Alcune ragioni etico-pragmatiche per desiderare un'altra vita," *Consecutio rerum* 2, no. 3 (2017): 344–45.

166. "The term 'form of life' refers to a culturally informed "order of human co-existence" that encompasses an "ensemble of practices and orientations" as well as their institutional manifestations and materializations." Rahel Jaeggi, "Towards an Immanent Critique of Forms of Life," *Raisons Politiques* 57, no. 1 (2015): 16.

167. "The critique of forms of life as I conceive it begins precisely where problems, crises, and conflicts arise, even if they are not overtly manifest." Jaeggi, "Towards an Immanent Critique of Forms of Life," 26.

168. "Such problems are not about normative claims made by some outside observer, but about the form of life's own claims, which it cannot satisfy." Jaeggi, "Towards an Immanent Critique of Forms of Life," 24. The form of life is thus not something rigid and absolute; rather, it is a strategy that changes through

time in relation to social mutations; therefore, it can be contrasted, reformed, and replaced with alternative visions and practices.

169. For a deeper study of these topics, which we can only refer to here, see among her others works Laura Pennacchi, *Il soggetto dell'economia: Dalla crisi a un nuovo modello di sviluppo* (Rome: Ediesse, 2015).

170. On this topic, in addition to the various theories of vulnerability we already referred to numerous times, see also Luigina Mortari, *Philosophy of Care* (Berlin: Springer, 2022), 4ff.

171. The reflection on care presupposes a "paradigm shift" in ethics, that is, "a particular-oriented shift within moral theory that tries to resist what Wittgenstein in the *Blue Book* calls 'the desire for generalities' (the desire for general rules of thinking and acting). This shift takes the form of the effort to valorize as relevant for morality the attention for the particular (particulars), for the ordinary details of human life, for the neglected aspects." Laugier, *Etica e politica dell'ordinario*, 47.

172. Laugier, "La cura: L'etica come politica dell'ordinario," *Iride* 23, no. 60 (2010): 296. See also Sandra Laugier, "L'etica di Amy: La cura come cambio di paradigma in etica," *Iride* 24, no. 2 (2011): 341: "Care is defined starting from the attention to the importance of the *non-visible* of things and moments, to the dissimulation that inheres in importance; it comes to help us when we are not capable of seeing."

173. Laugier, "La cura," 298.

174. Quoted in Laugier, "L'etica di Amy," 340.

175. Laugier, *Etica e politica dell'ordinario*: "At the core of the ethics of care is our ability (our disposition) to express ourselves morally which, as Cavell and Charles Taylor have shown in various ways, is rooted in the forms of life, in (Wittengenstein's) sense of a natural and social complex of expressions and connections with others. The form of life determines the ethical structure of an expression, and the latter in turn modifies and shapes the former."

176. Laugier, *Etica e politica dell'ordinario*, 45. See also Pascale Molinier, Sandra Laugier, and Patricia Molinier, *Qu'est-ce que le "care"? Souci des autres, sensibilité, responsabilité* (Paris: Payot, 2009); Sandra Laugier and Patricia Paperman, *Le souci des autres: Éthique et politique du "care"* (Paris: EHESS, 2006).

177. Luigina Mortari explicitly speaks of an "everydaly ethics of care" in Mortari, *Philosophy of Care*, 218.

178. One can in fact take care out of love only as long as love endures; and one can be an attendant caregiver only for some periods or times in life.

179. See Godbout, *World of the Gift*.

180. The expression is taken from Agnès Heller, *Beyond Justice* (Oxford: Blackwell, 1987), who proposes to "complete" the abstract ideal of justice through the notion of "good life," for which Heller presents an interesting and original version, as she considers righteousness (thanks to which one prefers to undergo

than to commit injustice) a fundamental element of the good life (one could see especially ch. 6). It is useless to say that it would be desirable to introduce, among the fundamental elements of the good life, also the perspective on care I have presented here.

Chapter Seven

1. Nussbaum, *Upheavals of Thought*.

2. "But if we follow Aristotle rather than Kant in thinking that the moral emotions themselves can be cultivated and made part of a good character, we will feel that the grudging way in which an unsympathetic person performs these duties is morally incomplete." Nussbaum, *Upheavals of Thought*, 400.

3. See what was said in chapter 1 in the present volume.

4. Edgar Morin, "Au-delà de la globalisation et du développement, société-monde ou empire-monde?," *Revue du MAUSS* 2, no. 20 (2004): 43.

5. Here it is sufficient to refer to Arnold Gehlen, *Man: His Nature and Place in the World* (New York: Columbia University Press, 1988).

6. Günther Anders, "Die Antiquiertheit des Hassens," in *Hass: Die Macht eines unerwünsch Gefühls*, ed. R. Khale, H. Menzner, and G. Vinnai (Reinbeck: Rowolt, 1985), 11–32.

7. Guido Cusinato remarks that "*care* [in English in the original] recalls the agricultural activity of cultivating and includes all those activities that promote the flourishing of life." Guido Cusinato, "Cura e nascita: Emotional sharing come fondamento delle relazioni di cura," in *Cura ed emozioni: Un'alleanza complessa*, ed. E. Pulcini and S. Bourgault (Bologna: Il Mulino, 2018), 154.

8. On the notion of mindfulness (which becomes popular as therapeutic practice starting in the 1970s thanks to the United States doctor Jon Kabat-Zinn), see, among others, Daniel J. Siegel, *The Mindful Brain: Reflection and Attunement in the Cultivation of Well-Being* (New York: Norton, 2007), and Zindel V. Segal, Mark G. Williams, and John D. Teasdale, *Mindfulness-Based Cognitive Therapy for Depression* (New York: Guilford Press, 2013).

9. Baruch Spinoza, *Ethics*, trans. Samuel Shirley (Indianapolis: Hackett, 1982), part 4.

10. On Spinoza's complex path through progressive transitions—from imagination to reason to intuitive knowledge—see Remo Bodei, *Geometria delle passioni: Paura, speranza, felicità, filosofia e uso politico* (Milan: Feltrinelli, 1991).

11. Antonio Damasio, *Looking for Spinoza: Joy, Sorrow, and the Feeling Brain* (London: Vintage, 2004).

12. "What is Spinoza's insight then? That mind and body are parallel and mutually correlated processes, mimicking each other at every crossroad, as

two faces of the same thing. That deep inside these parallel phenomena there is a mechanism for representing body events in the mind." Damasio, *Looking for Spinoza*, 217.

13. "Spinoza recommends the mental rehearsing of negative emotional stimuli as a way to build a tolerance for negative emotions and gradually acquire a knack for generating positive ones. This is, in effect, Spinoza as mental immunologist developing a vaccine capable of creating antipassion antibodies." Damasio, *Looking for Spinoza*, 275.

14. See Sergio Manghi, "Emozioni," in *Parole chiave: Per un nuovo lessico delle scienze sociali*, ed. Alberto Melucci (Rome: Carocci, 2000). Exemplary in this sense is Michel Maffesoli, *The Shadow of Dionysus: A Contribution to the Sociology of the Orgy*, trans. Cindy Linse and Mary Kristina Palmquist (Albany: State University of New York Press, 1992).

15. Thomas Nagel, "What Is It Like to Be a Bat?," in *Mortal Questions* (Cambridge: Cambridge University Press, 1991).

16. Peter Singer, *The Lives of Animals* (Princeton, NJ: Princeton University Press, 1999), 89.

17. See Mirko Alagna, *Atlanti: Immagini del mondo e forme della politica in Max Weber* (Rome: Donzelli, 2017), 52ff.

18. Peter Singer, *Writings on an Ethical Life* (New York: Harper Collins, 2000), xix. See also Virginia Held, "Care, Empathy and Justice: Comments on Michael Slote's Moral Sentimentalism," *Analytic Philosophy* 52, no. 4 (2011): 312–18, according to whom we must subject feelings to reflection and the examination of reason, and Frans de Waal, *Primates and Philosophers: How Morality Evolved* (Princeton, NJ: Princeton University Press, 2006).

19. Spinoza claims that "an emotion cannot be checked or destroyed except by a contrary emotion which is stronger than the emotion which is to be checked." See Spinoza, *Ethics*, part 4, proposition 7. This notion is effectively retrieved by Deleuze, for example, in this passage worth quoting at length: "Some sad passions are of course socially useful: among them fear, hope, humility, even remorse. But this only insofar as we do not live by the guidance of reason. It remains the case that every passion is in itself bad insofar as it involves sadness: even hope, even confidence. A City is so much the better the more it relies on joyful affections; the love of freedom should outweigh hope, fear and confidence. Reason's only commandment . . . is to link a maximum of passive joys with a maximum of active ones. For joy is the only passive affection that increases our power of action, and of all affections joy alone can be active. . . . The sense of joy is revealed as the truly ethical sense." Gilles Deleuze, *Expressionism in Philosophy: Spinoza*, trans. Martin Joughin (New York: Zone, 1992).

20. I advance here a partial correction of the thesis by Albert O. Hirschman, *The Passions and the Interests: Political Arguments for Capitalism before Its Triumph* (Princeton, NJ: Princeton University Press, 1977), who, with reference to modern

thought, identifies a common aspect to the various thinkers in their proposal of counterbalancing passions with interests.

21. As we have seen, in Anders, the matter is especially a temporal self-expansion: "We must grasp the events furthest in time, future events, and synchronize them with a point in time, the present, as if they occurred right now." See Günther Anders, *Die Antiquiertheit des Menschen* (Munich: Beck, 1956). The author is quoting from the Italian translation by L. Dallapiccola, *L'uomo è antiquato*, vol. 1, *Considerazioni sull'anima nell'epoca della seconda rivoluzione industriale* (Turin: Bollati Boringhieri, 2012), 266.

22. Anders, *L'uomo è antiquato*, 1:317.

23. Anders, *L'uomo è antiquato*, 1:283.

24. Arnold Gehlen, *Man: His Nature and Place in the World*, trans. Clare McMillan and Karl Pillemer (New York: Columbia University Press, 1988), 152. On ascesis in Gehlen, see the special journal issue devoted to *L'uomo, un progetto incompiuto*, vol. 2, *Antropologia filosofica e contemporaneità*, ed. A. Gualandi, *Discipline Filosofiche* 13, no. 1 (2003).

25. "The point, in brief, is to transform the critique conducted in the form of necessary limitation into a practical critique that takes the form of a possible transgression. . . . That criticism is no longer going to be practiced in the search for formal structures with universal value, but rather as a historical investigation into the events that have led us to constitute ourselves and to recognize ourselves as subjects of what we are doing, thinking, saying." Michel Foucault, "What Is Enlightenment?," in *The Foucault Reader*, ed. Paul Rabinow (New York: Pantheon Books, 1984), 45–46.

26. Michel Foucault, "The Subject and Power," in *Michel Foucault: Beyond Structuralism and Hermeneutics*, ed. Hubert Dreyfus and Paul Rabinow (Chicago: University of Chicago Press, 1982), 216.

27. Michel Foucault, "Technologies of the Self," in *Technologies of the Self: A Seminar with Michel Foucault*, ed. Luther H. Martin, Huck Gutman, and Patrick H. Hutton (Amherst: University of Massachusetts, 1998), 17.

28. "Ascesis is not a way of subjecting the subject to the law; it is a way of binding him to the truth." Michel Foucault, *The Hermeneutics of the Subject: Lectures at the Collège de France*, trans. Graham Burchell (New York: Palgrave MacMillan, 2005), 317.

29. Foucault, *Hermeneutics of the Subject*, 10.

30. "It is a matter of placing the imperative 'know thyself'—which to us appears so characteristic of our civilization—back in the much broader interrogation that serves as its explicit or implicit context: What should one do with oneself? What work should be carried out on the self? How should one 'govern oneself' by performing actions in which one is oneself the objective of those actions, the domain in which they are brought to bear, the instrument they employ, and the subject that acts?" Michel Foucault, "Subjectivity and Truth,"

in *Ethics: Subjectivity and Truth*, trans. Robert Hurley et al. (New York: New Press, 1997), 1:87.

31. Foucault, "Technologies of the Self," 35.

32. Foucault, "Technologies of the Self," 18.

33. Foucault, "What Is Enlightenment?," 47.

34. Important for this theme is the influence of Pierre Hadot, *Philosophy as a Way of Life: Spiritual Exercises from Socrates to Foucault*, trans. Michael Chase (Malden, MA: Blackwell, 1995).

35. Michel Foucault, *The Use of Pleasure*, vol. 2 of *The History of Sexuality*, trans. Robert Hurley (New York: Vintage, 1990), 31.

36. See Michel Foucault, *Care of the Self*, vol. 3 of *The History of Sexuality*, trans. Robert Hurley (New York: Vintage, 1988).

37. See *Colloqui con Foucault*, ed. Duccio Trombadori (Rome: Castelvecchi, 1999), 34ff.

38. Michel Foucault, *The Birth of Biopolitics*, trans. Graham Burchell (New York: Picador, 2008).

39. Foucault, *Hermeneutics of the Subject*, 24.

40. Sloterdijk clearly warns against possible misunderstandings, clarifying that the "subversive principle" of acrobatics "lies not in the 'height' of haughtiness, the *hyper* of *hybris* or the *super* of *superbia*; it is concealed in the 'acro' of acrobatics. The word 'acrobatics' refers to the Greek term for walking in tiptoe (from *akros*, 'high, uppermost' and *bainein*, 'to go, walk'). It names the simplest form of natural anti-naturalness." Sloterdijk, *You Must Change Your Life*, 125.

41. Peter Sloterdijk, *Globes: Spheres II*, trans. Wieland Hoban (Los Angeles: Semiotex(e), 2014).

42. Sloterdijk, *You Must Change Your Life*, 437.

43. By "anthropotechnics" Sloterdijk means the set of practices human beings historically adopted to build a sustainable environment-world, that is, "all those ways of ordering, techniques, rituals, and customs with which human groups have taken their symbolic and disciplinary formation 'into their own hands.'" Peter Sloterdijk, *Not Saved: Essays After Heidegger*, trans. Ian Alexander Moore and Christopher Turner (Cambridge, UK: Polity, 2017), 126–27.

44. "Wherever one encounters members of the human race, they always show the traits of a being that is condemned to surrealistic effort. Whoever goes in search of humans will find acrobats." Sloterdijk, *You Must Change Your Life*, 13.

45. "Acrobatic existence de-trivializes life by placing repetition in the service of the unrepeatable. It transforms all steps into the first, because each one could be the last. It knows only one ethical action: the supervision of all circumstances through the conquest of the improbable." Sloterdijk, *You Must Change Your Life*, 207.

46. "Since the global catastrophe began its partial unveiling, a new manifestation of the absolute imperative has come into the world, one that directs

itself at everyone and nobody in the form of a sharp admonition: 'Change your life!' Otherwise its complete disclosure will demonstrate to you, sooner or later, what you failed to do during the time of portents!" Sloterdijk, *You Must Change Your Life*, 444.

47. Sloterdijk, *You Must Change Your Life*, 299.

48. Sloterdijk, *You Must Change Your Life*, 4.

49. Sloterdijk, *You Must Change Your Life*, 441.

50. Sloterdijk, *You Must Change Your Life*, 446.

51. Sloterdijk, *You Must Change Your Life*, 448.

52. Sloterdijk, *You Must Change Your Life*, 195.

53. Sloterdijk, *You Must Change Your Life*, 195.

54. Sloterdijk, *You Must Change Your Life*, 452.

55. And he adds, "The helpless whole is transformed into a unity capable of being protected. A romanticism of brotherliness is replaced by a cooperative logic. Humanity becomes a political concept." Sloterdijk, *You Must Change Your Life*, 451–52.

56. "The care of the self is actually something that always has to go through the relationship to someone else who is the master, there is no care of the self without the presence of a master." Foucault, *Hermeneutics of the Subject*, 58. And also, "You make your examination of conscience to a friend, to someone dear to one and with whom you have intense affective relations." Foucault, *Hermeneutics of the Subject*, 163. In other words, the aesthetics of existence of Cynics, Stoics, and Epicureans, from whom Foucault draws inspiration, implies a relational dimension that nevertheless seems to be circumscribed to specific figures. See Pierre Hadot, *What Is Ancient Philosophy?*, trans. Michael Chase (Cambridge, MA: Harvard University Press, 2004).

57. Sloterdijk, *You Must Change Your Life*, 194.

58. Sloterdijk, *You Must Change Your Life*, 192.

59. Sloterdijk adds that, "by noting that their psyche is populated with confused notions, it occurs to them how desirable it would be to arrive at the other side of the tumult of notions so that they are not simply visited by muddled thoughts, but develop logically stable ideas." Sloterdijk, *You Must Change Your Life*, 194.

60. Sloterdijk, *Rage and Time*.

61. The entire quotation is worth reproducing: "One must probably return to the basic conception of philosophical psychology found in the Greeks, according to which the soul does not rely on eros and its intentions with regard to the one and the many. Rather, the soul opens itself equally to the impulses from thymos. While eroticism points to ways leading to those 'objects' that we lack and whose presence or possession makes us feel complete, thymotics discloses ways for human beings to redeem what they possess, to learn what they are able to do, and to see what they want." Sloterdijk, *Rage and Time*, 15–16.

62. Sloterdijk, *Rage and Time*, 114.

63. See Peter Sloterdijk, *Bubbles*, vol. 1 of *Spheres*, trans. Wieland Hoban (Los Angeles: Semiotext(e), 2011).

64. On this point, I share the interpretation by Antonio Lucci, *Un'acrobatica del pensiero: La filosofia dell'esercizio di Peter Sloterdijk* (Rome: Aracne, 2014), 229ff.

65. Sloterdijk offers a rich range made of ten types. See Sloterdijk, *You Must Change Your Life*, 276ff.

66. Sloterdijk, *You Must Change Your Life*, 229.

67. Lucci, *Un'acrobatica del pensiero*, 131ff.

68. It would be interesting to compare this point with the post-humanist perspective that, on the grounds of a critique of anthropocentrism, considers alterity and the need for alterity as the constitutive dimension of the human and the foundation of a "self-decentered" or, better, "anthropo-decentered" subject. See Roberto Marchesini, *Post-human: Verso nuovi modelli di esistenza* (Turin: Bollati Boringhieri, 2002).

69. As Anders remarks, it is not by accident that a "history of sentiments" has never been written. See Anders, *L'uomo è antiquato*.

70. Anders, *L'uomo è antiquato*, 1:316.

71. Anders's thought here reveals a convergence with Sloterdijk's as it grasps, in the urgency of the current times—*we cannot go on in this manner*—the motivation radically to change our way of being in the world.

72. Anders, *L'uomo è antiquato*, 1:317.

73. I have addressed this theme broadly in Pulcini, *Care of the World*, part 2.

74. Anders, *L'uomo è antiquato*, 1:282.

75. Anders, *L'uomo è antiquato*, 1:282.

76. Anders, *L'uomo è antiquato*, 1:284.

77. "Works of art produce feelings, and exactly specific feelings, which could not occur without the created objects, which could not subsist independently of the structure of the objects, that is, as mere condition of the soul." See Anders, *L'uomo è antiquato*, I, 320.

78. Anders, *L'uomo è antiquato*, 1:321.

79. This notion recurs frequently in Arendt's work. See especially Arendt, *The Human Condition*.

80. The representational role of imagination is asserted by Arendt in the seminars on Kant's *Critique of Judgement*; the role I propose to call "transformational" emerges instead in Hannah Arendt, "Lying in Politics," in *Crises of the Republic* (New York: Harcourt, 1972), 3–47.

81. "We saw that an 'enlarged mentality' is the condition *sine qua non* of right judgment: one's community sense makes it possible to enlarge one's mentality. Negatively speaking, this means that one is able to abstract from private conditions and circumstances, which, as far as judgment is concerned, limit and inhibit its exercise. Private conditions condition us; imagination and

reflection enable us to *liberate* ourselves from them and to attain the relative impartiality that is the specific virtue of judgment." Hannah Arendt, *Lectures on Kant's Political Philosophy* (Chicago: University of Chicago Press, 1982), 73.

82. Arendt, "Lying in Politics," 5.

83. This aspect is emphasized, with specific reference to Arendt, by Chiara Bottici: "As the faculty to make present what is potentially absent, it is at the very basis of the possibility of action. As she points out at the beginning of 'Lying in Politics,' a characteristic of human action is that it always begins something new in the world. . . . This capacity to begin something new depends, in its turn, on our capacity to mentally remove ourselves from where we physically are located and imagine that things might well be different from what they actually are. This capacity to change facts, or to act, therefore fundamentally depends on imagination." Chiara Bottici, "Imaginal Politics," *Thesis Eleven* 106, no. 1 (2011): 60–61. This theme is also addressed in Chiara Bottici, *Imaginal Politics: Images beyond Imagination and the Imaginary* (New York: Columbia University Press, 2014).

84. Anders, *L'uomo è antiquato*, 1:283, 318.

85. Anders, *L'uomo è antiquato*, 1:284.

86. According to Anders, when we listen to a symphony, "our soul is dilated, it takes up a breadth of understanding we ourselves could not lend to it." Anders, *L'uomo è antiquato*, 1:319.

87. With respect to this, I have already referenced the interpretation by Sophie Bourgault, "Cura come attenzione," which clearly underlines the non-sentimentalist aspect of Weil's conception of love.

88. See some rather unequivocal claims on this: "In a perfect friendship these two desires are completely absent. The two friends have fully consented to be two and not one, they respect the distance which the fact of being two distinct creatures places between them." Simone Weil, *Waiting for God*, trans. Emma Craufurd (New York: Harper and Row, 1973), 205.

89. See Adriana Cavarero, *Inclinations: A Critique of Rectitude*, trans. Amanda Minervini and Adam Sitze (Redwood, CA: Stanford University Press, 2016).

90. Leonardo da Vinci, *Saint Anne, the Virgin, and the Child with Lamb* (approx. 1510–1513).

91. Emotions are nothing except the mark and testimony of our constitutive incompleteness. They "involve judgments about important things, judgments in which, appraising an external object as salient for our own well-being, we acknowledge our own neediness *and* incompleteness before parts of the world that we do not fully control." Nussbaum, *Upheaval of Thought*, 19.

92. Laura Boella claims that "e-motion literally means 'to put into motion (*ex-movere*),' to put outside oneself. Based on this root, 'being upset, being moved' refer to a motion triggered by something that is outside oneself and leads outside oneself." See Laura Boella, *Il coraggio dell'etica: Per una nuova immaginazione morale* (Milan: Cortina, 2012), 150.

93. I address this topic in Elena Pulcini, "Emotional Subjects: Taking Care of the Future," in *Contemporary Italian Women Philosophers: Stretching the Art of Thinking*, Silvia Benso and Elvira Roncalli, ed. (Albany: State University of New York Press, 2021), 123–41.

94. See Michael Tomasello, *Why We Cooperate* (Cambridge, MA: MIT Press, 2009).

95. "We are condemned to incompleteness" is the formula in which we can perhaps sum up the core of the thought of Edgar Morin, *Connaissance, Ignorance, Mystère* (Paris: Fayard, 2017).

96. See Dario Forti, Franco Natili and Giuseppe Varchetta, *Il soggetto incompiuto: Psicosocioanalisi dell'individuo, dell'organizzazione e della polis* (Milan: Guerini e Associati, 2018).

97. On these topics, see the excellent interpretation by Sergio Manghi, *Il soggetto ecologico di Edgar Morin: Verso una società mondo* (Trent: Erickson, 2009). For Manghi, Morin's point of greatest radicality lies in his attribution of the quality of *subject* not only to the human being but also to any living being so as to rethink the human condition entirely, without separating it from the context of natural history and planetary ecology. As a side remark, we note that this opens to an unprecedented vision of the relation human-nature-world.

98. This suggestive expression is from María Zambrano, *Hacia un saber sobre el alma* (Madrid: Alianza Editoriale, 2000), 112. Guido Cusinato shows the important implications of this for a vision of the human being as animated by the constitutive and unlimited tension toward completion. See Cusinato, "Cura e nascita," 153–82.

99. Guido Cusinato, *Periagoge: Teoria della singolarità e filosofia come esercizio di trasformazione* (Verona: QuiEdit, 2017), 332.

100. On "sharing emotions," see Cusinato, *Periagoge*, chs. 6–7, 263–82, and Cusinato, "Cura e nascita," 166ff., where Cusinato takes into account the recent debate on the topics—for example, Michael Tomasello, *Origin of Human Communication* (Cambridge, MA: MIT Press, 2008), and Dan Zahavi, "You, Me and We: The Sharing of Emotional Experiences," *Journal of Consciousness Studies* 22, no. 1–2 (2015): 84–101—but also advances his own peculiar vision, based on Scheler, of the sharing of emotions. Regarding emotions, he underlines their solidarity element as well as the process of self-transcendence of the self that preludes to the recognition of the other, "as it is only in the encounter with the other that [the self] finds the space to sate its hunger to be born fully." I am, in turn, completely in agreement with this vision; yet I want to insist on the *unpredictable* character of emotional sharing as well as its not only involuntary but also unconscious nature.

101. Cusinato, *Periagoge*, especially ch. 9, "Practices of Awakening and Germinative Feelings," 311–73.

102. I reproduce here some definitions that underscore the radicality of the transformation expressed in the word "metamorphosis": *Dizionario Zingarelli:*

"Cambiamento, mutamento radicale [radical change, mutation]"; *Cambridge Dictionary*: "A complete change of character, appearance, or condition"; *Oxford Dictionary*: "metamorphosis (from something) (into something) (formal), a process in which somebody/something changes completely into something different"; *Oxford Learner's Dictionaries*: "A process in which someone or something changes completely into something different > the metamorphosis of a caterpillar into a butterfly."

103. I will quote only three meaningful passages: "To be another, another, another. As another, you could see yourself again, too," Elias Canetti, *The Secret Heart of the Clock: Notes, Aphorisms, Fragments, 1973–1985*, trans. Joel Agee (New York: Farrar, Straus and Giroux, 2005), 70; "What if one would have to completely enter another's life in order to see *oneself?*," Canetti, *The Secret Heart of the Clock*, 96; and "How much I would like to listen to myself as a stranger, without recognizing myself, and only find out later that it was I," Elias Canetti, *The Human Province* (New York: Seabury Press, 1978). For a brilliant reconstruction of this notion that runs through the entirety of Canetti's production, see Leonard Mazzone, *Il principio possibilità: Masse, potere e metamorfosi nell'opera di Elias Canetti* (Turin: Rosenberg & Sellier, 2017), according to whom "metamorphosis translates a process of the subject's liberation that actualizes itself in alliance with the other's life. In opposition to the notions of survival, paranoia, and anti-change that allow Canetti to dissect the body of power on the ground of their shared necrophilia metamorphosis is configured as a process of symbiotic, transparent, and dynamic liberation of a subject in transformation because in relation with living alterity."

104. Manghi, *Emozioni*, 11ff.

105. The merit of proposing this perspective, which partly owes to René Girard's thought and finds confirmation in the discoveries of the neurosciences, goes to Pierre Dumouchel, *Emotions: Essai sur le corps et le social* (Paris: La Découverte, 1999) and, in Italy, to Sergio Manghi's *Emotions* as well as his "Legame emozionale, legame sociale: Prefazione," in the Italian translation of Dumouchel, *Emozioni: Saggio sul corpo e il sociale* (Milan: Medusa, 2008).

106. See Hartmut Rosa, *Resonance: A Sociology of Our Relationship to the World*, trans. James Wagner (Cambridge, UK: Polity, 2021).

107. As Bataille claims, "*Secretly or not*, it is necessary to *become other*, or else cease *to be*"; here the "becom[ing] other" refers especially, and contextually to Bataille's reflection, to the need to take leave from the Enlightenment-style rationality and its servile attitude. See Georges Bataille, *The Sacred Conspiracy: The Internal Papers of the Secret Society of Acéphale and Lectures to the College of Sociology* (London: Atlas, 2018).

108. See Levinas, *Otherwise than Being*, 86ff.

109. The inner "principle of contestation" is the expression with which Maurice Blanchot alludes to a self that is open and exposed to alterity, starting

precisely from the perception of an internal difference constitutive of the self. See Maurice Blanchot, *The Unavowable Community*, trans. Pierre Joris (Barrytown, NY: Station Hill Press, 1988).

110. As we have already seen, the wound refers to *vulnus* and therefore to vulnerability.

111. For an overview of the varied galaxy of virtue ethics, I refer to two helpful syntheses: Rosalind Hursthouse, "Virtue Ethics," in *Stanford Encyclopedia of Philosophy*, https://plato.stanford.edu/entries/ethics-virtue/; Nafsika Athanassoulis, "Virtue Ethics," in the *Internet Encyclopedia of Philosophy*, https://www.iep.utm.edu/virtue/. For a synthesis of the fundamental features of virtue ethics, see Rosalind Hursthouse, *On Virtue Ethics* (Oxford: Oxford University Press, 1999) and the monographic issue of the journal *Teoria* 38, no. 2, ed. Angelo Campodonico and Maria Silvia Vaccarezza (2018). For Hume's perspective which, more than other approaches, is attentive to the theme of emotions, see Roger Crisp and Michael Slote, eds., *Virtue Ethics* (Oxford: Oxford University Press, 1997).

112. Hume, *Treatise of Human Nature*, 3.1.3.

113. See Daniel Statman, *Moral Luck* (Albany: State University of New York Press, 1993), and also, even though it does not acknowledge the specificity of virtue ethics, Martha Nussbaum, *The Fragility of Goodness: Luck and Ethics in Greek Tragedy and Philosophy* (Cambridge: Cambridge University Press, 1986).

114. Interesting is, from my perspective, the attention that some authors reserve for the issue of motivations when they claim that virtue ethics can be brought back and explained on the basis of the agents' motivational features. According, for example, to Slote, an agent-based virtue ethics "*understands right-ness in terms of good motivations and wrongness in terms of the having of bad* (or *insufficiently good*) *motives.*" Michael Slote, *Morals from Motives* (Oxford: Oxford University Press, 2001), 14. Slote, however, does not explain how to distinguish good from bad motivations. As I argued earlier, this distinction ought to be entrusted, first of all, to a critical-reflective analysis of our emotions.

115. "Most people who can truly be described as fairly virtuous, and certainly markedly better than those who can truly be described as dishonest, self-centered and greedy, still have their blind spots—little areas where they do not act for the reasons one would expect." Hursthouse, "Virtue Ethics," 1.1. This does not exclude, however, as claimed by some authors who belong to the Aristotelian trend of virtue ethics, that we can defend the idea of a unity of virtues, for which through *phronesis* we could potentially extend virtue to ever new areas of experience. See for example Daniel Russell, *Practical Intelligence and the Virtues* (Oxford: Oxford University Press, 2009).

116. These criticisms, which are partly legitimate, come from deontological and consequentialist theories.

117. "Hume's ethics, unlike Kant's, make morality a matter not of obedience to universal law but of cultivating the character traits which give a person 'inward

peace of mind, consciousness of integrity' . . . and at the same time make that person good company to other persons. . . . To become a good fellow-person one doesn't consult some book of rules; one cultivates one's capacity for sympathy, or fellow feeling." Annette Baier, *Moral Prejudices: Essays on Ethics* (Cambridge, MA: Harvard University Press, 1995), 54.

118. "Virtue ethics focuses especially on the state of character of individuals, whereas the ethics of care concerns itself especially with caring *relations*." Held, *Ethics of Care*, 19.

119. "Originary anthropological movement, generativity actualizes itself in four stages: to desire (without which nothing is possible), to bring to the world (to give birth, to initiate something that was not there), to take care (without which nothing can last), and, finally, to let go (to pass the baton). These are moments that regenerate us as capable and new subjects; we find testimony of them in art, in collaborative work, in volunteer work, in some entrepreneurship, and in craftsmanship." See Chiara Giaccardi and Mauro Magatti, *Generativi di tutto il mondo unitevi! Manifesto per la società dei liberi* (Milan: Feltrinelli, 2014).

120. See Giaccardi and Magatti, *Generativi di tutto il mondo unitevi!*

121. "This is why ethics is the experience of the impossible." Gayatri Spivak, preface to Mahasweta Devi, *Imaginary Maps* (London: Routledge, 1995), xxv. This aspect is underscored by Caterina Botti, who alludes especially to the role of imagination. See Botti, *Cura e differenza*, 194ff. See also Boella, *Il coraggio dell'etica*, 185ff.

122. See the transciption of the lecture by Chiara Giaccardi (with Mario Magatti), "Generativi di tutto il mondo unitevi!," held at the Circoli Dossetti as part of the Corso di formazione alla politica 2014–15: https://www.circolidossetti.it/chiara-giaccardi-con-mauro-magatti-generativi-di-tutto-il-mondo-unitevi/. Giaccardi continues as follows: "This transitivity is also an inter-temporality, which is what has been interrupted in the time out of joint of contemporaneity, where what holds true is only an instant disconnected from the other. Transitivity is receiving and giving, but it is also the before and after, the past and the future, the legacy and the promise, loyalty and hope. These are all constellations of meaning that have to do with this dimension in which we are the protagonists but in which, as it were, everything comes before and everything also goes beyond ourselves."

123. See especially chapters 5 and 6 in the present volume.

124. By directors Gianfranco Rosi (2016) and Emanuele Crialese (2011) respectively.

125. See Martha Nussbaum, *Political Emotions: Why Love Matters for Justice* (Cambridge, MA: Harvard University Press, 2013).

126. It suffices here to refer to the "whipped up masses" that are pushed by the passion of resentment against sacrificial victims, not in order to reestablish social cohesion (as in the perspective proposed by René Girard) but rather to

guarantee the survival of power through exemplary expulsions. On these topics, see Leonard Mazzone, *Il principio possibilità: Masse, potere e metamorfosi nell'opera di Elias Canetti* (Turin: Rosenberg & Sellier, 2017), especially ch. 5.

Index

Agape, 61, 63, 186n77

Alterity, 28, 74, 81, 98, 99, 135, 141–144, 164n11, 181n72, 199n68, 202n103, 202n109

Altruism, 17, 18, 24, 63, 66, 71, 102, 113, 140

Anders, Günther, 90, 97, 98, 105, 111–113, 126, 129, 133, 136–139, 144

Anesthesia (of fear), 112, 116, 137

Anthropocene, 108, 115

Apocalypse, 112, 113

Arab Spring, 3, 53

Archetype (of responsibility and care), 99

Arendt, Hannah, 19, 20, 41, 42, 78, 116, 118, 119, 122, 138, 139, 153

Aristotle, 52, 53, 125, 145

Ascetic(s), 5, 129, 130, 131, 133, 135, 136, 139–141, 144, 146

Attendant care, 64–66, 68, 120

Attention (as emotion), 4, 26, 31, 33, 58, 61, 64, 74, 86, 108, 116, 120, 122, 124, 126, 140, 146, 174n16, 174n17, 174n18

Automatism, 104, 137

Autonomy, 2, 23, 27, 30, 31, 37, 63, 67, 100, 132, 140, 144

Baier, Annette, 29, 104, 146

Barry, Brian, 91, 93, 104

Beck, Ulrich, 96, 97, 105

Benevolence, 10, 39

Bentham, Jeremy, 93, 182n8

Boltanski, Luc, 24, 77, 78, 178n29

Butler, Judith, 99, 100, 185n58, 185n63

Capabilities (approach), 33–35, 37, 39, 72, 167n5

Capitalism, 28, 65, 77, 150

Care work, 59, 64, 65, 67, 68

Caregiver, 24, 65–68

Catastrophe, 70, 73, 132, 133, 150–152, 197n46

Cavarero, Adriana, 140, 141

Charity, 13, 41, 66, 84

Choice, 23, 26, 36, 43, 45, 59, 64, 92, 94–96, 98, 104, 108, 144, 145

Circle(s) of concern, 40, 66, 68, 70

Circles of empathy, 74, 75, 107

Climate change, 28, 55, 90, 91, 108, 112, 119

Communitarian, 95, 97, 101, 134

Community, 31, 41, 42, 78, 89, 95–97, 101, 104–108, 182n9, 190n136, 199n81

Competition, 9, 16, 48

Conflict, 3, 21, 28, 29, 31, 54, 55, 81, 85, 90–92, 95, 144, 145, 147, 163n3, 170n53

Constitutive dependency, 27–29, 103
Contagion, 14, 16, 17, 81, 102, 151
Conversion, 85, 130, 132–135, 139, 142, 148, 150
Cooperation, 30, 31, 34–36, 68, 76, 77, 86, 108, 128, 141, 153, 171n61
Cruelty, 45, 55, 107
Culture, 80, 83, 119, 143

de Waal, Frans, 16, 72, 157n11
Death, 74, 96, 99, 110, 120, 150, 185n58
Debt, 4, 84, 97, 101–106, 117, 124
Decreation, 61, 140
Defense (of rights), 3, 4, 30, 33, 45, 63, 67
Deleuze, Gilles, 126, 195n19
Democracy, 3, 124
Deontological, 92, 99, 122, 145, 203n116
Dependence, 25, 27–29, 33, 34, 36, 37, 66, 67, 98, 99, 101–103, 120, 122, 134, 166n57
Derangement, 112
Derrida, Jacques, 82, 83, 86, 118, 180n68
Descartes, Renée, 186n66
Descending reciprocity, 104
de-Shalit, Avner, 91, 95–97, 107, 183n32, 183n33, 183n34
Destiny, 19, 61, 62, 73, 96, 97, 101, 105, 106, 112, 146, 151
Difference, 49, 58, 79, 81, 85, 93
Dignity, 3, 33–37, 39, 45, 52–54, 62, 65, 67, 85, 86, 91, 140, 165n24, 167n5, 173n89
Dilation (of psyche and self), 139
Disability, 33, 34, 36, 37, 67, 176
Disabled (the), 33, 60, 64, 65, 67
Disgust, 4, 39, 64, 66–68
Distribution (of resources), 4, 30, 31, 32, 46, 93, 94

Division (of labor), 4, 30–32, 37, 62

Ecological (crisis, disaster), 20, 70, 90, 97, 98, 108, 110, 112, 116, 120, 148, 149, 152, 189n119
Ecological conscience, 91
Egoism, 9, 18, 50, 55, 63, 147, 157n11
Elderly (the), 60, 64, 65, 67
Empathic care, 58, 188n107
Empathic consciousness, 2
Engagement, 20, 21, 40, 42, 53, 85, 86, 137, 163
Enlightenment, 43, 107, 202n107
Entropy, 73
Envy, 3, 16, 48–54, 80, 93, 153, 170n52, 170n58, 171n59
Equality, 4, 25–27, 30, 33, 37, 49, 54, 63, 78
Equity, 13, 25, 32
Eros, 61–64, 129, 135, 198n61
Ethics of sympathy, 13, 16, 17, 141
Eudaimonistic (judgement, goal), 40, 145
Everyday(ness), 68, 74, 124, 150

Fairness, 33, 93, 124, 168n26
Fear (for the other), 99, 110
Fear (for the world), 110, 111, 147
Fellow-feeling, 12, 41
Femicide, 62
Form(s) of life, 121–123, 192n163, 192n165, 192n166, 192n167, 192n168, 193n175
Foucault, Michel, 129–133, 135, 139, 144, 198n56
Fragility, 66, 99, 100, 101, 113, 122, 145, 150
Frankfurt, Harry, 17, 63
Freedom, 30, 33, 45, 48, 54, 81, 131, 134, 146, 152, 153, 172n82, 191n149, 195n19

Freud, Sigmund, 111, 126, 129, 134
Future generations, 4, 28, 70, 72, 83, 89–99, 104–112, 114, 115, 117, 119, 120, 123, 146

Generosity, 3, 4, 10, 13, 14, 18, 19, 45, 61, 168n34, 188n102
Giddens, Anthony, 62
Gift, 4, 79, 83, 84, 101–105, 117, 124, 176n2, 180n61, 180n62
Gilligan, Carol, 1, 2, 23–27, 29, 31, 32, 37, 59, 63, 163n3, 165n29
Givenness, 41, 138
Globalization, 31, 67, 69–71, 90, 97, 104, 164n6
Gosh, Amitav, 112
Gratitude, 19, 61, 84, 86, 180n60
Grief, 99, 185n58
Guilt, 19, 63, 85, 101, 109, 119, 162n84

Habermas, Jürgen, 28, 46, 169n41
Happiness, 12, 16, 18, 93, 94, 130
Harm, 90, 107, 170n58, 172n71, 183n33
Hatred, 41, 80, 84, 153, 160n55
Hedonistic calculus, 93
Hegemony, 2, 8, 9, 29, 121, 134, 140
Held, Virginia, 2, 20, 24, 25, 28–32, 59
Heuristic (of fear), 99, 112
Hobbes, Thomas, 9, 110, 129
Homo creator, 98
Homo empathicus, 73
Homo faber, 72, 98, 105, 111, 113
Homo oeconomicus, 8, 9, 18, 45, 72, 98, 108, 121, 122
Honneth, Axel, 46, 47, 54
Hope, 76, 124, 153, 195n19, 204n122
Hospitality, 82–84, 86, 87, 147, 152, 179n40, 179n55, 179n56, 180n68

Hume, David, 8, 10–16, 18, 19, 37, 71, 73, 107, 128, 145, 188n102
Humiliation, 1, 20, 44, 45, 51, 68, 80, 84, 89

Ignorance (veil of), 35, 49, 92
Imagination, 12–15, 18, 107, 112, 114, 129, 137–139, 160n48, 200n 83
Immunitarian, 72, 79–82, 86, 133
Impartial (spectator, evaluator), 13, 14, 17, 30, 50, 54, 55, 66, 73, 75, 108, 169n38
Impartiality, 23, 25, 29, 30, 35, 43, 50, 55, 78, 92, 124, 200n81
Indebted(ness), 101, 102, 106, 109
Independence, 2, 25, 34, 67
Indifference, 1, 72, 79, 83, 85, 93, 122, 147, 148, 150
Indignados, 3, 53
Indignation, 3, 19, 20, 43, 45, 48, 50–55, 57, 75–77, 85, 100, 109, 116, 173n1
Indirect reciprocity, 104, 187n92
Injustice, 3, 4, 25, 28, 39, 43–47, 49, 50, 52, 53, 55, 57, 58, 75, 76, 109, 116, 117, 160n41, 169n44, 169n46, 170n51, 170n52, 173n92
Interdependence, 2, 29, 31, 34, 36, 99, 100, 103–105, 122, 124, 166n57
Intergenerational justice, 92–95, 97, 104, 107
Intergenerational responsibility, 90, 103, 119
Interiority, 126, 134, 142, 151
Intrinsic value, 102, 114, 179n58
Involuntary, 141, 143, 201n100
Involvement, 26, 31, 57, 78, 85, 86, 163n92
Islamic fundamentalism, 52, 80

Jamieson, Dale, 91, 108, 115, 182n14

Jonas, Hans, 19, 90, 91, 97–101,
  105, 108, 110–114, 133, 184n55,
  190n126
Joy(ful), 8, 12, 40, 51, 127, 129,
  195n19
Just anger, 3, 76, 80, 85, 179n46
Just envy, 51

Kant, Immanuel, 8, 194n2
Kittay, Eva, 2, 25, 33, 34, 36, 37, 59,
  66, 67
Korsgaard, Christine, 17, 177n13

Lacan, Jacques, 102
Latour, Bruno, 151
Laugier, Sandra, 59, 122, 123,
  166n41, 192n163, 193n175
Leadership, 62, 76
Levinas, Emmanuel, 98, 99, 101,
  141, 144, 164n11
Liberal (theories, thought), 2, 8–10,
  23, 28, 29, 32–34, 37
Love of the world, 116

Mandeville, Bernard, 41
Marion, Jean-Luc, 102
Market (the), 9, 48, 65, 152
Mauss, Marcel, 54, 84, 102–104,
  157n12, 180n61
Metamorphosis, 5, 141, 142, 144–
  146, 148, 149, 151, 153, 154,
  201n102, 202n103
Modernity, 2, 18, 41, 70, 79, 98,
  101, 121, 129, 131, 135, 136, 140,
  143
Moral psychology, 1, 10, 114, 125,
  145, 155n3
Moral sentimentalism, 8, 10, 18, 20,
  37, 58, 71, 107, 155n4
Morin, Edgar, 126, 141, 201n97
Mourning, 99
Murdoch, Iris, 116, 122

Mutual advantage(s), 34, 36, 102
Mutual recognition, 71, 172n82,
  179n58

Nancy, Jean-Luc, 81
Neediness, 40, 67, 141, 167n5,
  200n91
Negative passion(s), 84, 110, 114,
  127, 154
Nietzsche, Friedrich, 19, 40, 41,
  48, 50–52, 69, 118, 130, 170n58,
  191n149
Normative, 1, 3, 17, 45–47, 82, 83,
  92, 94–96, 107, 120, 122, 125,
  130, 171n66, 192n163, 192n168
Nussbaum, Martha, 2, 7, 8, 10, 16,
  18, 19, 25, 32–37, 39, 40, 42,
  43, 46, 53, 63, 66, 77, 125, 153,
  173n10

Obligation, 71, 72, 74, 75, 78,
  89–97, 103–106, 120
Optimism, 107, 120

Paideia (of the passions), 5, 110,
  117, 129, 139, 145, 147, 151
Parfit, Derek, 92, 94
Parrhesia (truth-telling), 134
Passmore, John, 90, 93
Philia, 61, 63, 140
Pity, 39, 41, 42, 66, 77–79, 84,
  167n12, 178n29
Plasticity (of emotive life), 19, 126,
  144
Pogge, Thomas, 31, 35
Possessive individualism, 8, 9, 12, 136
Potentialities, 52, 55, 60, 72, 73, 97,
  128, 142–144, 151
Poverty, 1, 28, 34, 74–78, 120
Powerless(ness), 48, 51, 80, 84, 85
Private (the), 4, 26, 27, 29–31, 59,
  60, 62, 63, 68, 104, 199n81

Prometheus, 105, 190n126
Promise, 118–120, 122, 123,
 191n149, 191n151, 204n122
Public (space, sphere), 26–28, 30, 31,
 41, 42, 55, 59, 62, 78, 153

Rage (see also wrath), 19, 52, 53, 76,
 80, 134, 135, 162n84
Rationalism, 10, 33
Rationality, 2, 7, 9, 25, 27, 50,
 159n38, 202n107
Rawls, John, 2, 28, 29, 31–35,
 37, 43, 46, 49, 50, 92–94, 101,
 166n52, 168n26, 169n41, 171n61
Reciprocity, 4, 14, 82–84, 95, 101–
 104, 140, 141, 179n58, 187n89
Reflective sympathy, 14, 17, 73
Reflectivity, 17, 109
Relationality, 2, 141, 142, 146, 147
Remuneration, 60, 65, 67
Renault, Emmanuel, 3, 45–47,
 169n41, 169n44, 170n 51
Resentment, 4, 14, 16, 24, 48–54,
 64, 66, 68, 80, 81, 84, 85, 147,
 150, 153, 171n61, 204n126
Resistance, 131, 136, 139, 144, 145,
 148, 153
Resonance, 143
Responsible subject, 99
Ressentiment, 51
Revenge bank, 80
Ricoeur, Paul, 98, 100–102, 118, 141,
 164n11, 185n66
Rifkin, Jeremy, 72, 75
Rosa, Hartmut, 143, 148

Sacrifice, 36, 61–63, 67, 75, 170n58,
 182n8
Sad passion(s), 51, 52, 54, 127, 129,
 148, 195n19
Sad(ness), 12, 40, 173n10, 195n19
Sartre, Jean-Paul, 20

Scheler, Max, 10, 14, 16, 51, 141,
 201n100
Self-conscious emotions, 19, 110
Self-control, 5
Self-denial, 61
Self-destruction, 73, 105, 108,
 110–112
Self-exercise, 139
Self-interest, 9, 18, 29, 36, 59, 93,
 97
Self-love, 9, 45, 63, 64, 129, 169n39
Self-transcendence, 96, 117, 139,
 141, 142, 144, 146, 191n146,
 201n100
Self-transformation, 130–134, 137,
 139, 141, 144, 147
Sen, Amartya, 2, 9, 10, 18, 43–46,
 50, 55, 128, 166n52, 168n26
Seriousness, 40
Shame, 15, 19, 39, 85, 109, 117,
 119, 147
Simmel, Georg, 63, 64, 79, 83,
 174n21
Slote, Michael, 16, 37, 58, 74, 107,
 155n2, 173n5, 188n107, 203n114
Sloterdijk, Peter, 5, 19, 43, 52,
 53, 80, 129, 131–135, 139, 144,
 197n40
Smith, Adam, 8–15, 17, 18, 43, 45,
 50, 55, 71, 77, 78, 108, 128, 145,
 160n46, 168n34, 173n92
Social choice theory, 43, 104,
 168n27
Solidarity, 20, 21, 25, 30, 42, 45, 72,
 76, 77, 89, 101, 106, 149, 150,
 154, 201n100
Sontag, Susan, 42, 77, 85
Sorrow, 12, 13, 65, 162n76
Sovereign(ty), 5, 98–102, 118, 129,
 135, 136, 140, 144, 146, 164n11,
 191n149
Speed, 70, 90, 92

Spivak, Gayatri, 147
Stein, Edith, 11, 58
Stranger (the), 71, 74, 79–81, 85, 87, 108, 160n54, 174n14, 179n40, 181n72
Sympathy, 10–18, 20, 23, 37, 40, 58, 71–73, 84, 85, 107, 141, 158n25, 160n55, 165n25, 204n117
Technology, 98, 105, 136
Thymotic passions, 43, 45, 52, 134, 135
Transgenerational community, 95–97, 107
Tronto, Joan, 2, 25–29, 59
Trust, 10, 30, 31, 46, 65, 75, 77, 90, 103, 104, 108, 126, 128, 138

Universalization, 59
Utilitarianism, 18, 92–94, 157n12

Veil of ignorance, 35, 49, 92

Vengeance, 48–51, 80
Violence, 14, 30, 31, 53, 62, 66, 67, 70, 77, 80, 81, 84, 85, 100, 180n62, 185n63
Virtue ethics, 14, 20, 108, 133, 145, 146, 203n114
Voluntary, 143
von Hayek, Friedrich, 48
Vulnerability, 4, 25–27, 34, 40, 57, 66, 67, 73, 99, 100, 102, 104, 105, 112, 113, 122, 124, 141, 142, 149–151, 164n11, 185n56, 187n94, 203n110

Weil, Simone, 20, 41, 61, 84, 121, 140, 141, 174n18
Wittgenstein, Ludwig, 122, 192n163, 193n171
Wrath (see also rage), 45, 52

Zambrano, María, 126, 142, 201n97

About the Author

Elena Pulcini (1950–2021) taught social philosophy at the University of Florence. Her work focuses on the passions and individualism, the social pathologies of modernity, and forms of social bonds. Her thought explores women's subjectivity. She proposes a philosophy of care for the global age that is also developed in and through her interest in the philosophical-social implications of the ecological crisis. Her most recent works, some of which have been translated into other European languages, include: *L'individuo senza passioni: Individualismo moderno e perdita del legame sociale* [The individual without passion: Modern individualism and the loss of social ties] (2001); *Il potere di unire: Femminile, desiderio, cura* [The power to unite: The feminine, desire, care] (2003); *La cura del mondo: Paura e responsabilità nell'età globale* [Care of the world: Power and responsibility in the Global Age] (2009; awarded the Premio di Filosofia "Viaggio a Siracusa"); *Invidia: La passione triste* [Envy: The sad passion] (2011); *"Specchio, specchio delle mie brame . . .": Bellezza e invidia* ["Mirror, mirror, on the wall . . .": Beauty and envy] (2017); and *Responsabilità, uguaglianza, sostenibilità: Tre parole-chiave per interpretare il futuro* [Responsibility, equality, and sustainability: Three key words with which to interpret the future] (with Salvatore Veca and Enrico Giovannini, 2017). She was the editor of *Filosofie della globalizzazione* [Philosophies of globalization] (with Dimitri D'Andrea, 2001), *Umano post-umano: Potere, sapere, etica nell'età globale* [Human post-human: Power, knowing, and ethics in the global age] (with Mariapaola Fimiani and Vanna Gessa Kurotschka, 2004), and *Cura ed emozioni: Un'alleanza complessa* [Care and emotions: A complex alliance] (with Sophie Bourgault, 2018).